Mathematical Cognition

A Volume in Current Perspectives
on Cognition, Learning, and Instruction
Series Editor: James M. Royer, *University of Massachusetts*

Mathematical Cognition

edited by

James M. Royer
University of Massachusetts

INFORMATION AGE
PUBLISHING

80 Mason Street • Greenwich, Connecticut 06830 • www.infoage.com

Library of Congress Cataloging-in-Publication Data available

Mathematical cognition / edited by James M. Royer.
     p. cm. – (Current perspectives on cognition, learning, and instruction)
Includes bibliographical references.
  ISBN 1-930608-34-9 (pbk.) – ISBN 1-930608-35-7 (hardcover)
  1. Mathematics–Study and teaching (Preschool) 2. Mathematics–Study and teaching (Primary) 3. Cognition in children. I. Royer, James M., 1941- II. Series.
  QA135.6 .M375 2002
  372'.7–dc21

                                            2002011599

Printed in the United States of America

LIST OF CONTRIBUTORS

Martha Carr

Department of Educational Psychology
University of Georgia
mcarr@coe.uga.edu

Allan Feldman

School of Education
University of Massachusetts Amherst
afeldman@educ.umass.edu

David C. Geary

Department of Psychological Sciences
University of Missouri
GearyD@Missouri.edu

Sharon Griffin

Jacob Hiatt Center for Urban Education
Clark University

Hillary Hettinger

Department of Educational Psychology
University of Georgia
hhetting@coe.uga.edu

Mary K. Hoard

Department of Psychological Sciences
University of Missouri

David Klein

Department of Mathematics
California State University, Northridge
david.klein@csun.edu

Richard E. Mayer

Department of Psychology
University of California, Santa Barbara
mayer@psych.ucsb.edu

John Pegg   Centre for Cognition Research in Learning
                                and Teaching
                             University of New England
                             Australia
                             jpegg@metz.une.edu.au

James M. Royer   Department of Psychology
                             University of Massachusetts, Amherst
                             royer@psych.umass.edu

Loel Tronsky   Hampshire College

CONTENTS

A BRIEF OVERVIEW OF RECENT DEVELOPMENTS IN MATHEMATICAL COGNITION AND INSTRUCTION

James M. Royer

It is always interesting to ask the question of where specific cognitive abilities come from. This question has been asked most often about language. Whereas it is apparent that many species appear to innately possess the ability to signal, and several species have developed large labeling vocabularies and the ability to string together simple requests, strong arguments have been made that the symbolic utilization of language is uniquely human (e.g., Chomsky, 1980).

Interestingly, it appears that rudimentary mathematical ability is also possessed by many sub-human species, though higher-level arithmetic appears to be unique to humans. Dehaene (in press) presents the evidence supporting this assertion. He argues that the human ability for arithmetic has a specific cerebral substrate that is partially under genetic control and that precursors of this arithmetic ability can be found in animals. Specifically, rats, pigeons, parrots, chimpanzees, and raccoons have been shown to be able to perform mathematical operations such as the discrimination of the numerosity of set. In addition, Dehaene (in press) reviews evidence showing that monkeys in the wild can perform simple addition computa-

Mathematical Cognition, pages ix–xi
Copyright © 2002 by Information Age Publishing

tions (e.g., $1+1$, $2-1$) and that monkeys in captivity can be trained to acquire and generalize the strategy of arranging cards depicting numbers of objects from smaller to larger sets.

Dehaene (in press) argues that simple mathematical ability is common to many species, but it only humans that can represent number symbolically, and it is only humans that can turn rudimentary abilities into sophisticated mathematical representations and operations. The development of the human capacity for mathematical cognition is strongly mediated by educational experience, and part of the story of how this development occurs is told in the chapters contained in this volume.

The book begins with a chapter by Sharon Griffin that describes early mathematical capabilities and the instructional events encountered by young children that can enhance or inhibit the further development of those abilities. This chapter is followed by a chapter written by Martha Carr and Hillary Hettinger describing the development of strategies that are used to solve mathematical problems. As was the case with Griffith's chapter, Carr and Hettinger provide a detailed description of the interplay between cognitive capabilities and the instructional events that shape and enhance those abilities.

The chapters on the early development of mathematical competence are followed by a chapter by Richard Mayer that describes the cognitive processes involved in mathematical problem solving by the mature learner. Mayer portrays mathematical problem solving as involving four cognitive processes that are active in a cognitive system that is constrained by capacity limitations. These capacity limitations and other cognitive limitations are explored in greater detail in the chapter by David Geary and Mary Hoard which reviews the literature on the difficulties experienced by students who have mathematical learning disabilities. Their chapter begins with an overview of the background characteristics exhibited by students with mathematical disabilities, moves to an examination of the theoretical models that link mathematical development and mathematical disabilities, and closes with an examination of the cognitive and memory deficits that occur among students with math learning disabilities.

Both the Mayer chapter and the Geary and Hoard chapter point out the important role that working memory plays in mathematical cognition. The chapter by Loel Tronsky and James Royer summarizes the research on the role of working memory in mathematical functioning and it explores the theoretical reasons for the relationship between the two.

The final section of the book considers topics that are much more educational in nature. Allan Feldman discusses mathematics instruction from the constructivist perspective that has strongly influenced some of the recent policy perspectives on mathematics instruction. The perspective is not without controversy, however, as David Klein's chapter illustrates. Klein traces the history of math instruction in the 20th century, and in particular highlights the California controversy that has come to known as the "math wars."

The book closes with a chapter by John Pegg on math assessment. Pegg reviews various aspects of traditional approaches to the assessment of math competency and then presents an interesting description of a new approach to assessment that is strongly motivated by neo-Piagetian theory.

REFERENCES

Chomsky, N. (1980). On cognitive structures and their development: A reply to Piaget. In M. Piattelli-Palmarini (Ed), *Language and learning: The debate between Jean Piaget and Noam Chomsky* (pp. 35–54). Cambridge MA: Harvard University Press.

Dehaene, S. (in press). Précis of "The number sense." *Mind and Language.*

CHAPTER 1

THE DEVELOPMENT OF MATH COMPETENCE IN THE PRESCHOOL AND EARLY SCHOOL YEARS

Cognitive Foundations and Instructional Strategies

Sharon Griffin

ABSTRACT

Three questions are addressed in the present paper: What is math competence? How does it develop? How can it be fostered in school settings? It is suggested that   progress in answering these questions has been hindered because we lack an adequate definition of what math competence is. When the knowledge that lies at the heart of it is more clearly defined, it becomes easier to chart how this knowledge develops across the childhood years (from birth to 10 years) and how it can be fostered in school settings. Drawing on recent research in neuroscience, cognitive development, math education, and instructional design, specific answers to each question are

Mathematical Cognition, pages 1–32

1

provided. The knowledge structures that underlie math competence at four age-levels (4, 6, 8, and 10 years) are described. Tools to assess this knowledge are presented and instructional strategies that have proven effective in teaching this knowledge and in enhancing math competence are also described.

INTRODUCTION

What is math competence? How does it develop? How can it be fostered in school settings? In the present chapter, I provide one set of answers to these questions. Although the last question, in particular, has recently assumed greater prominence in the American national consciousness than has been the case for most of the previous century, the set of questions I have posed here is not new. Indeed, in the research literature that has accumulated over the past century (see, in particular, Piaget, 1952, 1954, 1963, 1970; also see Griffin & Case, 1997, for a review of current research) and in every curriculum manual that has been produced over the same time period to teach math in schools, a range of answers is available.

Although curriculum manuals focus explicitly and ostensibly on the last question posed above—how math competence can and should be taught— the selection of learning objectives to be addressed at each grade level and the design of lessons to help teachers "teach" each objective is invariably guided by some sense (or some model) of what children are capable of learning at each age/grade level and the sorts of knowledge it is important that they acquire. Thus, answers to the first two questions—What is math competence? How does it develop?—are embedded, at least implicitly, in every curriculum guide. During the past decade, answers to these questions have been made much more explicit in a set of principles and standards for school mathematics that was developed by the National Council of Teachers of Mathematics (NCTM, 1989, 2000) on the sensible assumption that, if teachers have a clearer idea of the knowledge they are expected to teach at each grade level and the manner in which this knowledge develops, they will have an easier time teaching it and will achieve greater success in the process.

In contemplating the wealth of knowledge that is available in the field and what I might add in this chapter that would be new, and important, and capable of moving the field forward, I was struck by two competing reflections. The first was that it is no longer necessary to justify an interest in the questions raised in this chapter, to explain their significance to our nation's well being, or to motivate the math education community to pay more attention to the subject. In broad sectors of our society, in our schools, in our research communities, and in our legislative bodies, there is now ample recognition that math competence is important for entry into the work force (Hunt, 1996) and for informed participation in a demo-cratic society. There is also ample recognition that our nation is still failing to achieve this for a significant proportion of our children (NAEP 1983, 1988, 1993).

My second reflection, which came hard upon the first, was that, given the unprecedented level of attention this issue has received during the past decade, we ought to be seeing more progress on this front. A clear direc-tion for reform—one that is grounded in research on how children think and learn—has been available since 1989 (NCTM, 1989, 2000). Through-out the 1990's, resources to improve mathematics education have been made available in public sectors of our society (e.g., federal, state, and municipal budgets) and in private sectors (e.g., business and foundations). A national will to improve the teaching of math (and reading) in our nation's schools is also apparent in our society, as witnessed by the promi-nent role that "the education issue" played in the last presidential race. What then is the problem? Why are the desired changes so slow in being realized?

One answer to this question is that change takes time and, indeed, there are signs of progress—small beacons of light—in schools across the nation. However, there may also be a deeper reason for our lack of progress, one that could hinder improvement for years to come. As I examined each of the questions to be addressed in this chapter and reviewed the available evidence, I came to face to face with a paradox in each, which points to one conclusion: We haven't yet gotten to the heart of the problem or defined it at the most basic level. In the remainder of this section, I give each paradox a name and a rough shape. In subsequent sections of this paper, as I address each of our leading questions in turn, I flesh out each paradox, define the nature of the problem more explicitly, and suggest a possible resolution.

The Definition Paradox

We can all recognize math competence when we see it and, given a bit of experience with individuals, we are all likely to know who has it and who doesn't, and who, for example, should be given the bill after a meal to fig-ure out the tip and to figure out how much each person owes. When it comes to defining what math competence is, however, what it consists of and what knowledge lies at the heart of it, I suspect that many of us, includ-ing the math teachers and educators among us, might be at a loss. Given the strong focus on enhancing this competence in our schools, it is para-doxical that a clear, crisp definition of what it is, of the knowledge that it entails, is not more readily available.

The absence of this knowledge is exemplified in a series of conversations I had with practicing elementary mathematics teachers who had agreed to serve as mentors for prospective teachers. In order to prepare my student-teachers to play a meaningful role in the classroom during their clinical experience, I asked each mentor teacher to tell me what math concepts she wanted her students to acquire during this period and which ones she considered the most important. To the dismay of both of us, this was not a meaningful question for many cooperating teachers and it was met at first with silence. While I considered how best to rephrase it, the teacher in question would often respond by describing performance objectives, "We're doing addition (or multiplication, or decimals, etc.)." When I asked next, "What is it about addition (or multiplication or decimals) that you want your students to understand?" the answer was once again couched in behavioral terms. It wasn't until I had several such conversations with several teachers that I realized that nothing in their training or in their professional experience had prepared them to ask the sorts of questions I was asking, let alone answer them.

To be sure, the Principals and Standards for School Mathematics (NCTM, 2000) is replete with answers to the definition question, with a different facet of what math competence entails addressed on each of the several hundred pages of this manual. This document, as well as state and district versions of it, is available in all the schools in which I have worked but it hasn't yet had the desired impact. For a reader who has yet to construct a definition of what math competence is, the hundreds of answers provided in these manuals make it exceedingly difficult to see the forest for the trees.

The Development Paradox

We know from pioneering work in cognitive neuropsychology and infant cognition that human infants are born with brain structures that are specifically attuned to numerical quantities and that have a long evolutionary history (Dehaene, 1997). These structures permit infants, for example, to distinguish a set of two objects from a set of three objects in the first few days of life (Antell & Keating, 1983); to match a set of three sounds to a set of three objects at six months (Starkey, Spelke, & Gelman, 1990); and to anticipate the results of transformations in small sets as early as five months; that is, to register surprise if two puppets are placed behind a screen in sequence and only one is present when the screen is raised and, conversely, to show the same surprise response if one puppet is withdrawn from two that have been placed behind a screen and two puppets are present when the screen is raised (Wynn, 1992). Whether one accepts the strong interpretation of these findings (i.e., that infants have an innate ability to represent number and to perform simple arithmetic) or prefers a weaker interpretation (i.e., that infants have a remarkable attunement to the magnitude of small sets), it is clear that a strong foundation for number sense is present in the earliest months of life.

Dehaene (1997) suggests that a quantitative representation, inherited from our evolutionary past, underlies our intuitive understanding of number. He proposes further that these quantitative representations may take the form of analog magnitudes—line segments for example—with a different group of neurons involved in coding different quantities so that if you think of the quantity that is about six, for instance, a certain population of neurons will light up (reported in Kunzig, 1997). While the latter claim is speculative at this point, it is clear that the foundations of number sense that have just been described are independent of language and are supported by brain structures that are dedicated to spatial processing (i.e., the parietal regions) and that are at least partially independent of the brain structures (i.e., the left temporal lobe) that support verbal processing (Dehaene & Cohen, 1995).

In the remaining preschool years, young children expand the quantitative competencies that have just been described; acquire language and with it, the ability to count; and become capable of demonstrating a range of math competencies—numerical estimation, comparison, simple addition and subtraction—that all emerge spontaneously without much explicit instruction. In a subsequent section, I suggest that many of the competencies just mentioned and the foundations for a true "number" sense are made possible by a major revolution in children's thought that occurs around the age of five years when their schemas for counting and their schemas for global quantity comparisons are merged into a single superordinate structure (Griffin & Case, 1997). For now, it is sufficient to point out that children's math competence, and the cognitive and neurological structures that support it, is flourishing and fairly well developed before they start their formal schooling at age six. Most young children take great delight in these achievements and are eager to demonstrate their competence to anyone who will listen as they show, for example, how high they can count, how well they can add, or how cleverly they can solve "an even harder number question" that an adult might pose.

Given this promising start, one might expect that children's math competence and confidence would grow by leaps and bounds when they are exposed to 12 or more years of formal mathematics instruction in school. Alas this is not the case, at least for the majority of high-school graduates who choose elementary or middle school teaching as a profession. To illustrate the fruits of math instruction in U.S. schools, I once again draw on my own experience with prospective teachers because it provides a compelling example. The following quote is a compilation of sentiments expressed by a number of students over a number of years, but it captures the dominant pattern. Note that all students represented in this sample have done well enough in their math courses in high school, as well as on the quantitative portion of the college entrance exams, to gain admittance to a competitive University.

> I know I have to teach math to be a teacher and I really want to be teacher but I have to tell you that I am afraid of math and not very good at it, and the thought of having to teach it really scares me, so I will need all the help I can get in this course and I promise to work as hard as I can. I really hated math for most of the time (or the whole time) I was in school. I know I could do the problems that I will have to teach if you reminded me of the formulas because I did them when I was in school. But I don't really understand why I use them, for fractions in particular, so please, if you possibly can, give me a placement in the early grades. I really like little kids and I think I could do a good job at that level.

What has happened to change the picture children present at five years of age into the picture these young adults present 15 years later? The changes implied in these descriptions feel like arrested development. Given the forward momentum that development typically acquires once it gets rolling, enabling it to overcome a host of obstacles as it seeks to realize its potential, the changes that have just been described could be painted in blacker terms, as negative development, posing a serious paradox that begs for a solution. Although I am not the first to make this point (see, for example, Hiebert, 1986; Dehaene, 1997), given that the problem persists, it bears repeating.

The Instruction Paradox

This paradox has already been flagged in the preceding discussion. All that is necessary here to give it a shape is to acknowledge the caveats that are typically provided when this issue is raised, and to restate it. During the past decade, a host of reasons have been provided to explain the poor performance of American children on international comparisons of mathematics achievement. They include the composition of our society and the great diversity in language, socioeconomic status, and cultural traditions that exist; our commitment to universal education for all children in our society; our belief that schools should be extensions of our communities and, accordingly, that health and human issues (e.g., social and emotional issues) deserve just as much attention as formal training in academic disciplines; the structure of the school day and the frequent interruptions that occur as children are pulled out of the classroom for a range of special programs and services.

A reason that is less commonly cited can be added to this list. Our commitment to local control of schooling has effectively prevented wide-scale research on curriculum effectiveness because the curriculum in use in each school, in each district, in each state is unique: chosen by that community for its purposes. It can and often is changed at will if a new approach appears more promising, creating challenges not only for program evaluation but also for students moving up through, or into, a particular system, who may experience extreme contrasts in the forms of instruction they are exposed to from one year to another.

Although all of these reasons have merit, they don't override the basic paradox. Given the wealth of our nation, our intellectual and technological expertise, and our commitment to education, we ought to be able to craft (or adopt) a form of mathematics instruction for our schools that is more effective, for more of our children. I suggested earlier that the paradoxes exist (and persist) because we haven't yet gotten to the heart of the problem. In the remaining sections of this paper, I examine each of the three questions posed in this paper at the most basic level possible, in an effort to uncover a truth or a pattern that lies at its core.

WHAT IS MATH COMPETENCE?

Any answer to the question of what math competence is, rests, fundamentally, on the way we define the discipline itself. Although a formal definition of mathematics may not be readily available to most of us, on the basis of our own mathematics learning experiences we have all constructed a core set of intuitions regarding the nature of the subject, the optimal way to learn it, and the role the teacher should play as a teacher of this subject. These "core images" of the discipline are believed to exert a profound and often unconscious influence on the ways we define math competence, on the ways teachers interpret a broad range of information on the subject (e.g., texts and teaching tools), and on the approaches teachers adopt to teach it in their own classrooms (Griffin & Case, 1997).

The core image that has guided mathematics instruction for most of the past century can be summarized as follows: *Math is a fixed body of knowledge involving numbers, and their manipulation via rules and algorithms* (Jackson, 1986). With this view of mathematics, it is not surprising that teachers have focused their instruction on ensuring their children know the rules and how to apply them, and have treated numbers, essentially, as disembodied entities.

Although numbers and algorithms are clearly involved in the business of doing math, they are not, by a long shot, the whole story. In an effort to expand this view of the discipline and the form of instruction it inspired, the NCTM (1989) urged a move away from facts and procedures and toward an emphasis on number sense. This was widely accepted by the math education community as a move in the right direction but it posed a number of problems. Many teachers didn't know what number sense was, let alone how to teach it. This issue, too, has been systematically addressed over the past decade and three core features of number sense are now widely acknowledged: (1) can use procedures in a flexible fashion (e.g., can switch the order of addends to make computation easier); (2) can use benchmark values (e.g., when adding 18 and 19, can round each up to 20, add 20+20, and take 3 away from the sum); and (3) understands the magnitude of numbers (e.g., that 31 is larger than 29; that 1/3 is larger than 1/4).

Although these refinements on the core image of mathematics are a definite improvement on the earlier view, with the exception of the last feature (i.e., understands the magnitude of numbers), they still focus exclusively on numbers and algorithms and thus, miss the boat in a fundamental way. The argument I want to make here is that, contrary to popular belief, math is not *about* numbers. It is *about* quantity. And it's only when we know what something is about and what it can be used for that it gains any real meaning for us. Although this notion underpins many of the recommendations for reform in mathematics education (NCTM, 2000), many teachers have yet to grasp this fundamental fact. By ignoring the quantity component in our views and in our descriptions of the discipline, we are essentially treating math as a meaningless endeavor. This is especially problematic given the findings from cognitive neuropsychology that were reported in the previous section. If children's earliest intuitions about numbers are rooted in quantitative representations and are supported by brain structures dedicated to spatial processing, as the evidence strongly suggests (Dehaene, 1997), we are essentially cutting our children off at the knees when we teach math in school as a discipline that is divorced from quantity.

To lay a foundation for a solution and a possible resolution of the paradoxes described in previous sections, a new core image of the discipline is needed: one that explicitly captures the quantity component. Something like the following may offer a start: *Math is a set of conceptual relations between quantities and numerical symbols.* If an image such as this could be made salient in the teacher's perceptions of the discipline, they would have a much greater chance of implementing the recommended reforms and of creating their own. It would encourage teachers to ask a different set of questions in their classrooms (e.g., "What are numbers?" as opposed to "What are the rules for manipulating numbers?") and to create a different set of practices: ones that focus on constructing and discovering relationships between quantities and numbers (as opposed to knowing and applying rules) and ones that provide a rich forum for children to examine alternative ways of describing and recording these relationships (as opposed to finding the right answer or using the right rule). (See Griffin & Case, 1997, for a more detailed description of this image and the practices it supports.)

Evidence that this image is not yet salient in the conceptions of many teachers is provided in the ways they themselves approach mathematical problem solving. In a study conducted by Post et al. (1991), only 50% of middle school teachers achieved success on the following problem: Order from smallest to largest: 2/3, 5/8, 1/4, 3/5, 3/4, 3/8. The failure of the remaining 50% suggests that, for these teachers, the numbers in the problem were not associated with particular quantities, did not have a magnitude that could be visualized or imagined and thus, could not be easily rank-ordered by size. Many teachers also failed to use procedures they were familiar with (i.e., converting numbers to decimals or to equivalent fractions) as a fall back option, suggesting that the central request of the problem—to connect numbers to quantities—was one that did not hold a great deal of meaning.

An even more compelling example is provided by the problem illustrated in Figure 1.1. In this problem, the quantities to which the numbers are to be connected are made available in the problem situation. The quantities are easy enough for a child to see and to label (e.g., the big square, the shaded part of the big square). And yet, an even larger propor-

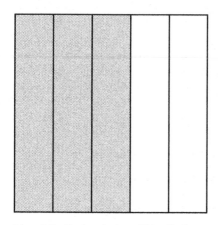

For each problem, identify the whole and identify the part asked for:
    (a) Can you see 3/5 of something?
    (b) Can you see 5/3 of something?
    (c) Can you see 3/5 of 5/3?
    (d) Can you see 2/3 of 3/5?
    (e) Can you see 1 ÷ 3/5?

Figure 1.1.   Can you see 3/5 problem.

tion of teachers are unable, not only to solve the problems posed, but even to make sense of the questions (Post et al., 1991). If 3/5 is seen as a quantity—something that is less than one whole and somewhat bigger than one-half—it is easy to see 3/5 in the figure: It is the shaded part of the big square (taken to be the whole in this case). Similarly, if 5/3 is seen as a quantity—something that is greater that one whole by about two-thirds—it is easy to see 5/3 in the figure: It is the big square (with the shaded part taken to be the whole in this case). In short, the essential task in this set of problems is connecting numbers to quantities. The fact that this task is so difficult for so many educated adults suggests that they have had little experience constructing or discovering these relationships, i.e., engaging meaningfully in the business of doing math.

To conclude this section, I offer my own core image of the discipline (Figure 1.2). It was suggested to me years ago by Robbie Case (personal communication) and it has scaffolded my own understanding of what math competence is, how it develops, and how it can best be fostered in school settings. As illustrated in Figure 1.2, mathematics comprises three worlds: the world of real quantities that exist in space and time; the world of counting numbers (i.e., spoken language); and the world of formal symbols (e.g., written numerals and operation signs). Math competence rests fundamentally on the construction of a rich set of relationships among these worlds. As described in the following section and illustrated with dotted lines in the figure, in the course of development the first set of relationships children construct is between the world of real quantities and the world of counting numbers. It is only when this is successfully achieved and this integrated knowledge network is connected to the world of formal symbols, that this formal world gains any meaning. To teach math competence, it is imperative that these three worlds be continually available in the learning experiences

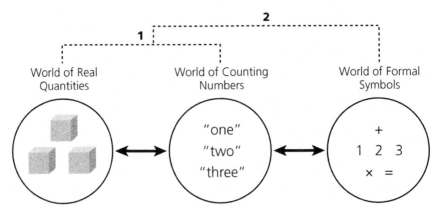

Figure 1.2.   Core image of mathematics.

provided in order to give students a rich set of opportunities to discover and to construct relationships among them, at higher and higher levels of complexity. This is discussed in greater detail in the final sections of this paper.

HOW DOES MATH COMPETENCE DEVELOP?

The development of math competence rests, fundamentally, on the development of cognitive structures that permit a child to interpret the world of quantity and number in increasingly sophisticated ways, to acquire new knowledge in this domain (e.g., to benefit from learning opportunities provided in school), and to solve the range of problems that the domain presents. For the past 15 years, in cognitive developmental research conducted with Robbie Case and informed by neo-Piagetian theory (Case, 1985, 1992), I have examined the knowledge structures of children who succeed in school. Our subjects were the typical subjects of developmental research, drawn from university lab schools and suburban communities: i.e., children who have had a reasonable level of exposure to the opportunities our society offers. Drawing on our own research and that of several other investigators (e.g., Fuson, 1988; Gelman, 1978; Ginsburg & Russell, 1981; Resnick, 1983; Siegler & Robinson, 1982) we identified a set of central conceptual structures for four age levels (4, 6, 8, and 10 years) that we believe underlies successful learning of arithmetic (Case & Griffin, 1990; Griffin, Case, & Siegler, 1994; Griffin, Case, & Capodilupo, 1995; Griffin & Case, 1996, 1997; Case, Griffin, & Kelley, 1999).

In the publications just cited, we have described these structures in increasingly complex ways to illustrate our growing understanding of the complex knowledge networks each entails, and to present evidence that these structures are, as hypothesized (a) central to children's performance on a broad range of quantitative tasks, and (b) foundational for future learning. My goal in this chapter is to describe each structure in much simpler terms in order to illuminate (a) the sorts of things children can and cannot do with each structure (e.g., the sorts of problems children are capable of solving), and (b) the math concepts it would make sense to teach at each age/grade level to ensure that the learning experiences that are provided are finely tuned to children's growing understanding.

To achieve this, I provide two forms of information to scaffold my discussion. The first is an abstract image of the four structures, which provides a broad overview of the developmental progression and the form these structures assume at each successive age level (Figure 1.3). The second is a set of developmental tests—the Number Knowledge test, the Time Knowledge test, and the Money Knowledge test—that were used in our research to identify and define these structures. These tests provide concrete illustra-

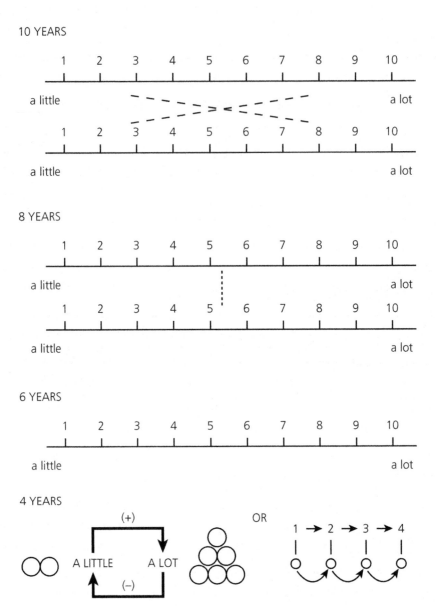

Figure 1.3.   Development of children's central conceptual structure for whole numbers from 4 to 10 years of age.

tions of the sorts of problems children are capable of solving, at four age levels, in three quantitative domains—the domains of number, time, and money—and they are presented here in their entirety for the age levels under consideration (Tables 1.1, 1.2, and 1.3). In the ensuing discussion, I refer first to the figure and use it to provide a brief overview of the manner in which these structures develop. In the more detailed descriptions of each age level structure that follow, I draw heavily from items on the developmental tests, as well as from Siegler and Robinson's (1982) balance beam task, to illustrate the competencies children are able to demonstrate at each age level and to flesh out the bare-bones description of these structures that is provided in the figure.

The developmental tests that are presented here were originally developed in the 1980s (see Case & Griffin, 1990; Griffin, Case, & Sandieson, 1992) to test central postulates of neo-Piagetian theory. They have been substantially modified over the years on the basis of our research and subjected to developmental scaling techniques to ensure that all items at each age level are ones that reflect age level capabilities; i.e., the majority of children at that age level and at all higher age levels achieve success on these items while the majority of children at younger age levels fail these items. The versions presented here are the current versions of these tests and, with the exception of minor differences in Level 0 items on the Number Knowledge test, were used in the research reported in the final section of this paper.

Table 1.1.   Number Knowledge Test

Level 0 (4-year old level): Go to Level 1 if 3 or more correct.

1	Can you count these chips and tell me how many there are? (Place 3 counting chips in front of child in a row)
2a	(Show stacks of chips, 5 vs. 2, same color). Which pile has more?
2b	(Show stacks of chips, 3 vs. 7, same color). Which pile has more?
3a	This time I'm going to ask you which pile has less. (Show stacks of chips, 2 vs. 6, same color). Which pile has less?
3b	(Show stacks of chips, 8 vs. 3, same color). Which pile has less?
4	I'm going to show you some counting chips (Show a line of 3 red and 4 yellow chips in a row, as follows: R Y R Y R Y Y). Count just the yellow chips and tell me how many there are.
5	Pick up all chips from the previous question. Then say: Here are some more counting chips (Show mixed array [not in a row] of 7 yellow and 8 red chips). Count just the red chips and tell me how many there are.

Level 1 (6-year-old level): Go to Level 2 if 5 or more correct.

1	If you had 4 chocolates and someone gave you 3 more, how many chocolates would you have altogether?
2	What number comes right after 7?
3	What number comes two numbers after 7?
4a	Which is bigger: 5 or 4?
4b	Which is bigger: 7 or 9?

Table 1.1.   Number Knowledge Test (Cont.)

5a	This time, I'm going to ask you about smaller numbers. Which is smaller: 8 or 6?
5b	Which is smaller: 5 or 7?
6a	Which number is closer to 5: 6 or 2? (Show visual array after asking question)
6b	Which number is closer to 7: 4 or 9? (Show visual array after asking question)
7	How much is 2+4? (OK to use fingers for counting)
8	How much is 8 take away 6? (OK to use fingers for counting)
9a	(Show visual array - 8 5 2 6 - and ask child to point to and name each numeral). When you are counting, which of these numbers do you say first?
9b	When you are counting, which of these numbers do you say last?

Level 2 (8-year-old level): Go to Level 3 if 5 or more correct

1	What number comes 5 numbers after 49?
2	What number comes 4 numbers before 60?
3a	Which is bigger: 69 or 71?
3b	Which is bigger: 32 or 28?
4a	This time I'm going to ask you about smaller numbers. Which is smaller: 27 or 32?
4b	Which is smaller: 51 or 39?
5a	Which number is closer to 21: 25 or 18? (Show visual array after asking the question)
5b	Which number is closer to 28: 31 or 24? (Show visual array after asking the question)
6	How many numbers are there in between 2 and 6? (Accept either 3 or 4)
7	How many numbers are there in between 7 and 9? (Accept either 1 or 2)
8	(Show card 12 54) How much is 12+54?
9	(Show card 47 21) How much is 47 take away 21?

Level 3 (10-year-old level):

1	What number comes 10 numbers after 99?
2	What number comes 9 numbers after 999?
3a	Which difference is bigger: the difference between 9 and 6 or the difference between 8 and 3?
3b	Which difference is bigger: the difference between 6 and 2 or the difference between 8 and 5?
4a	Which difference is smaller: the difference between 99 and 92 or the difference between 25 and 11?
4b	Which difference is smaller: the difference between 48 and 36 or the difference between 84 and 73?
5	(Show card, "13, 39") How much is 13 + 39?
6	(Show card, "36, 18") How much is 36 – 18?
7	How much is 301 take away 7?

Table 1.2.   Time Knowledge Test

Level 0 (4-year-old level): Go to Level 1 if 3 or more correct.

1   Suppose your parent tells you that you can play with your favorite toy for one minute. Is that a long time or a short time?

2   Now I'm going to draw 2 lines. Watch me. [Make 2 lines of equal length, drawing one very slowly and the other very quickly]. Which one took a long time to make?

3a   Which is longer: one hour, one minute, or are they the same?

3b   Which is shorter: one hour, one minute, or are they the same?

4   Can you tell me something that happens early in the morning at your house?

5   This clock says 2 o'clock. See the hour hand is here? Now I'm going to change it. [Demonstrate in front of child.] Now it says 5 o'clock. [Change again to 3 o'clock in full view of child.] Can you tell me what time this is?

Level 1 (6-year-old level): Go to Level 2 if 3 or more correct.

1a   Suppose I tell you I'll come to your house at 6 o'clock. I get there at 5 o'clock. Am I early or late?

1b   Suppose I tell you I'll come to your house at 3 o'clock. I get there at 4 o'clock. Am I early or late?

2a   [Show analog clock reading 4:00] What time is this?

2b   [Show analog clock reading 4:30] What this is this?

3a   [Show analog clock reading 9:00] What time is this?

3b   [Show analog clock reading 9:30] What time is this?

4   [Show analog clock reading 6:00] If it's 6 o'clock now, how long until 7 o'clock?

5   Pretend you're taking a car trip and the car clock says 3 o'clock. [Show analog clock reading 3:00] You ask your mother, "How much longer till we get there?" and your mother says, "Two hours". What time will it be when you get there?

Level 2 (8-year-old level): Go to Level 3 if 3 or more correct.

1   Suppose I wait in line for 30 minutes, and then I wait for another 30 minutes. How long have I waited altogether? [If child says 60 minutes, ask "Can you think of another way to say that?"]

2a   Which is longer: 1 hour and 50 minutes or 2 hours and 1 minute?

2b   Which is longer: 2 hours and 5 minutes or 1 hour and 45 minutes?

3   [Show analog clock reading 2:15] What time is this?

4   [Show analog clock reading 4:10] What time is this?

5   [Show analog clock reading 3:40] If it's 3:40 now, how long until 4 o'clock?

6   [Show analog clock 6:10] If it is 6:10 now, how long until 7:00 o'clock?

Level 3 (10-year-old level):

1   If it is 7:20 now, how long until 9:45?

2   If it is 10:50 now, how long until 11:25?

Table 1.2.   Time Knowledge Test (Cont.)

3	[Show child analog clock reading 1:08] What time is this?
4	[Show child analog clock reading 2:58] What time is this?
5	It took John 90 minutes to go to school from home. It took him only an hour and a half to come home from school. Can you explain why?
6a	Which is longer: two hours or 90 minutes?
6b	Which is longer: 70 minutes or an hour and five minutes?
7	If you leave on a trip at 8:40 and the trip takes 30 minutes, what time will you arrive?

Table 1.3.   Money Knowledge Test

Level 0 (4-year-old level): Go to Level 2 if 3 or more correct.

1a	Which is worth more: a dollar or a penny?
1b	Which is worth less: a dollar or a penny?
2a	Does a car cost a lot or a little?
2b	Does a piece of gum cost a lot or a little?
3a	If you buy a toy that costs a lot and you give the man a little, will he ask you for more money or will he give you some back?
3b	If you buy a toy that costs a little and you give the man a lot, will he ask you for more money or will he give you some back?
4	Here's one bunch of pennies [show 2 pennies] and here's another bunch [show 8 pennies]. Which bunch is worth more?
5	Here's one set of dollars [show 5 $1 bills] and here's another set [show 2 $1 bills]. Which is worth more?

Level 1 (6-year-old level): Go to Level 2 if 3 or more correct.

1	I'm going to show you some money. [Show $5, $1, $2.] Which is worth the most?
2	If I give you this [show $5 bill] and this [show 2 $1 bills] how much money did I give you altogether?
3	Suppose you go to a store to buy a candy and you want to buy this candy. [Show real piece of candy with price on it.] This candy costs 5 cents but you only have 4 cents. How much more money do you need to buy the candy?
4	This time you want to buy this candy. [Show real piece of candy with price on it.] This candy costs 7 cents and you give the owner 10 cents. How much change do you get back?
5a	[Show a dime and a nickel.] Which is worth more?
5b	[Show a dime and a penny.] Which is worth less?
6a	[Show 1 $5 bill and 2 $1 bills.] Which is worth more?
6b	[Show 3 $1 bills and 1 $5 bill.] Which is worth less?

Table 1.3.   Money Knowledge Test (Cont.)

Level 2 (8-year-old level): Go to Level 3 if 2 or more correct.

1	[Show no objects.] If I give you a dime and then I give you 6 more cents, how much have I given you altogether?
2	[Show a $5 bill with 1 cent and a $1 bill with approximately 21 cents.] Which is worth more?
3	[Show bike picture with price tag.] Suppose you want to buy this bike. It costs $60.00. You have $45.00. How much more money do you need?
4a	[Show a nickel and a dime.] Which is closer to 8 cents [show a nickel and 3 pennies] a nickel or a dime?
4b	[Show a quarter and a dime.] Which is closer to 19 cents [show a dime, a nickel and 4 pennies]: a quarter or a dime?

Level 3 (10-year-old level):

1	If I give you 2 quarters and then I give you 4 quarters, how much is it worth altogether? [How many cents have I given you?]
2a	[Show visual array.] Which closer to $25.35: $20 or $30?
2b	[Show visual array.] Which is closer to $46.45: $46 or $47?
3a	[Show visual array.] Which is closer to $40: $29.95 or $61.05?
3b	[Show visual array.] Which is closer to $15: $9.95 or $19.95?
4a	[Show two groups of coins.] Suppose you have a quarter and a dime and I have 4 dimes. Who has more money: you (child) or me (tester)?
4b	[Show two groups of coins.] Suppose you have 3 quarters and I have 5 dimes and 2 nickels. Who has more money: you (child) or me (tester)?
5	Your hot lunch cost $3.45 and you gave the cook a $20 bill and 2 quarters. How much change should you receive?

Turning now to the figure, the developmental progression it was meant to capture can be summarized as follows. At four years of age, children have two structures available—a schema for making global quantity comparisons (e.g., saying which of two quantities is a lot or a little) and a schema for counting small sets of objects (e.g., saying the counting words as you touch each object in turn)—which are not yet linked. At this age, therefore, they are able to apply one *or* the other of these structures at any one time. At six years, these two "precursor" structures have become integrated into a single super-ordinate structure in which numbers, conceptualized as an ordered series of number words, are intimately linked to quantities and used to determine which of two quantities is a little or a lot. At this age, therefore, they know that small number indicate a little, and big numbers indicate a lot, and each counting word they say up in the sequence means that a set has been increased by one. At eight years, this single integrated structure is differentiated into two such structures, allowing children to use numbers to make quantity determinations along two quantitative variables (e.g., tens and ones in the number system; hours and minutes in the time system; dollars and cents in the money system). At 10 years, the two components of the differentiated structure are more fully integrated, allowing children to make compensations along one quantitative variable to allow for changes along the other.

Figure 1.3 also reflects, albeit invisibly, core assumptions of the general theory (i.e., Central Conceptual Structure theory; see Case & Griffin, 1990; Case & Okamoto, 1996) on which this developmental progression was based. Three assumptions that have particular relevance for education are worth mentioning here before we turn to a detailed description of each structure.

1. In keeping with most other modern theories of intellectual development, it is assumed that a major reorganization occurs in children's thought around the age of five years when cognitive structures that were constructed during the previous stage are hierarchically integrated. This marks the beginning of a new stage of development in which the higher-order unit of thought that was created by this process is itself gradually differentiated (between the ages of 7 and 9 years) and progressively elaborated (between the ages of 9 and 11 years). The complex structure that is thus created provides a building block for the next stage of development that occurs around 11 years.

2. Important changes in cognitive structures are presumed to occur about every two years during this period of development. The ages provided in the figure mark the mid point of these stages and are meant to indicate, for example, that children acquire the 4-year-old structure sometime between the ages of three and five years and the 6-year-old structure sometime between the ages of five and seven years, etc.

3. The theory assumes that the developmental pattern illustrated in the figure is typical for the majority of children in developed societies (e.g., 60%). This means that 20% of children may show a faster rate of development than is indicated in the figure and 20% may show a slower rate. For all children, however, development is presumed to proceed according to the sequence shown, with each higher-order structure dependent on the acquisition of the previous structure.

The 4-year-old Structures

By the age of four years, children have constructed two structures—a global quantity schema and an initial counting schema—that are the culmination of their development in this domain in the preschool years and that provide the building blocks for the major reorganization that follows.

Global Quantity Schema

At four years of age, children's understanding of quantity shows a marked advance over the understandings demonstrated in infancy and described in a previous section. They are now able to recognize, as well as to describe, global differences in quantity along a number of variables. As illustrated by Level 0 items on the developmental tests (Tables 1.1, 1.2, and 1.3), they can tell which of two stacks of chips has more or less (Number Test); which of two time units (e.g., an hour and a minute) is longer or shorter (Time Test); and which of two monetary units (e.g., a dollar and a penny) is worth more or less (Money Test). When presented with two stacks of weights on a balance scale, they are also able to tell which is heavier or lighter and which side of the beam will go down (Balance Beam Task). At this age, children rely on perception rather than counting to make these determinations and, if the differences between the sets are not perceptually salient, the sets are judged to be equivalent (i.e., "the same"). At this age, children can also recognize that a set gets bigger if one or more items are added and smaller if one or more items are taken away but, once again, they rely on perceptual features rather than counting to make these determinations. See Tables 1.1–1.3, Level 0, for additional examples of 4-year-old quantitative competencies.

Initial Counting Schema

By the age of four years, children have also acquired some fairly sophisticated counting skills. They know that each number word occurs in a fixed and necessary sequence; they know that each number word must be assigned to one and only one object in a set; and they know that the last number word said indicates the size of the set. They can rote count from one to five (or one to ten) with ease and, when shown a mixed array of seven yellow and eight red chips, they can count just the red chips and tell how many there are (Number Test, Level 0). Although children have these counting competencies at their disposal, they don't typically use them at this age to make the quantity determinations described above. It is as if their counting schemas and their global quantity schemas are stored in two separate files (or two separate regions of the brains) that are not yet connected. All this changes when children make the progression to the next developmental stage.

The 6-year-old Structure

By the age of six years, children have integrated their global quantity schema and their initial counting schema into a super-ordinate structure—a single "mental counting line" (see Figure 1.3)—that gives them tremendous leverage in making sense of the quantitative world and that is called, for this reason, a *central conceptual structure for whole numbers*. With this higher-order knowledge structure, children come to realize that numbers that are higher up in the counting sequence indicate larger quantities than numbers that are lower down and that numbers themselves have magnitude (e.g., 9 is bigger than 7; see Number Test, Level 1). They also realize that a question about addition or subtraction can be answered, in the absence of any concrete set of objects, simply by counting forward or backward along the counting string. Thus, they are able to handle hypothetical verbal statement such as "if you had four chocolates and someone gave you three more" (Number Test, Level 1) with ease, simply by starting at four and counting up three more. They do not even need to see the objects that are involved or know anything else about them. These simple understandings actually betoken a major revolution in children's understanding which changes the world of mathematics from something that can only occur "out there" to something that can occur inside their own heads and under their own control.

As this change takes place, children begin to use their counting skills in a wide range of other contexts. In effect, children realize that counting is something one can do to determine the relative value of two object or two sets on a wide variety of dimensions. For example, they realize that the counting numbers (and their associated symbols) can be used to read the hour hand on the clock to tell what time it is (Time Test); to judge which of three bills that are identical in size (a $5 bill, a $1 bill, and a $2 bill) is worth the most (Money Test); and to figure out that, even though a nickel is bigger than a dime, a dime is worth more (Money Test). Unlike 4-year-olds, they also spontaneously apply their counting skills to stacks of weights on the balance scale that look similar in size (e.g., 5 versus 4) to determine which has the most and which side of the beam will go down (Balance Beam Task). See Tables 1.1–1.3, Level 1, for additional examples of 6-year-old competencies. Although these changes are impressive, at this age children are able to apply their number understandings to only one quantitative dimension at a time.

The 8-year-old Structure

By the age of eight years, children have differentiated their central conceptual structure into a double "mental counting line" (see Figure 1.3) which permits them to represent two quantitative variables in a loosely coordinated fashion. With this more complex structure, they are able to understand place value (e.g., to represent the tens dimension and the ones dimension in our base ten system and work with these dimensions in a coordinated fashion); to mentally solve double-digit addition problems (e.g., 12+54); and to tell which of two double-digit numbers (e.g., 69 or 71) is bigger or smaller (Number Test, Level 2). In solving the last problem mentioned, they are able to avoid the mistake that is commonly made by younger children; that is, to focus exclusively on the "ones" value, to judge 9 to be bigger than 1 and to choose 69 as the answer. This new structure also permits children to read hours *and* minutes on a clock (Time Test); to solve problems that involve two monetary dimensions such as dollars *and* cents (Money Test); and to solve balance beam problems in which distance from the fulcrum, as well as number of weights, must be computed to judge which side of the beam will go down (Balance Beam Task). See Tables 1.1–1.3, Level 2, for additional examples of 8-year-old competencies.

The 10-year-old Structure

By the age of 10 years, children have elaborated their 8-year-old structure into a fully integrated structure which permits them to represent two quantitative variables in a well-coordinated fashion and/or to handle three quantitative variables. With this new structure—the culmination of development in this stage—they acquire a well-developed understanding of the whole number system and are able, for example, to perform mental computations with double-digit numbers that involve borrowing and carrying (e.g., 13 + 39) and to solve arithmetic problems involving triple-digit numbers (Number Test, Level 3). With this new structure, they are also able to translate from one time dimension (e.g., hours) to another (e.g., minutes) to determine which of two times (e.g., two hours or 90 minutes) is longer (Time Test); to translate from one monetary dimension (e.g., quarters) to another (e.g., dimes and nickels) to determine who has more money (Money Test); and to solve Balance Beam problems in which number of weights and distance from the fulcrum both vary and some compensation between these variables is required to determine which side of the beam will go down. See Tables 1.1–1.3, Level 3, for additional examples of 10-year-old competencies.

The developmental progression that has just been described suggests that significant change occurs in children's central conceptual structure for whole numbers over the age range of 4 to 10 years, permitting them to solve an increasingly sophisticated set of problems in a variety of quantitative domains. How can we account, therefore, for the developmental paradox that was described in an earlier section? If a majority of children in our society start their formal schooling at age 6 with a well developed central conceptual structure for whole number and if that structure is progressively enhanced over the next four years, as the preceding discussion suggests, why do so many of our children emerge from high school feeling weak and largely incompetent in math? Two sets of findings and one conjecture provide a possible answer for this puzzle.

First, although the pattern just described is typical for the majority of children who succeed in school math and who have had a reasonable level of exposure to the opportunities our society presents, there are many children—a majority in some communities—who are exceptions to this rule. There is now ample evidence to suggest that a substantial minority of American children—living most frequently in low socioeconomic (SES) communities—start school without the central conceptual structure in place (Griffin, Case, & Siegler, 1994; Case, Griffin, & Kelley, 1999). If opportunities for children to connect their understanding of quantity to their understanding of number are not provided in school (as was suggested in a previous section), and if such a connection is actively discouraged by an exclusive focus on numbers referents, these children may be lost from the start. Although they may master the rules, math may seem from the start like a meaningless endeavor.

Second, the foundations for the development progression that was just described were laid in the preschool years and are thus relatively independent of schooling. Factors that have been proposed to account for the early development of math competence and to support it include a variety of specific experiences provided at home, such as opportunities to count and relate sets numerically, and the presence of board games in the home (Starkey, Klein, & Sloan, 1993). The foundations for the next stage of development—mastery of the rational number system—are laid in the school age years (i.e., between 6 and 10 years) and are thus highly dependent on schooling. If schools don't provide opportunities for children to link these numbers (e.g., fractions) to quantities and to construct, for example, the central conceptual structure for rational numbers (Moss & Case, 1999), this set of connections may not be acquired. Our society provides fewer supports for this conceptual endeavor than was the case for whole number understanding.

Third and finally, there is evidence in children's performance on the developmental tests (Tables 1.1–1.3) that the sorts of instruction children are exposed to during the school age years are not well attuned to their growing understanding of number and thus, may hinder rather than support this development. Three examples are provided here to illustrate this point.

> *Example 1:*   Although all children use their fingers at a certain point in their development to solve single-digit mental arithmetic problems (Number Test, Level 1), some children do so surreptitiously, hiding their fingers under the table and blushing if this act is witnessed. The belief that it is wrong to use fingers for this sort of task deprives them of the full use of the tools God or nature gave them to represent quantities, to count the quantities displayed, and to make sense of numbers.

> *Example 2:*   When solving double-digit mental arithmetic problems such as 12 + 54 (Number Test, Level 2), many more children fail to use their understanding of tens and ones to compute the answer by, for example, rounding the 12 to 10; adding 10 to 54; and then adding 2. Instead they try to create a mental image of the numbers stacked on top of each other in the typical worksheet format they have been exposed to in school. They then add the numbers in the first column, remember the sum, add the numbers in the second column, remember the sum, and add the two sums together to get the answer. This procedure not only deprives them of full use of a conceptual structure (i.e., the 8-year-old structure) they are able to apply on other tasks, it also makes this task exceedingly cumbersome to solve and makes errors in computation much more likely.

> *Example 3:*   Although children's cognitive development makes it easy for them to learn to tell the time by hours and minutes when they are 7–8 years old and in grade 2 (described in a previous section), many teachers spend an inordinate amount of time attempting to teach this skill to first graders because it is mandated by state or district curriculum guidelines. This practice not only deprives students of meaningful instruction that is better attuned to their level of understanding, it also exposes them to needless frustration and failure in the process.

Taken together, the three explanations that have been provided for the developmental paradox in the foregoing discussion point to one conclusion: the need to provide more opportunities to connect numbers and quantities in school, in rich and meaningful ways, and in ways that are finely attuned to children's growing understanding. This is the subject of the next section of this paper.

HOW CAN MATH COMPETENCE BE FOSTERED IN SCHOOL SETTINGS?

In the previous sections, a number of "first principles" of math learning and cognitive development have been implied or explicitly mentioned. To provide an interim summary of these principles and to highlight the theoretical foundations for the instructional strategies that are described next, five of the important ones are listed below.

1. Mathematics comprises three worlds: the world of real quantities, the world of counting numbers, and the world of formal symbols.
2. Math competence rests, fundamentally, on the construction of a rich set of relationships among these worlds.
3. Math knowledge is constructed by the individual, through exploration and active participation in physical and social environments, and with the help of a mentor or guide who can point out salient features.
4. Development proceeds in an invariant sequence, by a process of differentiation and hierarchic integration in which new forms of thought (e.g., the central conceptual structures for whole number) build on and incorporate previous forms of thought.
5. Individuals use their current forms of thought to make sense of the experiences they are exposed to.

Three broad strategies for instruction that can be derived from this list are described next, as well as several specific strategies that can be subsumed under each broad category. Each instructional strategy (or principle) is illustrated with examples from an early mathematics program for young children called Number Worlds (Griffin & Case, 1995; Griffin, 1996, 1997, 2000) that was created to teach the central conceptual structures for whole number and to provide a set of activities for four grade levels (PreK–2) that would enable teachers to put the instructional strategies described below into practice.

Instructional Strategies to Foster the Development of Math Competence

Provide a rich set of activities that expose children to the three worlds of math and that provide opportunities for them to construct relationships among them, at higher and higher levels of complexity.

As may be seen, this strategy flows directly from Principles 1 and 2 above. The Line Land activities that were created for each level of the

Number Worlds program provide a good example of this strategy. It was reasoned that, if children represent number and quantity in the form of a "mental counting line" (as the research suggests), then it makes sense to expose them to a variety of external forms of this sort of representation if one wants to foster the development of this conceptual structure and the understandings it implies. The games and props that were created for this purpose allow children, for example: (a) to move their own bodies along a life-size, numbered Teddy Bear path at the pre-K level; (b) to move a pawn, which serves as a representation of self, along a game-board path numbered from 1 to 10, at the kindergarten level; (c) to move a Magic Shoe pawn that enables them to leap over ten houses in a single bound, along a neighborhood game board displaying a row of 100 numbered houses, at the grade one level; and (d) to move a deliveryman pawn up floors and along corridors on the Hotel game-board, which shows 100 numbered rooms stacked in floors of 10 units each, at the grade two level. As children move through these spatial environments to solve problems posed by the games, they have ample opportunity to discover properties of the number system because this system is fixed in these spatial environments and displayed in a prominent fashion.

As children move through these spatial environments, they are also required by the rules of each game to count out loud—so other players can be sure they don't cheat—and to talk about (e.g., predict, explain) their movements—so they become proficient at using the standard linguistic terms (e.g., the language of distance) for describing quantities in this context. Finally, in most games at the grades one and two levels, children are required to create a written record of their actions (e.g., to use the formal symbol system to record their movements and transactions) that can be used, for example, to determine the winner or to determine who landed on the secret number. As these examples illustrate, this series of games provides ample opportunity for children to construct relationships among the worlds of quantity, counting numbers, and formal symbols, at higher and higher levels of complexity. Note that, although other games and activities included in the program serve the same purpose, they expose children to several other ways of representing number (e.g., as a group of objects, as a dot-set pattern, as a position on a scale). The specific instructional strategies that have been illustrated in this example can be summarized as follow:

- *Representational Congruence.* The props used to accompany these activities should be congruent with (a) the structure of the formal mathematics system, and (b) the structure of children's mental representations of this system.

- *Representational Diversity:* The props used to accompany these activities should expose children systematically to the major ways numbers are represented, talked about, and used in different contexts.
- *Spatial and Numerical Correspondence:* Spatial and numerical operations should correspond with one another.

Provide plenty of opportunity for children to actively explore the concepts you want them to learn and to discuss these ideas in a social context.

This strategy flows directly from Principle 3 above. As was illustrated in the foregoing discussion, most of the activities included in the Number Worlds program are set in a game format. This requires that small groups of 4–5 children work together collaboratively to achieve the game goal and that each child actively participates (e.g., by taking his or her turn, by moving through the environments as the game directs, and by describing his or her movements orally and/or in writing as the game directs). Children are generally motivated to do all of these things because the games are fun and because they want to win. Mathematical communication is not only required by the rules of each game, it is also supported by three devices: Dialogue Prompts provided in the teacher's guide; Question Cards included with the game props; and a Wrap-Up period at the end of each lesson, where children describe what they did that day and what they learned. The specific instructional strategies that have been described here can be summarized as follows:

- *Physical, Social and Verbal Interaction:* The activities should provide opportunities for children to actively interact with the materials and to use the knowledge they are constructing in a variety of ways (e.g., to solve game problems, to communicate with peers).
- *Mathematical Communication:* There should be a good deal of verbal communication about the activities and their mathematical properties.
- *Mathematical Notation:* The mathematical notation system should be represented and used.

Provide a carefully graded sequence of activities that allow children to use their current understandings to construct new understandings at the next level up.

This strategy flows directly from Principles 4 and 5 above. The sequence of activities that was created for the Number Worlds program was also guided by the developmental research reported in a previous section, which provided a finely grained portrait of the manner in which children acquire mathematical understandings and the forms these understandings assume at different age levels. Thus, activities in the pre-K program allow children to use their 4-year-old conceptual structures and to acquire foundational knowledge for the 6-year-old structure. Activities in the kindergarten program allow children to construct and to consolidate the 6-year-old central conceptual structure, etc. Within each grade level program, activities have also been classified at three levels of developmental complexity. Finally, the entire PreK–2 program was designed to provide a seamless sequence of activities that permits children to start at a level that is comfortable for them, and to move through the normal developmental progression at a rate they can keep pace with. The specific instructional strategies that have been illustrated in this example can be summarized as follows:

- *Developmental Sequencing:* The activities should be sequenced in their normal order of developmental acquisition.
- *Developmental Appropriateness:* The program should allow children to move through the normal process of development at a rate they can keep pace with.
- *Conceptual Bridging:* Each activity should provide a "conceptual bridge" between children's current understandings of number and quantity and the central numerical understandings the programs are designed to teach.

Program Effects

The question that naturally arises is: Does a program such as Number Worlds, which is solidly grounded in cognitive developmental theory and research, make a difference in children's math learning and achievement? To answer this question, three groups of children were followed for a three-year period, from the beginning of kindergarten to the end of grade two. The treatment group, drawn from a low SES community, received the Number Worlds program for the entire period; a control group from a low SES community and a normative group from a more advantaged population received a variety of other programs. The Number Knowledge Test (Table 1.1) was administered to all children at the beginning of kindergarten and at the end of each successive grade. A variety of other tests, including the Time Test (Table 1.2) and the Money Test (Table 1.3) were administered to all children as well, at the end of grade two.

The results indicate that the treatment and the control groups started kindergarten at a distinct disadvantage to the normative group. As illustrated in Figure 1.4, their conceptual understanding of number was closer to the 4-year-old level (Level 0 on the Number Test) than to the 6-year-old level (Level 1) at the beginning of school, suggesting that they had not yet acquired the central conceptual structure for whole numbers. By the end of kindergarten and at the end of each successive year, the performance of the treatment group was indistinguishable from the normative group and,

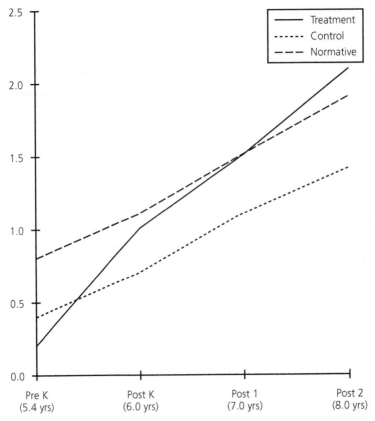

Figure 1.4.   Mean developmental level scores on Number Knowledge test at 4 time periods.

in absolute terms, higher than the normative group at the end of grade two. By contrast, the performance of the control group lagged further and further behind. The same pattern that was found on the Number Test at the end of grade two (illustrated in Figure 1.4) was found on the Time Test as well; namely: the treatment group demonstrated competencies in this domain that were indistinguishable (but higher in absolute terms) from those demonstrated by the normative group, and that were significantly superior to those demonstrated by the control group. On the Money Test, the competencies demonstrated by the treatment group were superior to both other groups. Note that the treatment group had received no instruction in time or money concepts during this period, and exposure to dial representations and to money had been carefully avoided.

Finally, on a Formal Notation Test, which presented children with arithmetic problems (e.g., double-digit subtraction problems, a multiplication problem) that were formally notated in a typical worksheet format, the treatment group outperformed the normative group and this group, in turn, outperformed the control group. These results provide strong evidence that the Number Worlds program enabled a group of at-risk children to acquire the knowledge it was designed to teach; namely: the conceptual understandings of number and quantity implied in the central conceptual structures and assessed on the Number Knowledge Test. The results also show that children who acquired these understandings were able to use them to solve problems on a range of other tasks (e.g., Time Test, Money Test, Formal Notation Test) and in a variety of content domains (e.g., time, money) where no formal instruction had been explicitly provided. This set of findings thus provides strong evidence that the knowledge implied in the central conceptual structures does, indeed, underlie math competence and is essential for its development.

CONCLUSION

The goal of the present paper was to address three questions: What is math competence? How does it develop? How can it be fostered in school settings? A close examination of these questions revealed a paradox at the heart of each which may explain why the desired reforms in mathematics education have been so slow in being realized. In the answers that were provided in this chapter, a resolution for each paradox was offered. For the "definition paradox" it was suggested that our current definition of mathematics fails to capture the essence of what math is and what it is about. Math is not *about* number, it is *about* quantity, and a definition that captures this, such as "math is a set of conceptual relations between quantities and symbols," may go a long way toward helping us teach math more effectively in school.

For the "development paradox," it was suggested that the disjunction between the competence and confidence children demonstrate at the start of school and the lack of both many young adults experience at the end of their formal schooling may be partially explained by the learning experiences they have been exposed to. If these experiences were better attuned to the essential nature of the discipline and to the cognitive structures children have available at different ages to make sense of this discipline, this disjunction may be avoided and increased competence realized.

Finally, it was suggested that the "instruction paradox" may be resolved by implementing forms of math instruction that remedy the problems just mentioned. Research findings on the effectiveness of one such program (i.e., Number Worlds), that provides ample opportunity for children to construct links between quantities and numbers, and that is finely attuned to children's developing understandings, provide evidence that at-risk children can acquire the knowledge needed to thrive in school math, and to compete successfully with their more affluent peers. This program, as well as others that are currently available (see, e.g., Carpenter & Fennema, 1992; Fuson, 1997; Hiebert, 1997; Resnick et al., 1990), demonstrates that it is possible to achieve increased levels of math competence in our nation's schools if appropriate forms of instruction are provided.

AUTHOR NOTE

Address correspondence to: Sharon Griffin, Department of Education, Clark University, 950 Main St., Worcester, MA 01610. Phone: (508) 793-7778; Fax: (508) 793-8864.

REFERENCES

Antell, S.E., & Keating, D.P. (1983). Perception of numerical invariance in neonates. *Child Development, 54,* 695–701.

Carpenter, T.P., & Fennema, E. (1992). Cognitively guided instruction: Building on the knowledge of students and teachers. *International Journal of Research in Education, 17*(5), 457–470.

Case, R. (1985). *Intellectual development: Birth to adulthood.* New York: Academic Press.

Case, R. (1992). *The mind's staircase: Exploring the conceptual underpinnings of children's thought and knowledge.* Hillsdale, NJ: Erlbaum.

Case, R., & Griffin, S. (1990). Child cognitive development: The role of central conceptual structures in the development of scientific and social thought. In E.A. Hauert (Ed.), *Developmental psychology: Cognitive, perceptuo-motor, and neurological perspectives* (pp. 193–230). North-Holland: Elsevier.

Case, R., Griffin, S., & Kelley, W. (1999). Socioeconomic gradients in mathematical ability and their responsiveness to intervention in early childhood. In D. Keating & C. Hertzman (Eds.), *Developmental health and the wealth of nations.* New York: Guilford.

Case, R., Griffin, S., & Kelley, W. (2001). Socioeconomic differences in children's early cognitive development and their readiness for schooling. In S.L. Golbeck (Ed.), *Psychological perspectives on early childhood education.* Hillsdale, NJ: Erlbaum.

Case, R., & Okamoto, Y. (1996). The role of central conceptual structures in the development of children's thought. *Monographs of the Society for research in Child Development, 61* (Serial No. 246).

Dehaene, S. (1997). *The number sense.* New York: Oxford University Press.

Dehaene, S., & Cohen, L. (1995). Towards an anatomical and functional model of number processing. *Mathematical Cognition, 1,* 83–120.

Fuson, K. (1988). *Children's counting and concepts of number.* New York: Springer-Verlag

Fuson, K. (1997). Snapshots across two years in the life of an urban Latino classroom. In J. Hiebert (Ed.), *Making sense: Teaching and learning mathematics with understanding.* Portsmouth, NH: Heinemann

Ginsburg, H.P., & Russell, R. (1981). Social class and racial influence on early mathematical thinking. *Monographs of the society for research in child development, 46* (Serial No. 193).

Griffin, S. (2000). *Number worlds: Preschool level.* Durham, NH: Number Worlds Alliance, Inc.

Griffin, S. (1998). *Number worlds: Grade two level.* Durham, NH: Number Worlds Alliance, Inc.

Griffin, S. (1997). *Number worlds: Grade one level.* Durham, NH: Number Worlds Alliance, Inc.

Griffin, S., & Case, R. (1995). *Number worlds: Kindergarten level.* Durham, NH: Number Worlds Alliance, Inc.

Griffin, S., & Case, R. (1996). Evaluating the breadth and depth of training effects when central conceptual structures are taught. *Society for Research in Child Development Monographs, 59,* 90–113.

Griffin, S., & Case, R. (1997). Re-thinking the primary school math curriculum: An approach based on cognitive science. *Issues in Education, 3*(1), 1–49.

Griffin, S., Case, R., & Capodilupo, A. (1995). Teaching for understanding: The importance of central conceptual structures in the elementary mathematics curriculum. In A. McKeough, I. Lupert, & A. Marini (Eds.), *Teaching for transfer: Fostering generalization in learning* (pp. 121–151). Hillsdale, NJ: Erlbaum.

Griffin, S., Case, R., & Sandieson, R. (1992). Synchrony and asynchrony in the acquisition of children's everyday mathematical knowledge. In R. Case (Ed.), *The mind's staircase: Exploring the conceptual underpinnings of children's thought and knowledge* (pp. 75–97). Hillsdale, NJ: Erlbaum.

Griffin, S., Case, R., & Siegler, R. (1994). Rightstart: Providing the central conceptual prerequisites for first formal learning of arithmetic to students at-risk for school failure. In K. McGilly (Ed.), *Classroom lessons: Integrating cognitive theory and classroom practice* (pp. 24–49). Cambridge, MA: Bradford Books MIT Press.

Hiebert, J. (1997). *Making sense: Teaching and learning mathematics with understanding.* Portsmouth, NH: Heinemann.

Hiebert, J. (1986). *Conceptual and procedural knowledge: The case of mathematics.* Hillsdale, NJ: Erlbaum.

Hunt, E. (1996). *Will we be smart enough? A cognitive analysis of the demands of the workplace in the year 2000.* New York: Russell Sage, Inc.

Jackson, P. (1986). *The practice of teaching.* New York: Teachers College Press.

Kunzig, R. (1997). A head for numbers. *Discover magazine, 18* (7) 108–115.

Moss, J., & Case, R. (1999). Developing children's understanding of rational numbers: A new model and experimental curriculum. *Journal for Research in Mathematics Education, 30*(2), 122–147.

National Assessment of Educational Progress. (1983). *The third national mathematics assessment: Results, trends, and issues.* Denver, CO: Education Commission of the States.

National Assessment of Educational Progress. (1988). National Center for Educational Statistics, U.S. Department of Education, Office of Educational Research and Improvement, Washington, DC.

National Assessment of Educational Progress. (1993). *Can students do mathematical problem-solving?* Education Information Branch, U.S. Department of Education, Office of Educational Research and Improvement, Washington, DC.

National Council of Teachers of Mathematics. (1989). *Curriculum and evaluation standards for school mathematics.* Reston, VA: NCTM

National Council of Teachers of Mathematics. (2000). *Principles and standards for school mathematics.* Reston, VA: NCTM.

Piaget, J. (1952). *The child's conception of number.* New York: Norton.

Piaget, J. (1954). *The construction of reality in the child.* New York: Basic Books.

Piaget, J. (1963). *The psychology of intelligence.* Paterson, NJ: Littlefield, Adams.

Piaget, J. (1970). *Science of education and the psychology of the child.* New York: Viking Press.

Post, T., Harel, G., Behr, M., & Lesh, R. (1991). Intermediate teachers' knowledge of rational number concepts. In E. Fennema, T. Carpenter, & S. Lamon (Eds.), *Integrating research on teaching and learning mathematics.* Albany: State University of New York Press.

Resnick, L. B. (1983). A developmental theory of number understanding. In H.P. Ginsburg (Ed.), *The development of mathematical thinking* (pp. 110–152). New York: Academic Press.

Resnick, L. B., Bill, V., & Lesgold, S. (1990). Developing thinking abilities in arithmetic class. In A. Demetriou, M. Shayer, & A. Afklides (Eds.), *The modern theories of cognitive development go to school.* London: Routledge

Siegler, R.S., & Robinson, M. (1982). The development of numerical understanding. In H.W. Reese & Lipsitt (Eds.), *Advances in child development and behavior.* New York: Academic Press.

Starkey, P., Klein, A., & Sloane, K. (1993). *Preparation for the transition to kindergarten: The Head Start Family Math Project.* Paper presented at the Second National Head Start Research Conference, Washington, DC.

Starkey, P., Spelke, E.S., & Gelman, R. (1990). Numerical abstraction by human infants. *Cognition, 36,* 97–127.

Wynn, K. (1992). Addition and subtraction by human infants. *Nature, 358,* 749–750.

CHAPTER 2

PERSPECTIVES ON MATHEMATICS STRATEGY DEVELOPMENT

Martha Carr and Hillary Hettinger

ABSTRACT

This chapter reviews different types of mathematics strategies and their development. The factors that affect the development of strategy use are then discussed. These factors include conceptual knowledge, the semantic structure of the problem, working memory, contextual effects, fluency, and procedural knowledge. Several theoretical perspectives to the development of mathematics strategies including perspectives from cognitive psychology, constructivism and social constructivism, are then presented. Finally, implications of this research and theory for education are outlined.

INTRODUCTION

Mathematics is seen more and more as a problem solving activity as opposed to the rote calculation skills that have been traditionally thought to comprise mathematics. As a result, the focus of mathematics education is shifting from

Mathematical Cognition, pages 33–68

the instruction of algorithms and simple computation to the instruction of problem solving skills, including the instruction of strategies for problem solving. Children are seen as needing a variety of strategic approaches that will allow them to be flexible in their mathematics problem solving (Davis, 1992). One goal of educational researchers and cognitive psychologists, therefore, is to determine the factors influencing children's acquisition of strategies and the changing role of these factors in the development of strategies. This chapter will present current theoretical approaches to strategy development and discuss the individual factors that are believed to influence the development and form of mathematics strategies.

Research on strategy development is important because strategies provide the means by which children and adults can organize and process increasingly complex information. Specifically, the amount and complexity of the information children must deal with increases at a higher rate than the maturation of the cognitive system. Even in adulthood, our cognitive systems cannot handle the amount of information to which we are exposed without some means of strategically organizing and manipulating that information. Strategies allow us to create symbolic representations of our experiences and to reorganize and compile information into larger, logical units. As we move into the information age and are faced with ever increasing amounts of information, strategies will become more important for making sense of our world.

Research on strategy development also provides insight into the potential diversity of strategy development in response to environmental demands. We are just beginning to learn how strategies develop as a function of individual differences in working memory, contextual influences, domain knowledge, fluency, and problem structure. In observing how strategies emerge within different contexts we can better understand which characteristics of strategy use are "hard wired" in through biology and which characteristics can be manipulated by changing the context within which they are learned.

Mathematics strategies in this chapter will be defined broadly as any method used to solve a mathematics problem. This definition is more in line with Ashcraft's (1990) definition of strategies as "how they are performed mentally." It is less in line with the definition of strategy by Bisanz and LeFevre (1990) who prefer a more constrained use of the term so as to discriminate strategies from other cognitive procedures. Our definition of strategy is similar to that of Bisanz and LeFevre, however, in that we view strategies as flexible and goal-oriented. Strategies must be used with a specific outcome in mind and there must be a selection of possible strategic approaches.

Factors considered to be important for strategy development and use, including procedural knowledge, conceptual knowledge, procedural fluency, context, and the semantic structure of the problems will be discussed. Next, three theoretical perspectives on strategy development will be explored, including cognitive psychology, Piagetian constructivist and social constructivist perspectives. Research from each perspective provides insight into the role and relative importance of different factors as predictors of the development and use of strategies. Finally, we will examine the literature on how strategy development may differ as a function of a learning disability and gender. First, in order to provide a framework for the chapter, the development of strategies for arithmetic, multiplication, division, algebra, and geometry will be outlined briefly.

The Development of Strategies

Addition and subtraction strategies. During the preschool and kindergarten years, addition and subtraction strategies are initially external representations of number through the use of counters or fingers. Early addition strategies utilizing external representations include *counting-all* in which the child represents each number in the problem, counts each set, and then counts both sets together. Children *count-on* using counters or fingers by stating one number of the addition problem and counting on the second number (Carpenter & Moser, 1984). Children also use counters or fingers to represent numbers when first learning to subtract. Children may initially represent all of the numbers and then remove the subtrahend. For example, for 4 − 1, the child may use counters to represent four, remove one counter, and then count the remainder. Children can *add-on* by putting out counters to represent the subtrahend and then adding and counting additional counters until the minuend is reached. Finally, children can use a *matching* procedure in which counters representing the minuend and the subtrahend are lined up next to each other. The answer is determined by counting the unmatched counters in the minuend (Carpenter & Moser, 1984).

As children progress through kindergarten and first grade, they become increasingly able to use strategies in which they mentally count numbers instead of physically representing them with fingers or counters. Children *count-on* for addition mentally, and mentally *add-on* and *count-back* for subtraction. Second grade children have also been found to use addition to solve subtraction problems by inversely representing the problem (Siegler, 1987). In later elementary school years, children begin to retrieve answers to addition and subtraction problems and to use *decomposition* strategies that require children to retrieve answers to basic math facts (Carpenter & Moser, 1984). Solution of basic mathematics facts by adults is primarily through retrieval (Ashcraft, 1992).

Multiplication strategies.   The types of strategies children use to solve multiplication problems are thought to reflect their conceptual knowledge of mathematics. Three types of strategy groupings (semantic structures that underlie strategies) have been proposed to underlie multiplication strategies (Kouba, 1989; Mulligan & Mitchelmore, 1997). The first set of strategies, *direct counting*, includes modeling with counters using a one by one count. This approach to solving multiplication problems is one of the earliest developing strategic approaches. The second strategic approach is *repeated addition* in which numbers are counted in sets (e.g., 2, 4, 6, 8) without the use of counters or fingers. Finally, the third strategic approach is the use of *multiplicative calculation* in which the answer is drawn from memory or through derived facts. The third approach is typically the last approach to be developed by children.

Strategies involved in working with fractions.   As children work with fractions in late elementary school and middle school, their strategic approaches to problem solving develop and change. Children move from a *distribution strategy*, in which they mark and cut all the pieces and redistribute all of the pieces into even groups, to a *mark-all strategy*, in which all of the pieces are marked but only the pieces that require cutting are cut, to a *preserved-pieces strategy*, in which only the pieces that need to be cut are marked and cut (Lamon, 1996). In later grades, children use more advanced strategies for solving fraction problems (Smith, 1995). The strategies Smith observed included *parts strategies*, similar to those described by Lamon, that focused on measuring and partitioning wholes into equal size parts. In addition, Smith (1995) identified *components strategies* that require the student to make inferences about the relationships within and between the numbers in a fraction, so that 1/2 and 4/8 are viewed as the same because 1 and 2 are related the same way as 4 and 8. *Reference point strategies* use a reference point on the number line (typically 1 or 0) to compare two fractions. Neither the components or reference point strategies give an exact answer, but rather are used to find the order of fractions involved in the problem. Finally, the *transform strategy* involves transforming fractions into equivalent forms, typically by using the fraction algorithm taught in school. Smith found that competent students used all four strategies depending on problem type, but predominantly used the transform and components strategies.

Algebra problem strategies.   Students typically take one of three strategic approaches to solving algebra problems. They use either reduce, isolation or substitution strategies. The *substitution strategy* is a trial-and-error approach in which variables are replaced by numbers with the goal of balancing the equation (Sleeman, 1984). For the *reduce strategy*, students' goal is to clear the parentheses by carrying out indicated operations (Mayer, 1982). For the *isolation strategy*, the student attempts to solve the problem by moving all the Xs to one side and all the numbers to the other side (Mayer, 1982). The types of strategies students use depends on the type of problem with the isolation strategy being used more commonly on equation problems and the reduce strategy being used on word problems (Mayer, 1982).

Geometry strategies.   In geometry, strategy development tends to move from concrete to the abstract and from a hit-or-miss, haphazard approach to approaches based on an emerging conceptual understanding of geometry. Students may initially apply general strategies such as guessing or estimating, move on to strategies in which they partition lines into sections, and then transition to developing abstract representations that do not involve physical partitioning (Clements, Battista, Sarama, Swaminathan, & McMillen, 1997). For example, Clements et al. (1997) found three types of strategies used to solve geometric problems including: (1) a simple trial-and-error process in which the children filled in the spaces of the geometric shape, (2) a strategy in which students began to construct units and to operate with the units to complete the geometric shape, and (3) a strategy in which the units were subsumed under superordinate units.

Variability in Strategy Use

There is considerable variability in children's strategy use even when they enter kindergarten. Some children come to kindergarten already using counters to count, other children are able to do so with limited instruction, and some children require considerable instruction in the use of counters to count-all (Baroody, 1987). As children progress through school, they acquire a repertoire of strategies including retrieval and the use of manipulatives. While elementary school children tend to use counting strategies, they are able to use retrieval when they are dealing with less difficult problems (Kaye, Post, Hall, & Dineen, 1986; Siegler, 1987). Fast counting strategies and retrieval efficacy emerge as speed increases with age and practice. Professional mathematicians use a variety of strategies to solve problems, many of them invented rather than taught (Dowker, 1992).

Children also differ in the abruptness with which they shift strategies. Children who are more varied in their strategy use are more gradual in their strategy shifts than children who possess only a few strategies (Alibali, 1999). When children are instructed to use a specific strategy, however, they tend to abruptly shift to the instructed strategy as the dominant strategy (Alibali, 1999). Likely, as children acquire a more diverse selection of strategies and become more expert in their mathematics they become more selective in how and when they apply these strategies.

Table 2.1. Points at Which Mathematics Strategies Predominate

	Early Elementary Grades	Middle Elementary Grades	Later Elementary Grades	Middle School	High School	Adulthood
Addition/Subtraction Strategies	Strategies involving counters or fingers, including *counting-all* (kindergarten and first grade), *counting-on, adding-on,* and *matching* (later first grade)	*Mental counting* without physical representation, *inverse representation* of the problem (second grade)	*Retrieval* of basic math facts, *decomposition* of difficult problems into manageable parts (third grade)	Retrieval and decomposition	Retrieval and decomposition	Retrieval and decomposition
Multiplication Strategies	*Direct counting,* using counters (first grade)	*Repeated addition* in which numbers are counted mentally in sets (second grade)	*Multiplicative calculation* (third grade)	Retrieval	Retrieval	Retrieval
Strategies Involved in Working with Fractions			*Distribution* (fourth grade), *mark-all* (fourth and fifth grades)	*Preserved pieces strategies* (sixth through eighth grades), *component, reference point,* and *transform* strategies (upper middle grades)		
Algebra Strategies				*Reduce, isolation, or substitution* strategies		
Geometry Strategies			Trial and error, constructing and operating on units		Abstract representations	

This emerging variability in strategy use is dependent on a number of factors including brain maturation, a better conceptual understanding of mathematics including the procedures used to solve mathematics problems, and experiences that promote the development of strategies. In some cases, children can acquire a variety of new strategies through instruction. For example, a child who counts-on can be taught to count-up for subtraction. In other cases, children's acquisition of new strategies is limited by an immature working memory or lack of conceptual knowledge. For example, many beginning first graders are unable to count-on without using manipulatives because they have yet to develop sufficient working memory to maintain two number lines simultaneously. With maturity and the development of fluent and sophisticated knowledge about mathematics, individuals become able to construct novel strategic approaches to problem solving. Strategy development in the expert mathematician becomes a part of the problem solving process and reflects a deep understanding of the problem and potential ways of solving that problem. Table 2.1 presents information about the points at which strategies are most commonly used.

FACTORS AFFECTING STRATEGY DEVELOPMENT

We know about when mathematics strategies develop and the order in which they develop, but we know less about why and how strategies develop in the way they do. A number of factors including conceptual knowledge, working memory, contextual effects, semantic structure of the problem, fluency, and procedural knowledge are thought to influence how and when mathematics strategies develop. Although studies of these factors have tended to examine the factors individually, it is becoming increasingly evident that these factors interact with each other. For example, conceptual knowledge and procedural knowledge act together in an iterative manner to promote strategy development (Rittle-Johnson, Siegler, & Alibali, 2001).

Conceptual Knowledge

A child's ability to do addition and subtraction is dependent on more than making associations between addends and solutions. Children develop rules for addition and subtraction and apply these rules to novel problems (Baroody, 1989). For example, when children understand that a given number can be broken down into smaller numbers (the part-whole scheme) they are then able to construct and use decomposition strategies

(Putnam, DeBettencourt, & Leinhardt, 1990). Related to this, children need an explicit understanding of inversion in order to use decomposition strategies (Bryant, Christie, & Rendu, 1999).

Conceptual knowledge used for one area of mathematics can be used to bridge two areas of mathematics and can provide a conceptual basis for problem solving in a new area. For example, when young children are initially exposed to multiplication and division they may use manipulatives to solve the problems (Carpenter, Ansell, Franke, Fennema, & Wiesbeck, 1993). Children may also use their semantic models for addition and subtraction as a basis for their multiplication strategies including: (1) direct counting, an extension of addition in which children use manipulatives to represent sets of numbers, (2) repeated addition, in which equal size sets of numbers are created and counted, and (3) multiplicative operations in which children use derived facts or retrieval from memory (Mulligan & Mitchelmore, 1997). Similar models for division were documented including direct counting, repeated subtraction, and repeated addition. Children also use multiplicative operations as a basis for division strategies (Mulligan & Mitchelmore, 1997).

Conceptual knowledge, however, does not always predate the emergence of new strategies and is not always prerequisite to strategy development. Baroody (1987) found that an understanding of commutativity was not necessary for the use of strategies that disregard order (e.g., counting-on). These strategies may initially emerge in an effort to save time with no real initial understanding of commutativity. While the development of conceptual knowledge likely underlies the development of some strategies, it is just as likely that conceptual understanding follows, and emerges out of, the procedural knowledge for a strategy (Rittle-Johnson et al., 2001).

Semantic Structure of Problem

The bulk of the work examining the impact of the semantic structure of problems on mathematics strategy use has focused on math word problems. Much of this work has involved mathematics problem solving in older children and adults, but work with young children indicates that even for simple addition and subtraction word problems, semantic structure influences the types of strategies used by children (Verschaffel & de Corte, 1993). Elementary school children, for example, who were given change addition problems (e.g., Susan has 2 apples and Paul gives Susan 3 more apples, how many apples does Susan have?) tended to use addition strategies in which they would first count out counters for the first addend and then add counters to the second addend to the first set of counters. When children were given compare problems (e.g., Pete has 3 apples, Ann has 7 apples. How many do they have together?), they would create a set of counters representing the first addend and a set of counters representing the second addend. They would then join the two sets and count the joined set for a total score. These two strategic approaches were thought by De Corte and Verschaffel (1987) to be derived from the semantic structure of the two different problems.

The semantic structure of the problem can mislead novices but provide critical information to experts about the best strategies to use for problem solving. More successful problem solvers focus on the semantic features of problems, construct appropriate models of the problem situation and select strategies appropriate for the situation (Hegarty, Mayer, & Monk, 1995). Less successful word problem solvers tend to focus on keywords and numbers but do not construct a conceptually based model of the problem. As a result, their strategies for solving word problems tend to be trial-and-error manipulations of numbers (Hegarty et al., 1995). Less successful word problem solvers also tend to use less effective strategies such as number position and guessing (Littlefield & Rieser, 1993).

Working Memory

Increasingly complex strategies require more working memory to process information. When children begin using the counting-on strategy, for example, they must simultaneously maintain and count on two number lines in memory. This requires more working memory space than a strategy for which the child only has to count using a single number line (Case & Okamoto, 1996). Thus, working memory limitations can significantly constrain the types of strategies children use to solve mathematics problems.

Strategies, in turn, can limit mathematics problem solving by taking up a significant amount of working memory, leaving little working memory to use for other activities including monitoring and planning. While counters can facilitate counting for young children who do not have an abstract representation of number, they can slow or interfere with the use of more advanced strategies (Boulton-Lewis, 1998). According to Boulton-Lewis (1998) when children are attempting to use a more advanced strategy while using counters they must map those representations onto their concrete representatives. This additional cognitive activity takes up working memory space that could otherwise be used to better represent the problem or monitor problem solving.

Word problems require considerable working memory because children must read and represent the problem, determine the best strategy for solving the problem and carry out that solution strategy in working memory. Working memory capacity becomes particularly important if the child is attempting to construct a representation of the problem and potential solution path because this creates additional demands on working memory. The ability of young children with immature working memories to solve word problems is therefore constrained because they are limited in their ability to construct a representation of the problem and in their ability to select and successfully use strategies (Romberg & Collis, 1985).

Contextual Effects

Context influences the strategies children use on several levels including the instructional experiences children have in their classrooms, the school systems they attend and their cultures. The research on contextual effects and strategy use indicates that all children do not automatically develop the same strategies in the same invariant order. Instead, the strategies children use depend on the demands of the situation and whether those demands occur as a function of cultural (e.g., money systems) or classroom practices (e.g., a focus by teachers on surface features of problems versus the semantic structure underlying the problem).

Different schools and cultures value different strategic approaches to mathematics and emphasize these strategies in their classrooms. Carroll (1996) found that children attending a suburban school used more derived facts and mental strategies than children attending an urban school. Children in the urban school, in contrast, were more likely to use the standard written algorithms to solve multidigit problems (Carroll, 1996). While Americans typically do not teach decomposition strategies, the Dutch routinely teach these strategies to children and as a result, decomposition strategy use is much more common in the Netherlands (Beishuizen, 1993). Flemish schools, in contrast, tend to focus on memorizing basic mathematics facts in the early school years. As a result, children are less likely to develop and use of mental counting strategies (Verschaffel & de Corte, 1993).

Children's conceptual understanding and strategies for multiplication, division, addition and subtraction develop as a function of classroom instruction (Fischbein, Deri, Nello, & Marino, 1985). Even when children are capable of using a strategy, they may not use it because it is not supported within their classroom. Stern (1992), for example, found that the short cut strategy emerged only when instruction was organized so that children could see the value of the strategy. Specifically, Stern (1992) found that children frequently did not use the shortcut strategy of eliminating values that cancel each other out in the equation (e.g., $a + b - b$). Instead, children typically treated the problem $a + b - b$ the same way they would treat the problem $a + b - c$. Stern (1992) found that when children were given blocks of problems such as a + b − b they were more likely to discover and use the shortcut strategy than when these problems were presented in the same frequency but distributed among problems for which this strategy would not be effective. This indicates that if a certain strategy is desired, a teacher should systematically create situations that promote the use of the desired strategies.

Fluency (Reaction Time)

Practice using strategies results in an increase in both speed of processing and accuracy (Geary, 1987). In addition to increased retrieval from memory, the speed with which children can use other strategies including counting strategies, decomposition strategies and algorithms in third and fourth grade is also affected by practice (Goldman, Mertz, & Pellegrino, 1989; Hitch, Cundick, Haughey, Pugh, & Wright, 1987). One reason for the connection between speed of processing and accuracy is that speed is an indicator of the strength of association between a problem and its answer, particularly in the case of retrieval. Improved fluency is also an indicator of the child's familiarity with the procedures of a strategy and the capacity of the child to accurately carry out the strategy. Furthermore, as children increase their speed of processing there is a decrease in the demands on attention in working memory (Hitch et al., 1987). The combination of more consolidated procedural routines as well as stronger associations between particular problems and their answers improves children's strategy use and provides opportunities for children to develop more advanced conceptual and strategy knowledge.

Procedural Knowledge

Good strategy use is not possible unless the child has a good understanding of the procedures needed to perform the strategy. The ability to successfully solve mathematics problems is dependent on the ability to perform a number of procedural subskills that comprise the strategy (Nesher, 1986). These subskills can be as basic, as in the case of naming number words in the correct sequence (Gelman & Gallistel, 1978), or as complex as exemplified by counting-on strategies where children must possess procedures for simultaneously maintaining and counting on two number lines. As children attempt more complex problems, more complex procedural knowledge is required in the form of algorithms that allow children to solve multidigit problems requiring borrowing or carrying.

The procedural knowledge that comprises strategies, and conceptual knowledge about those procedures are interdependent (Hiebert & Lefevre, 1986) in that many strategies require conceptual knowledge about number and counting. For example, the ability to use the counting-on strategy emerges out of an understanding of cardinality (Fuson, 1992b). The decomposition strategy requires the understanding that individual numbers can be broken into smaller numbers and recombined. This understanding is necessary for children to develop procedures to transform and compare the parts to the whole in a problem (Putnam et al., 1990).

All of the factors discussed above likely play a role in development of mathematics strategies. Differences in the types of problems we are given, differences in classroom instruction, differences in conceptual and procedural knowledge, and different opportunities to practice strategies will result in individual and group differences in the types of strategies that emerge and variability of strategy use. The next question to be addressed is how these factors interact during the development of mathematics strategies. Theories from several different theoretical perspectives, including cognitive psychology, constructivist theory and social constructivist theory, have offered explanations for how and why mathematics strategies emerge. Each perspective focuses on different aspects of strategy development and, as a result, provides us with different insights into strategy development.

THE COGNITIVE PSYCHOLOGY PERSPECTIVE

Research on strategy development from the perspective of cognitive psychology examines the variability of strategies, the adaptiveness of strategic thinking to new situations, the processes that underlie strategy change, individual differences in the ways strategies change, and children's emerging ability to generalize strategies to new and different tasks (Siegler, 1996). A theory of mathematics strategies must explain how and why mathematics strategies vary over time, over tasks, and within and between children. Similarly, the theory must explain how children select strategies for particular problems, the mechanisms for acquiring new strategies and discarding old strategies, and the processes for generalizing strategies to new tasks. Finally, theories of strategy development must explain how and why individual differences develop in strategy use.

Siegler's Overlapping Waves Theory

For many years, researchers studying mathematics strategies believed that children of a certain age used a single strategy to solve a given problem, which they would discard as they learned another, more efficient one. Strategic development was often studied by focusing on changes in these solitary strategies over long periods of time, and models of strategy development often matched the invariant stage-like models used to describe development in general. Recent research by Robert Siegler and his colleagues (Siegler, 1996), however, has painted a much more complicated picture of children's strategy use, one which describes strategic variability within individual children and within each child's strategy use on an individual problem. The question of mathematics strategy development, therefore, shifts from describing the order of strategy development to describing the factors that influence children's selections. Strategy selection is dependent on a number of factors including children's confidence in their ability to retrieve an answer from memory, problem characteristics, and individual styles.

When a child is given a mathematics problem and he or she is able to retrieve the answer with confidence, retrieval is the strategy of choice. The point at which a child is confident in his or her ability to recall is dependent on the strength of association between the problem and the answer. A child who has repeatedly and correctly practiced a problem and answer combination (e.g., 7 + 5 = 12) will have a strong association between the problem (7 + 5) and the answer (12) in comparison to a child who has practiced retrieving the answer to 7 + 5 but who has not been accurate. Confidence is also based on individual style, with some individuals (perfectionists) needing to be much more confident than other individuals (Kerkman & Siegler, 1997). If the child is not sufficiently confident in his or her ability to retrieve the answer he or she will select from "back-up strategies" such as counting-on or decomposition strategies.

Strategies are also selected based on children's ability to evaluate the usefulness of a particular strategy for a particular problem. Good strategy users have similar confidence criteria to not-so-good strategy users but are better at selecting the best strategy and calculating answers to problems (Kerkman & Siegler, 1997). The nature and goals of the problem and the difficulty and novelty of the problem also influence which strategies children will select from their repertoire of strategies. More difficult or novel problems are more likely to elicit backup strategies, such as the use of counters, instead of retrieval.

Strategy use adapts and changes over time with more effective strategies being selected with greater frequency as the child experiences success with these strategies. Less effective strategies are selected less often, leading to their gradual decline in frequency. Chen and Siegler (2000) hypothesize that this trajectory of development can be conceptualized in terms of five components of strategy discovery and change: (1) the child's acquisition of the new strategy, (2) the mapping of the strategy onto novel problems, (3) the strengthening of the strategy, (4) their refinement of choices among the useful and available strategies, and (5) the successful execution of the new strategy. This way of conceptualizing strategic change allows researchers to observe the course of the strategy as it moves from the base of the wave to the crest. Thus, as the use of each strategy rises and falls with development, a pattern of overlapping waves is formed, with each wave representing a specific strategy. Instead of being discarded, as in the case of older models of strategy development, old strategies continue to be present even after newer, more efficient strategies arise (Siegler, 1996). The overlapping waves theory is supported by research in mathematical and non-mathematical domains (Adolph, 1997; Rittle-Johnson, Bethany, & Siegler, 1999; Schauble, 1996; Siegler & Robinson, 1982).

Siegler and his colleagues have observed this strategic variability in several mathematical domains, including addition (Siegler & Robinson, 1982), subtraction (Siegler, 1987, 1989), and multiplication (Lemaire & Siegler, 1995; Siegler, 1988). As an example of this research, Siegler and Jenkins (1989) studied four- and five-year-olds' acquisition of the counting-on strategy over a period of eleven weeks. During this time, children were given several addition problems to solve individually, and information was obtained about their strategy use. Data from the study supported the overlapping waves theory in that all children used multiple strategies to solve the problems, including the counting-all strategy, the counting-on strategy, retrieval, and decomposition. There was great variety in the strategies children chose, with each individual child approaching the problems in a unique way. In addition, as the children gained practice in solving problems, their addition strategies became more complex, efficient and appropriate. Siegler and his colleagues also noted that throughout the development of addition, change occurs on multiple fronts: not only are the strategies changing, but speed, accuracy, automaticity, and range of problems to which the strategy can be applied also change.

Similar trajectories have been described for other mathematical domains. In the domain of multiplication, for example, the most common strategies used to solve problems include retrieval, repeated addition, representing/counting (using hatchmarks to represent each multiplicand), and relying on related problems. With experience, reliance on retrieval begins to dominate strategic choices. When presented with novel multi-digit problems, however, even experienced problem-solvers exhibit variability in their strategy use (Siegler, 1996).

This work provides us with an understanding of how increased fluency, procedural knowledge, and conceptual knowledge influence the selection of strategies and the emergence of new strategies. From this work we know that strategies do not emerge full blown to displace an existing strategy but, instead, emerge slowly as a function of practice and improved understanding of procedures and concepts.

THE CONSTRUCTIVIST PERSPECTIVE

Researchers working from a constructivist perspective believe that it is impossible to understand the development of mathematics strategies without understanding the nature of children's conceptualizations of number and counting (Steffe, 1992a, 1992b). Constructivist theorists view mathematics strategy development as embedded within developing schemes and cognitive structures about mathematics. Strategies develop as a function of children's emerging knowledge about mathematics, in particular, the internalization of number as a symbol and emergence of more abstract schemes about number.

According to von Glasersfeld (1991), a scheme consists of three parts: assimilation, activity, and the expected outcome. As an example, when a girl hears the problem, "Susan has five cookies. Paul has three cookies. Susan gives Paul two cookies. How many cookies does Paul have now?", the girl first assimilates the problem into a scheme that best resonates with the experience. The girl may assimilate the problem as an addition problem and count two and then continue to count three. When she has finished counting two and counting three, she reports the last number of the count (five). In this case, the assimilatory part of the scheme interprets the problem the girl has just heard as an addition problem, the activity is the counting that the girl does after she assimilates the problem, and the expected outcome is the answer (five). As can be seen in the example, the scheme that assimilates the problem determines the activity that will occur in response to the problem. The scheme also includes an expected outcome for each activity. In mathematics it can be a certain value, a given range of values, or any value at all.

Children are actively constructing schemes for mathematics as a function of their mathematical experiences. As children acquire more experience, their schemes become more abstract and more general. As an example, children initially realize that for the problems they have encountered, the order of presentation does not matter. So, they may realize that 3 + 5 and 5 + 3 both equal 8. Eventually after repeated experiences with such problems children may realize that order never matters for any addition problems. This knowledge is more abstract and generalized than their memories of specific episodes, such as the episode in which they encountered 3 + 5 and 5 + 3. This more abstract knowledge affects the types of strategies children use to solve mathematics problems. Children will count on from the larger addend regardless of its placement in the problem.

As children acquire more experience schemes differentiate and become more focused in their applications, so that a child's scheme related to order in mathematics (commutativity) may initially be applied to subtraction as well as addition problems. As children utilize the scheme and receive feedback about their answers they restrict commutativity to addition. Children become more accurate in the strategy use as they learn when they can and cannot apply certain strategies.

In addition to the development of more general rules for mathematics, children also internalize mathematics symbols. Young elementary school age children frequently cannot count without the use of manipulatives, such as fingers or counters. Constructivist theorists believe that this is because they have yet to develop an internal representation of number. For example, beginning first graders do not understand that the number five represents a count of five and cannot count a set of numbers mentally. The number five is believed to exist only in the activity of counting objects whether they are fingers or counters. As children develop schemes about numbers, they become increasingly able to represent number mentally. Children's strategies change from being entirely external with children counting exclusively using counters or fingers to internal with children being able to mentally count. The shift from external to internal representation is a qualitative shift in the schemes that underlie strategy use.

The process by which schemes develop and differentiate is called perturbation. Perturbation occurs in response to discrepancies between the expected outcome and the actual outcome, for example, when subtraction results in a larger number than is expected. A perturbation may also occur when a child realizes that he or she has assimilated an experience into the wrong scheme. For example, the child may realize that a math problem must be solved through subtraction instead of addition. Perturbations can drive the development of more accurate and advanced strategies as children discriminate among problems based on applicability of specific strategies. Children gradually become aware that counting up from the subtrahend in the problem $18 - 2$ is not as effective as counting down from 18.

It is through the development of schemes and the process of perturbation that children's strategies are developed and refined. Strategy development is a reflection of underlying schemes with significant changes in strategies (e.g., the developmental of mental strategies) being the product of qualitative as well as quantitative changes in schemes. Several constructivist theories have been proposed to explain the development of strategies including work by Karen Fuson, Les Steffe, and Robbie Case. Table 2.2 presents information on commonalities across the three constructivist approaches.

Sequencing, Cardinality, and Counting

Karen Fuson's (1992b) work focuses on how strategies develop out of the integration of different schemes about number into larger cognitive

Table 2.2. Constructivist Approaches to Mathematical Strategy Development

Model	Description	Stages of Developmental Progression			
		Early	Transitory	Middle	Late
Fuson (1992)	New strategies emerge as children integrate their schemes about number into larger cognitive structures. When cardinality, sequencing, and counting schemes merge, strategies shift to being internal.	Breakable Chain (manipulatives are necessary)		Numerical Chain (internal representation begins)	Bi-directional Chain (full internalization, allowing for decomposition strategies
Steffe (1992)	Children internalize strategies as they internalize number. Strategies become more flexible as the ability to unitize numbers develops. These emerging abilities occur as a function of changes in number schemes.	Perceptual Counting (manipulatives are necessary)	Figurative Counting (manipulatives are internally visualized)	Initial Number Sequence (internal representation begins)	Tacitly/Explicitly Nested (numbers can be internally manipulated, allowing for decomposition)
Case & Griffin (1990); Case et al. (1996)	Developmental changes in central conceptual structures are responsible for changes in mathematical strategies. These changes are largely dependent on the development of working memory.	Predimensional (manipulatives are necessary)	Unidimensional (internal representation of one number line)	Bidimensional (internal representation of more than one number line)	Integrated Bi-dimensional (novel relationships between numbers can be constructed, allowing for decomposition)

structures. The integration of schemes for cardinality, sequencing and counting is thought to be critical for the emergence of increasingly complex and advanced strategies. Strategies shift from using external representations to using internal representations as a function of the merging of the three schemes into a single cognitive structure.

Children initially understand cardinality, sequencing and counting as three separate activities. For example, a child might be able to say the number words but may not be able to count using the words or to recognize that the total number of objects in a set is the same as the last number in a count (cardinality). As children work with numbers they come to realize that the sequence of number words is used to count objects and that the last number of the count also represents the count for the entire set. As these three separate schemes become integrated into larger cognitive structures new strategies emerge. For example, children become able to begin a number count at a number other than one. This is possible because children realize that the number at which they begin to count comprises all the numbers in the count prior to it. So that for the problem 5 + 5, the child will begin to count at 5 with the full understanding that when he or she says "five" that word also represents the counts of one through four. The development of the counting cognitive structure is described by Fuson as progressing from a string level, to a numerical chain, to a bidirectional chain level. Each level of scheme integration beginning with the breakable chain is described below.

Breakable chain. The development of the breakable chain cognitive structure involves an integration of the scheme about counting with the scheme for sequence. Children must count using manipulatives to represent the numbers in their number sequence/count because they have not yet internalized number. Children have a scheme for cardinality so they can understand both that the number three in the problem 3 + 2 have both a cardinal meaning and is representative of the first number of a count. This allows children to begin a count from one of the addends (typically the larger addend) instead of using manipulatives. At this point, children will be observed using counting-on strategies using manipulatives.

Numerical chain. At this level, children have constructed an internal representation of number and the child no longer must use objects to represent his or her count. Having developed this capability, the number words in the sequence becomes the count with each number in the count being recognized as having cardinal meaning in itself. These changes allow children to keep track of the numbers while counting on the second addend, so that for the problem 3 + 2 the number three is represented mentally as a cardinal number and the child counts the numbers "4" and "5" while simultaneously keeping track of that count—"1" and "2". The child understands the second count as representing the counts of "4" and "5".

Bidirectional chain. At the next level, numbers are understood as embedded within larger numbers. The numbers are unitized in that children can combine and recombine numbers in any number of combinations, so that 5 + 2 can be partitioned as 4 + 3 or 6 + 1. This allows children to use decomposition strategies by combining and repartitioning numbers in a problem in ways that make the problem easier to solve, so that 89 + 99 can be recombined into the problem 88 + 100.

Fuson's work on the development of counting and cardinality suggests that as children's understanding of counting, number word sequencing and cardinality become integrated, children can use increasingly complex strategies in addition and subtraction. As children make sense out of mathematics they are, in turn, able to create strategies to manipulate these mathematical symbols. These strategies are seen to develop even when children are not encouraged to develop and use them in classrooms (Fuson, 1992a).

Steffe's Numerical Schemes

Steffe's work focuses on the stages of internalization of number and children's emerging ability to unitize numbers. As children internalize number, strategy use is also internalized in that children no longer rely exclusively on manipulatives to solve mathematics problems. Likewise, as children are able to unitize number their strategy use becomes more flexible in that numbers can be partitioned and repartitioned into new and different units for the purposes of calculation. These emerging abilities occur as a function of qualitative as well as quantitative changes in children's schemes about number. The levels of schemes including the perceptual counting scheme, the figurative counting scheme, the number sequence, and the tacitly and explicitly nested number scheme are described below.

Perceptual counting scheme. Children at this stage have number words (the number sequence), but do not yet have internal representations for the number words. At this level, in order to count children must use counters. Children must represent both addends in an addition problem though the use of counters or fingers. As they say each number word they must touch or move the object that represents that number word. Strategy use for children with the perceptual counting scheme is limited to strategies utilizing manipulatives, such as counters and fingers. Furthermore, children at this stage must count out all objects in a set in order to find a sum. They are unable to maintain a count in memory if the objects on which the count is based are not present.

Steffe (1992b) believes that the use of manipulatives provides opportunities for scheme development in that it allows children to reflect on the relationship between their counting activities and the end result of a group of counted objects. Children gradually come to realize that the last number they counted represents the entire counted set. Thus, strategies that utilize manipulatives logically lead to the development of an understanding about cardinality and counting.

Figurative counting scheme.   The figurative counting scheme allows children to rerepresent a remembered item repeatedly so that a child can mentally represent fingers or counters. A child may, for example, report thinking about counting fingers or counters (or toes) but this counting may not be apparent to an external observer. This scheme is transitional in that it is the beginning of the internalization of object concepts for number words. Internalization is the process by which children construct object concepts for the number words that they say during counting. At this point children will report strategies in which they visualize counting fingers or counters but do not actually put up their hands to count fingers or actively count counters.

The initial number sequence.   The initial number sequence emerges out of children's internalization of number. As children use their figurative counting schemes they become able to monitor their figurative counts. As a part of that process, they derive a more abstract representation of a number from the figurative objects. The initial number sequence is a truly abstract representation of number. The child does not need to visualize countable objects nor does the child require number words to represent numbers. The advent of the initial number sequence allows for the development of addition and subtraction schemes. Children can count-on and count-back but they cannot use strategies that require them to break up a number into component numbers. For example, a child could not break up $13 - 6$ into $13 - 3 = 10 - 3 = 7$.

Tacitly and explicitly nested number sequence.   The explicitly nested number sequence is characterized by the ability to embed and disembed numbers from the initial number sequence. It is also characterized by the ability to view a number in the number line both as a unit in itself and as a composite of other numbers. A child with the explicitly nested number sequence can take the number 49 and break it down into four tens and a nine. The child also realizes that 49 is a subunit of 50 and can be represented as $50 - 1$ in a problem. This ability to partition numbers into a number of subunits allows for the development of the decomposition strategies. Children can now take a problem such as $49 + 75$ and create different but equal segments to make it easier to solve a problem. The problem $49 + 75$ could be resegmented, for example, as $50 + 75 - 1$ or $25 + 75 + 24$.

Children with the explicitly nested number sequence understand that addition and subtraction are complimentary procedures. This allows the child to use addition-like strategies (counting-up) to solve subtraction problems and subtraction-like strategies to solve addition problems. A child with an explicitly nested number sequence will be able to solve the subtraction problem 46 – 41 by counting up 5 from 41 instead of counting down 41 from 46. Similarly, such a child could solve the problem 49 + 75 into 50 + 75 – 1. In sum, the emergence of the explicitly nested number sequence makes strategy use much more flexible than prior conceptualizations of number and counting.

The tacitly nested number sequence is a transitional stage in that it is characterized by the ability to segment and resegment numbers into different combinations, but the child is not aware of the relationships that he or she is creating and cannot explain why the new procedures work. It is not until the explicitly nested number sequence emerges that the child is able to explain why the strategies work.

Steffe's work indicates that higher level strategies emerge out of lower level strategies. The tendency to see strategies emerge in a specific order, for example, the tendency of children to use counting-all strategies before they use counting-on strategies, is a reflection on the developmental interdependence of these strategies. In this case, children must count-all if they have no internal representation of a number line. It is the development of the initial number sequence that allows children to move from counting-all objects to counting-on. The two types of strategies represent a qualitatively different representation of number.

Case's Theory of Intellectual Development

While Karen Fuson and Les Steffe assume that mathematics strategies develop out of emerging mathematical concepts, Robbie Case assumes development of central conceptual structures to be responsible for cognitive development and subsequently, for the development of mathematics strategies. Case's theory differs from other developmental theories in that he combines aspects of cognitive theory with Piagetian theory. Specifically, it is assumed that the merging and differentiation of the cognitive structures is dependent on the development of working memory.

Case and Griffin (1990) hypothesize that children possess basic conceptual structures that allow them to interpret and respond to a range of experiences. These conceptual structures progress through four general levels of development in which related conceptual structures are merged into more complex conceptual structures and these complex conceptual structures are differentiated from each other (Case, Okamoto, Griffin, McKeough, Bleiker, Henderson, & Stephenson, 1996). The development of more complex conceptual structures is dependent upon the maturation of working memory limits.

Four levels of development are hypothesized to occur including the predimensional, unidimensional, bidimensional, and integrated bidimensional levels. At each level, revisions in the conceptual structures allow for novel and adaptive ways of responding to the environment. For instance, children initially have separate cognitive structures for quantity and for numerosity that eventually merge into a single cognitive structure allowing children to see the relationship between quantity and numerosity.

Each level allows for new and different mathematics strategies to emerge. Children's mathematics strategies are initially limited to strategies for which they represent and count each number (e.g., counting-all) because they have not yet integrated the schemas for quantity and numerosity (predimensional level). As working memory matures, the schemas for quantity and numerosity merge and differentiate so that children are able to simultaneously hold and use two number lines in memory. This allows for the use of counting-on and counting-up strategies. By the time the child has reached the integrated bidirectional level, he or she is able to construct novel relationships among numbers on different number lines. This allows children to develop decomposition strategies.

From Case's perspective, strategy development is tied to the development of working memory. As working memory increases children are able to develop symbolic representations of numbers and, eventually, to simultaneously represent and manipulate these representations. It is the increased working memory capacity that, in part, allows for more sophisticated strategies and related conceptual knowledge to develop. Case also assumes that experience plays a role in the consolidation of the conceptual knowledge that underlies strategies. As children have repeated experiences with strategies they discriminate the important components of that strategy from incidental components and strategy use become more refined and fluent.

SOCIAL CONSTRUCTIVIST AND SITUATED COGNITIVE PERSPECTIVES

Research on the development of mathematics strategies from the perspective of social constructivist and situated cognition theory assumes that the development of mathematics strategies can be understood only within the context from which the strategies emerge. Strategies are tied to the mathematics goals created by the mathematical situations in which children find themselves. Mathematics strategies within the traditional classroom, for example, might be very different from mathematics strategies for activities outside of the classroom. As a result, the strategies that emerge out of the goals may differ considerably across contexts even for the same child.

Geoffrey Saxe (1995; Saxe, Dawson, Fall, & Howard, 1996) has proposed the Emergent Goals Framework as a means of observing and understanding the development of mathematics. The framework is based on the work of Piaget and Vygotsky in that it considers both the social interactions and activities within which the mathematical activity is embedded as well as the cognitions that the child brings to those interactions. Specifically, the framework includes four parameters including children's prior understanding, the conventions and artifacts of mathematics, social interactions, and the activity structures. The four parameters result in different emerging strategies as a function of their interactions.

The *Activity structure* refers to culturally prescribed activities whether they are the purchase of an item in a store, determining the price of an item to sell, or determining the answer to a word problem. The activity structure includes knowledge of what needs to be done and the motivation for doing it.

Social interaction refers to the contexts in which the strategies emerge and change. Social interactions can have a significant impact on goals and the strategies individuals use to achieve goals. For instance, scaffolding by a more expert learner may result in very different goals and strategies for those actions on the part of a learner. A more expert learner can scaffold a more advanced strategy for a novice or might provide a model for more advanced strategies.

Conventions and artifacts can refer to any tools used to accomplish the mathematics goal. In the case of Brazilian street vendors, the Brazilian currency is an artifact that affects the strategies the children use to calculate sale prices and change. In the case of the Oksapmin people, the convention of using body parts to calculate determine the types of strategies that develop to solve mathematical problems.

Prior understanding refers to the knowledge the learner brings to a mathematics situation. The limits of that knowledge affect the learner's ability to use conventions and artifacts, influence the types of social interactions, and influence their ability to participate in certain activity structures. A child with less expertise in division will be less able to solve some division problems presented in school, will have different interactions with peers and teachers than a more expert learner, and will be less able to take advantage of the tools and conventions typically used in the classroom setting to solve division problems.

These four parameters determine the types of mathematical strategies the learner will set for him or herself. In the traditional classroom setting a first grader may be presented with the problem 8 + 4 and given counters to solve that problem. If the child is unable to conceptualize number on an abstract level and he or she has been taught to count using counters the child will likely use the strategy of solving the problem via the use of the counters. A child with more advanced knowledge of number may not take advantage of the counters even though he or she has been instructed to use them. Instead, he or she may develop the goal of calculating the answer via the use of decomposition strategies.

The strategies that children set for mathematics change as their understanding of mathematics improves and as the context in which they do mathematics changes. Saxe (1982) found that as the Oksapmin of New Guinea moved to a money economy they developed and used more abstract strategies for calculating change as a function of the demands of the new economy. Furthermore, as children move from one mathematics topic to the next their strategies change as a function of the demands placed on them, so that as children are asked to solve mathematics problems that include variables they develop strategies for solving these problems. These strategies may be based on a good understanding of a variable or they may be based on memorized algorithms for solving algebra problems. Strategies are not static and change in response to changes in the environment and the child's understanding of mathematics.

Different contexts may result in children developing multiple arithmetic systems, including different sets of strategies, to be used in the different contexts within the same culture (Nunes, 1992). For example, Carraher, Carraher, and Schliemann (1985) examined the mathematics strategies of low income children in Brazil who both attended school and held street jobs where they would sell candy and other small items or provide services such as car washing. Carraher et al. (1985) examined the strategies the children used when they bartered for goods or services. They then asked the children to solve the same mathematics problems as those used during bartering but the problems had been converted into word problems and computational exercises the children typically encountered in school. The children used different strategies for calculating prices for their merchandise or services than they used to solve the pencil and paper problems presented to them (Carraher, Carraher, & Schliemann, 1987). Specifically, when children were bartering on the streets they tended to use grouping strategies such as decomposition for addition and subtraction and repeated grouping for multiplication. The same problems presented with pencil and paper resulted in the use of written algorithms.

Children may develop advanced strategies in one context that can be transferred to other mathematics contexts. In his work with Brazilian street vendors Saxe (1995) found that the grouping mathematics strategies children used to set prices and calculate change on the street were also used when these children were given pencil and paper computational tasks typical of classroom mathematics instruction. The street sellers did not use the algorithms typically used by school children to solve these tasks. Instead, they transferred the strategies they developed as street vendors to solve the classroom pencil and paper tasks.

Work from the social constructivist perspective has provided unique insight into how environmental demands can shape the development of mathematical symbol systems and the strategies that emerge out of these systems. Furthermore, this perspective on strategy use provides insight into the tremendous variation that can occur in strategy use. Even within the western culture or within a single culture there are differences in the types of strategies children develop and use.

STRATEGY DEVELOPMENT IN SPECIAL POPULATIONS

Children with Mathematics Disabilities

The research on mathematics learning disabilities has provided a consistent picture of the learning disabled student as developmentally delayed in their strategy use (e.g., Geary & Brown, 1991; Geary, Brown, & Samaranayake, 1991; Goldman, Pellegrino, & Mertz, 1988; Ostad, 1997), and in their strategic efficiency and automaticity (e.g., Goldman et al., 1988; Jordan & Montani, 1997). Geary et al. (1991), for example, reported several differences in mathematics strategy use in their study of mathematically normal and disabled first and second graders. They found that relative to the normal group, math disabled students relied on less sophisticated strategies (e.g., verbal counting) for solving mathematics problems. Learning disabled children rarely retrieved the answers from memory and when they attempted retrieval, the retrieved answer was more likely to be incorrect. In addition, relative to the normal group, who showed an increase in retrieval use and speed and a decrease in error, the learning disabled students' strategy choices and problem-solving speed changed little over the course of the ten-month study. In a related study comparing gifted, normal, and disabled third and fourth graders on the same dimensions (Geary & Brown, 1991), disabled students again showed developmental immaturity in their strategic functioning, leading Geary and his colleagues to conclude that the strategy development of mathematically disabled students was on a delayed path relative to their nondisabled peers. This developmental delay in mathematically disabled children's strategic functioning continues throughout the elementary school years. Ostad (1997) conducted a cross-sectional two-year study of the developmental changes in addition strategy use among first, third, and fifth grade children with math disabilities and found patterns similar to those in the studies conducted by Geary and his colleagues.

Other studies have indicated differences in mathematically disabled students' strategic efficiency and fluency (e.g., Jordan & Montani, 1997; Kirby & Becker, 1988). Kirby and Becker (1988) evaluated addition and subtraction problem solving in mathematically disabled, reading disabled and nondisabled fifth graders. The mathematically disabled students in their study did not differ from the other two groups in encoding or strategy use, but differed significantly in their efficiency, suggesting that learning disabled students' problem-solving abilities were harmed by their lack of fluency. Kirby and Becker suggested that the lack of significant difference in their study between the mathematically disabled and mathematically normal children's strategy choices may have been due to the use of relatively uncomplicated mathematical tasks. Jordan and Montani (1997) also found mathematically disabled children to lack fluency and efficiency in comparison to nondisabled children. In their study of math disabled, math/reading disabled, and nondisabled third graders, both disabled groups performed significantly worse on timed tests of word and number problems, indicating a lack of fluency.

While strategic differences in mathematically disabled and mathematically normal children's problem solving have been well documented, the underlying causes of the differences are not clear. Researchers have suggested information-processing and retrieval deficiencies as the cause of the differences (e.g., Cauzinille-Marmeche & Julo, 1998; Geary et al., 1991; Sovik, Frostrad, & Heggberget, 1999). Geary et al. (1991), for example, found that math disabled students have a shorter working memory span and that their working memory span was directly related to their number of counting errors. Presumably, the math disabled students' infrequent use of retrieval and high error rates when using counting strategies were due to poor working memory resources that prevented quick problem-solving. Other research by Swanson and Rhine (1985) found mathematically disabled students to perform significantly worse than normal students on tasks that required the reordering or abandoning of previous strategies, indicating a deficiency in the cognitive resources needed to deal with the transformations.

Other researchers have suggested additional factors underlying math-disabled students' strategic differences, including neuropsychological factors (Batchelor, Gray, & Dean, 1990), self-monitoring and metacognitive difficulties (Montague & Bos, 1990), and poor instruction (Garnett, 1992). Students who have both reading and math difficulties are put at a double disadvantage and demonstrate much less strategic ability than their math-disabled or non-disabled peers, even on pure number problems (Jordan & Montani, 1997; Sovik et al., 1999).

Although research describing the strategic distinction between math disabled and non-disabled students has been primarily conducted with elementary school-age children, studies comparing non-disabled and learning-disabled secondary students also indicate significant differences in the strategies of learning disabled students and average students. Strategic deficiencies in the early years often escalate as students move into adolescence and adulthood (Mercer & Miller, 1992), showing up in higher-level mathematics, such as algebra, where math-disabled students often find they lack the skills necessary to represent the problem, come up with a solution, and monitor their strategy choices (Hutchinson, 1987; Maccini, McNaughton, & Ruhl, 1999). Consequently, math disabled students in the secondary grades fall even farther behind and often require considerable remediation and intervention (Maccini et al., 1999).

Research on mathematics learning disabilities shows us how deficits in basic cognitive processes, such as retrieval, can stymie the development of mathematics strategies. Deficits in basic cognitive processes make it difficult for children develop fluency in their procedural skills and slow inefficient procedures, in turn, likely handicap the development of conceptual knowledge.

Gender Differences in the Development of Mathematics Strategies

Although gender differences in mathematics strategies are not pervasive, they have been found for some mathematics tasks. Gender differences in mathematics strategy use for addition and subtraction have been documented as early as the first grade (e.g., Carr & Jessup, 1997; Fennema, Carpenter, Jacobs, Franke, & Levi, 1998a; Waxman, 1987). In two studies of first grade students' strategy use, girls were found to prefer strategies involving manipulatives while boys were more likely to use retrieval to solve addition and subtraction problems (Carr & Jessup, 1997; Carr, Jessup, & Fuller, 1999). Fennema, Carpenter, Jacobs, Franke, and Levi (1998a) found a similar pattern in their longitudinal study of students' math strategy development from first through third grade. The girls in their study tended to use more concrete strategies involving manipulatives, such as counters, whereas boys were more likely to use decomposition strategies and retrieval. In all three studies, girls and boys showed similar success rates in solving the problems. Thus, differences in strategy use did not translate into differences in the total number of problems correctly answered.

Gender differences in strategy use have been found with older students but they are restricted to certain areas of mathematics. High achieving adolescent girls tend to rely on more conventional strategies to solve SAT-M problems whereas high ability boys are more willing to use unconventional mathematics strategies (Gallagher & De Lisi, 1994). No gender differences, however, were found in the strategies high school age girls and boys used to solve geometry problems with boys and girls being equally likely to use visual/spatial strategies and verbal-logical strategies (Battista, 1990).

Several interpretations of this phenomenon have been proposed. In an issue of *Educational Researcher* scholars offered possible explanations of the Fennema et al. (1998a) longitudinal study. Sowder (1998), a mathematics educator, suggested that the girls in the study understood the difficult strategies, but chose to describe their approach using more traditional strategies because of their relative ease of explanation. Hyde and Jaffee (1998), from a social psychology perspective, blamed the teachers' unconscious activation of gender stereotypes in their instruction for the differences. Feminist philosopher Nel Noddings (1998) provided yet another explanation, suggesting that strategic differences were due to girls being less interested in higher-level math concepts. It remains to be seen which of these interpretations, if any, explain why girls and boys prefer different strategic approaches to mathematics problem solving.

There are no gender differences in the development of working memory, therefore, maturational differences in working memory is an unlikely reason for these gender differences. At this point it is unclear whether differences in fluency, procedural knowledge, conceptual knowledge, or contextual effects are responsible for gender differences in strategy use. Nor do we know how these gender differences play out in terms of subsequent mathematics achievement.

IMPLICATIONS FOR EDUCATION

The theory and research on strategy development presented here has important implications for educators. Siegler's (1996) adaptive strategy choice model suggests that strategic development in children is variable, with same-age groups and individual children choosing a variety of strategies to solve a given problem. As children gain more practice with math problems, they begin to select more efficient and sophisticated strategies. This suggests that teachers should be flexible in the strategies they require children to use, giving them practice solving many different types of problems using many different types of strategies.

Children benefit from the direct instruction of strategies. Children given direct instruction in creating situational models of problems that focus on the semantic features of the problems are more likely to use such strategies and to abandon the less successful direct translation strategies for word problems that focus on surface features of problems (Mayer & Hegarty, 1996). Direct instruction of more complex strategies appears to help children develop a wider selection of strategies from which to choose. As a result, children become more efficient in their strategy use.

Teachers must keep in mind that good strategy use means that children must have a good conceptual understanding of the strategy. Research from a constructivist theoretical approach indicates that children construct more sophisticated strategies as they practice and play with a variety of math problems. More sophisticated strategies begin to emerge through a dynamic interaction between their growing conceptual awareness and experience with different types of problems.

Fuson's and Steffe's theories also suggest that young children's emerging numeric awareness is dependent on their use of manipulatives, such as counters. The use of such manipulatives encourages children to construct mental models that will be the building blocks for more complex strategies later. The value of the continued use of manipulatives after children have constructed an internal representation of number is questionable. The work of Fuson, Steffe, and Case indicate that as children begin to construct sophisticated strategies like decomposition, the use of visual aids like number lines may assist their growing awareness. Therefore, teachers can help children develop strategically by providing them manipulatives and other visual aids to work with as they practice a variety of math problems. The work of Boulton-Lewis (1997), however, suggests that manipulatives may overload children's working memory and make it more difficult for them to learn more complex mathematics. Given this, manipulatives can be recommended without reservation for children at the earliest stages of mathematics but teachers may want to be cautious in their use of manipulatives for older children. For older children, the use of manipulatives should be restricted to situations in which the children are having trouble understanding a mathematics concept or problem.

The social constructivist and situated cognition theoretical perspectives support a shift away from rigid, paper-pencil drills with the goal of having children apply their mathematical knowledge to real-world situations. Teachers need to be explicit about their goals for children's learning, providing authentic situations where children can construct and use strategies that are useful on problems they will encounter in their everyday lives. The use of authentic tasks will also help children understand the relationship between invented strategies, such as decomposition, and the standard algorithm taught in school (Boulton-Lewis, & Tait, 1994).

The research reviewed in this chapter also suggests that teachers need to be aware of the effect of gender and learning disabilities on mathematics strategy development. While few differences are shown in children's success in solving problems, the early differences in boys' and girls' strategy choices may dissuade girls from attempting or succeeding in higher-level math (Fennema & Peterson, 1985). Teachers must also be aware of the needs of learning disabled students. A number of instructional programs exist that are designed to address math disabled students' strategic needs (Thornton, Langrall, & Jones, 1997), and teachers should be encouraged to use these programs so that every student, regardless of developmental level, can reach his or her potential.

Finally, children of other nations repeatedly outperform children in the United States. This may be due, in part, to the more rigid instructional methods used by American teachers and the tendency of American teachers to focus on algorithms as the primary technique for computing answers to mathematics problems (Lee, 1998). The theory and research presented here suggests that children should be exposed to a number of different strategies and that when children possess a variety of strategies they are better able to deal with novel mathematical problems. Teachers need to keep in mind that as strategies emerge and are used by children, conceptual knowledge about counting and strategies also emerges. Strategy instruction provides more than means for solving problems, it also provides children with a different view of mathematics. The more diverse the potential views on a problem, the better the child will understand the problem and the strategy.

REFERENCES

Adolph, K.E. (1997). Learning in the development of infant locomotion. *Monographs of the Society for Research in Child Development, 62*(3), 1–140.

Alibali, M.W. (1999). How children change their minds: Strategy change can be gradual or abrupt. *Developmental Psychology, 35*(1), 127–145.

American Association of University Women. (1992). *How schools shortchange girls: A study of major findings on girls and education.* Washington, DC: American Association of University Women Educational Foundation.

Ashcraft, M.H. (1990). Strategic processing in children's mental arithmetic: A review and proposal. In D. F. Bjorklund (Eds.), *Children's strategies: Contemporary views of cognitive development* (pp. 185–211). Hillsdale, NJ: Erlbaum.

Ashcraft, M.H. (1992). Cognitive arithmetic: A review of data and theory. *Cognition, 44*(1–2), 75–106.

Baroody, A.J. (1987). The development of counting strategies for single-digit addition. *Journal for Research in Mathematics Education, 18*(2), 141–157.

Baroody, A.J. (1989). Kindergartners' mental addition with single-digit combinations. *Journal for Research in Mathematics Education, 20*(2), 159–172.

Batchelor, E.S., Gray, J.W., & Dean, R.S. (1990). Empirical testing of a cognitive model to account for neuropsychological functioning underlying arithmetic problem solving. *Journal of Learning Disabilities, 23*(1), 38–42.

Battista, M.T. (1990). Spatial visualization and gender differences in high school geometry. *Journal for Research in Mathematics Education, 21*(1), 47–60.

Beishuizen, M. (1993). Mental strategies and materials or models for addition and subtraction up to 100 in Dutch second grades. *Journal for Research in Mathematics Education, 24*(4), 294–323.

Bisanz, J., & LeFevre, J.A. (1990). Strategic and nonstrategic processing in the development of mathematical cognition. In D.F. Bjorklund (Ed.), *Children's strategies: Contemporary views of cognitive development* (pp. 213–244). Hillsdale, NJ: Erlbaum.

Boulton-Lewis, G. M. (1998). Children's strategy use and interpretations of mathematical representations. *Journal of Mathematical Behavior, 17*(2), 219–237.

Boulton-Lewis, G., Cooper, T., Atweh, B., Pillay, H., Wilss, L., & Mutch, S. (1997). Processing load and the use of concrete representations and strategies for solving linear equations. *Journal of Mathematical Behavior, 16*(4), 379–397.

Boulton-Lewis, G.M., & Tait, K. (1994). Young children's representations and strategies for addition. *British Journal of Educational Psychology, 64*(2), 231–242.

Bryant, P., Christie, C., & Rendu, A. (1999). Children's understanding of the relation between addition and subtraction: Inversion, identity, and decomposition. *Journal of Experimental Child Psychology, 74*(3), 194–212.

Carpenter, T.P., Ansell, E., Franke, M.L., Fennema, E., & Wiesbeck, ? (1993). Models of problem solving: A study of kindergarten children's problem-solving processes. *Journal for Research in Mathematics Education, 24*(5), 428–441.

Carpenter, T.P., & Moser, J.M. (1984). The acquisition of addition and subtraction concepts in grades one through three. *Journal for Research in Mathematics Education, 15*(3), 179–202.

Carr, M., & Jessup, D. L. (1997). Gender differences in first-grade mathematics strategy use: Social and metacognitive influences. *Journal of Educational Psychology, 89*(2), 318–328.

Carr, M., Jessup, D.L., & Fuller, D. (1999). Gender differences in first-grade mathematics strategy use: Parent and teacher contributions. *Journal of Research in Mathematics Education, 30*(1), 20–46.

Carraher, T.N., Carraher, D.W., & Schliemann, A.D. (1985). Mathematics in the streets and in schools. *British Journal of Developmental Psychology, 3*(1), 21–29.

Carraher, T.N., Carraher, D.W., & Schliemann, A.D. (1987). Written and oral mathematics. *Journal for Research in Mathematics Education, 18*(2), 83–97.

Carroll, W.M. (1996). Use of invented algorithms by second graders in a reform mathematics curriculum. *Journal of Mathematical Behavior, 15*(2), 137–150.

Case, R., & Griffin, S. (1990). Child cognitive development: the role of coentral conceptual structures in the development of scientific and social thought. In C.A. Hauert (Ed.), *Developmental psychology: Cognitive, perceptuo-motor, and neuropschological perspectives.* Amsterdam: Elsevier Science.

Case, R., & Okamoto, Y. (1996). The role of central conceptual structures in the development of children's thought. *Monographs of the Society for Research in Child Development, 61*(1–2).

Cauzinille-Marmeche, E., & Julo, J. (1998). Studies of micro-genetic learning brought about by the comparison and solving of isomorphic arithmetic problems. *Learning and Instruction, 8*(3), 253–269.

Chen, Z., & Siegler, R. S. (2000). Across the great divide: Bridging the gap between understanding of toddler's and older children's thinking. *Monographs of the Society for Research in Child Development, 65*(2, Serial No. 261).

Clements, D.H., Battista, M.T., Sarama, J., Swaminathan, S., & McMillen, S. (1997). Students' development of length concepts in a logo-based unit on geometric paths. *Journal for Research in Mathematics Education, 28*(1), 70–95.

Davis, R.B. (1992). Understanding "understanding." *Journal of Mathematical Behavior, 11*(3), 225–241.

Davis, H., & Carr, M. (2001). *Gender differences in strategy use: The impact of temperament.* Unpublished manuscript.

de Corte, E., & Verschaffel, L. (1987). The effect of semantic structure on first graders' strategies for solving addition and subtraction word problems. *Journal for Research in Mathematics Education, 18*(5), 363–381.

Dowker, A. (1992). Computational estimation strategies of professional mathematicians. *Journal for Research in Mathematics Education, 23*(1), 45–55.

Fennema, E., Carpenter, T.P., Jacobs, V.R., Franke, M.L., & Levi, L.W. (1998a). A longitudinal study of gender differences in young children's mathematical thinking. *Educational Researcher, 27*(5), 6–11.

Fennema, E., Carpenter, T.P., Jacobs, V.R., Franke, M.L., & Levi, L.W. (1998b). New perspectives on gender differences in mathematics: A reprise. *Educational Researcher, 27*(5), 19–21.

Fennema, E., & Peterson, P.L. (1985). Autonomous learning behavior: A possible explanation of gender-related differences in mathematics. In L.C. Wilkinson & C.B. Marrett (Eds.), *Gender influences in classroom interaction* (pp. 17–35). Orlando, FL: Academic Press.

Fischbein, E., Deri, M., Nello, M.S., & Marino, M.S. (1985). The role of implicit models in solving verbal problems in multiplication and division. *Journal for Research in Mathematics Education, 16*(1), 3–17.

Fuson, K.C. (1992a). Relationships between counting and cardinality from age 2 to age 8. In J. Bideaud, C. Meljac, & J.P. Fischer (Eds.), *Pathways to number: Children's developing numerical abilities* (pp. 127–149). Hillsdale, NJ: Erlbaum.

Fuson, K.C. (1992b). Research on learning and teaching addition and subtraction of whole numbers. In G. Leinhardt, R. Putnam &, R.A. Hattrup (Eds.), *Analysis of arithmetic for mathematics teaching* (pp. 53–187). Hillsdale, NJ: Erlbaum.

Gallagher, A.M., & De Lisi, R. (1994). Gender differences in Scholastic Aptitude Test: Mathematics problem solving among high-ability students. *Journal of Educational Psychology, 86*(2), 204–211.

Garnett, K. (1992). Developing fluency with basic number facts: Intervention for students with learning disabilities. *Learning Disabilities Research and Practice, 7*(4), 210–216.

Garnett, K., & Fleischner, J.E. (1983). Automatization and basic fact performance of normal and learning disabled children. *Learning Disability Quarterly, 6*(2), 223–230.

Geary, D.C. (1987). Cognitive addition: On the convergence of statistical and conceptual models. *Bulletin of the Psychonomic Society, 25*(6), 427–430.

Geary, D.C. (1990). A componential analysis of an early learning deficit in mathematics. *Journal of Experimental Child Psychology, 49*(3), 363–383.

Geary, D.C., & Brown, S.C. (1991). Cognitive addition: Strategy choice and speed-of-processing differences in gifted, normal, and mathematically disabled children. *Developmental Psychology, 27*(3), 398–406.

Geary, D.C., Brown, S.C., & Samaranayake, V.A. (1991). Cognitive addition: A short longitudinal study of strategy choice and speed-of-processing differences in normal and mathematically disabled children. *Developmental Psychology, 27*(5), 787–797.

Geary, D.C., Widaman, K.F., Little, T.D., & Cormier, P. (1987). Cognitive addition: Comparison of learning disabled and academically normal elementary school children. *Cognitive Development, 2*(3), 249–269.

Gelman, R., & Gallistel, C.R. (1978). *The child's understanding of number.* Cambridge, MA: Harvard University Press.

Goldman, S.R., Mertz, D.L., & Pellegrino, J.W. (1989). Individual differences in extended practice functions and solution strategies for basic addition facts. *Journal of Educational Psychology, 81*(4), 481–496.

Goldman, S.R., Pellegrino, J.W., & Mertz, D.L. (1988). Extended practice of basic addition facts: Strategy changes in learning-disabled students. *Cognition and Instruction, 51*(3), 223–265.

Hegarty, M., Mayer, R.E., & Monk, C.A. (1995). Comprehension of arithmetic word problems: A comparison of successful and unsuccessful problem solvers. *Journal of Educational Psychology, 87*(1), 18–32.

Hiebert, J., & Lefevre, P. (1986). Conceptual and procedural knowledge in mathematics: An introductory analysis. In J. Hiebert (Ed.), *Conceptual and procedural knowledge: The case of mathematics* (pp. 1–27). Hillsdale, NJ: Erlbaum.

Hitch, G., Cundick, J., Haughey, M., Pugh, R., & Wright, H. (1987). Aspects of counting in children's arithmetic. In J. A. Sloboda & D. Rogers (Eds.), *Cognitive processes in mathematics* (pp. 26–41). New York: Clarendon Press/Oxford University Press.

Hopkins, K.B., McGillicuddy-De Lisi, A.V., & De Lisi, R. (1997). Student gender and teaching methods as sources of variability in children's computational arithmetic performance. *Journal of Genetic Psychology, 158*(3), 333–345.

Hutchinson, N.L. (1987). Strategies for teaching learning disabled adolescents algebraic problems. *Reading, Writing, and Learning Disabilities, 3*, 63–74.

Hyde, J.S., & Jaffee, S. (1998). Perspectives from social and feminist psychology. *Educational Researcher, 27*(5), 14–16.

Jordan, N.C., & Montani, T.O. (1997). Cognitive arithmetic and problem solving: A comparison of children with specific and general mathematics difficulties. *Journal of Learning Disabilities, 30*(6), 624–634, 684.

Kaye, D.B., Post, T.A., Hall, V.C., & Dineen, J.T. (1986). Emergence of information-retrieval strategies in numerical cognition: A developmental study. *Cognition & Instruction, 3*(2), 127–150.

Kerkman, D.D., & Siegler, R.S. (1997). Measuring individual differences in children's addition strategy choices. *Learning & Individual Differences, 9*(1), 1–18.

Kirby, J.R., & Becker, L.D. (1988). Cognitive components of learning problems in arithmetic. *Remedial and Special Education, 9*(5), 7–16.

Kouba, V.L. (1989). Children's solution strategies for equivalent set multiplication and division word problems. *Journal for Research in Mathematics Education, 20*(2), 147–158.

Lamon, S.J. (1996). The development of unitizing: Its role in children's partitioning strategies. *Journal for Research in Mathematics Education, 27*(2), 170–193.

Lee, S-Y. (1998). Mathematics learning and teaching in the school context: Reflections from cross-cultural comparisons. In S.G. Paris & H.M. Wellman (Eds.), *Global prospects for education: Development, culture, and schooling* (pp. 45–77). Washington, DC: American Psychological Association.

Lemaire, P., & Siegler, R.S. (1995). Four aspects of strategic change: Contributions to children's learning of multiplication. *Journal of Experimental Psychology: General, 124*(1), 83–97.

Littlefield, J., & Rieser, J.J. (1993). Semantic features of similarity and children's strategies for identifying relevant information in mathematical story problems. *Cognition & Instruction, 11*(2), 133–188.

Maccini, P., McNaughton, D., & Ruhl, K.L. (1999). Algebra instruction for students with learning disabilities: Implications from a research review. *Learning Disability Quarterly, 22,* 113–126.

Mayer, R.E. (1982). Different problem-solving strategies for algebra word and equation problems. *Journal of Experimental Psychology: Learning, Memory, & Cognition, 8*(5), 448–462.

Mayer, R.E., & Hegarty, M. (1996). The process of understanding mathematical problems. In R.J. Sternberg & T. Ben-Zeev (Eds.), *The nature of mathematical thinking* (pp. 29–53). Mahwah: Erlbaum.

Mercer, C.D., & Miller, S.P. (1992). Teaching students with learning problems in math to acquire, understand, and apply basic math facts. *Remedial and Special Education, 13*(3), 19–35.

Montague, M., & Bos, C.S. (1990). Cognitive and metacognitive characteristics of eighth grade students' mathematical problem solving. *Learning and Individual Differences, 2*(3), 371–388.

Mulligan, J.T., & Mitchelmore, M.C. (1997). Young children's intuitive models of multiplication and division. *Journal for Research in Mathematics Education, 28*(3), 309–330.

Nesher, P. (1986). Learning mathematics: A cognitive perspective. *American Psychologist, 41*(10), 1114–1122.

Noddings, N. (1998). Perspectives from feminist philosophy. *Educational Researcher, 27*(5), 17–18.

Nunes, T. (1992). Ethnomathematics and everyday cognition. In D.A. Grouws (Ed.), *Handbook of research on mathematics teaching and learning: A project of the National Council of Teachers of Mathematics* (pp. 557–574). New York: Macmillan Publishing Co Inc.

Ostad, S.A. (1997). Developmental differences in addition strategies: A comparison of mathematically disabled and mathematically normal children. *British Journal of Educational Psychology, 67,* 345–357.

Putnam, R.T., DeBettencourt, L.U., & Leinhardt, G. (1990). Understanding of derived-fact strategies in addition and subtraction. *Cognition & Instruction, 7*(3), 245–285.

Rittle-Johnson, B., & Siegler, R.S. (1999). Learning to spell: Variability, choice, and change in children's strategy use. *Child Development, 70*(2), 332–348.

Rittle-Johnson, B., Siegler, R.S., & Alibali, M.W. (2001). Developing conceptual understanding and procedural skill in mathematics: An iterative process. *Journal of Educational Psychology, 93,* 346–362.

Romberg, T.A., & Collis, K.F. (1985). Cognitive functioning and performance on addition and subtraction work problems. *Journal for Research in Mathematics Education, 16*(5), 375–382.

Saxe, G.B. (1982). Developing forms of arithmetical thought among the Oksapmin of Papua New Guinea. *Developmental Psychology, 18*(4), 583–594.

Saxe, G.B. (1995). From the field to the classroom: Studies in mathematical understanding. In L.P. Steffe & J. Gale (Eds.), *Constructivism in education* (pp. 287–311). Hillsdale, NJ: Erlbaum.

Saxe, G.B., Dawson, V., Fall, R., & Howard, S. (1996). Culture and children's mathematical thinking. In R. . Sternberg & T. Ben-Zeev (Eds.), *The nature of mathematical thinking* (pp. 119–144). Mahwah: Erlbaum.

Schauble, L. (1996). The development of scientific reasoning in knowledge-rich contexts. *Developmental Psychology, 32*(1), 102–119.

Siegler, R.S. (1987). Strategy choices in subtraction. In J.A. Sloboda & D. Rogers (Eds.), *Cognitive processes in mathematics* (pp. 81–106). New York: Clarendon Press/Oxford University Press.

Siegler, R.S. (1988). Strategy choice procedures and the development of multiplication skill. *Journal of Experimental Psychology: General, 117*(3), 258–275.

Siegler, R.S. (1989). Hazards of mental chronometry: An example from children's subtraction. *Journal of Educational Psychology, 81*(4), 497–506.

Siegler, R.S. (1996). *Emerging minds: The process of change in children's thinking.* New York: Oxford University Press.

Siegler, R.S., & Jenkins, E. (1989). *How children discover new strategies.* Hillsdale, NJ: Erlbaum.

Siegler, R.S., & Robinson, M. (1982). The development of numerical understanding. In H.W. Reese & L.P. Lipsitt (Eds.), *Advances in child development and behavior* (Vol. 16). New York: Academic Press.

Sleeman, D. (1984). An attempt to understand students' understanding of basic algebra. *Cognitive Science, 8*(4), 387–412.

Smith, J.P. (1995). Competent reasoning with rational numbers. *Cognition & Instruction, 13*(1), 3–50.

Sovik, N., Frostrad, P., & Heggberget, M. (1999). The relation between reading comprehension and task-specific strategies used in arithmetical word problems. *Scandinavian Journal of Educational Research, 43*(4), 371–398.

Sowder, J.T. (1998). Perspectives from mathematics education. *Educational Researcher, 27*(5), 12–13.

Steffe, L.P. (1992a). Learning stages in the construction of the number sequence. In J. Bideaud , C. Meljac, & J. Fischer (Eds.), *Pathways to number: Children's developing numerical abilities* (pp. 83–98). Hillsdale, NJ: Erlbaum.

Steffe, L.P. (1992b). Schemes of action and operation involving composite units. *Learning & Individual Differences, 4*(3), 259–309.

Stern, E. (1992). Spontaneous use of conceptual mathematical knowledge in elementary school children. *Contemporary Educational Psychology, 17*(3), 266–277.

Svenson, O., & Broquist, S. (1975). Strategies for solving simple addition problems: A comparison of normal and subnormal children. *Scandinavian Journal of Psychology, 16*(2), 143–148.

Swanson, H.L., & Rhine, B. (1985). Strategy transformations in learning disabled children's math performance: Clues to the development of expertise. *Journal of Learning Disabilities, 18*(10), 596–603.

Thornton, C.A., Langrall, C.W., & Jones, G.A. (1997). Mathematics instruction for elementary students with learning disabilities. *Journal of Learning Disabilities, 30*(2), 142–150.

Verschaffel, L., & de Corte, E. (1993). A decade of research on word problem solving in Leuven: Theoretical, methodological, and practical outcomes. *Educational Psychology Review, 5*(3), 239–256.

von Glasersfeld, E. (1991). Knowing without metaphysics: Aspects of the radical constructivist position. In F. Steier (Eds.), *Research and reflexivity* (pp. 12–29). London: Sage.

Waxman, H.C. (1987). Investigating sex-related differences in mathematical problem-solving strategies of elementary school students. *Perceptual and Motor Skills, 65*, 925–926.

CHAPTER 3

MATHEMATICAL PROBLEM SOLVING

Richard E. Mayer

ABSTRACT

Everyone can and should become proficient in mathematics. Furthermore, to become proficient in mathematics means to build several different—but intertwined—strands of mathematical proficiency (or kinds of mathematical knowledge) that can be used to solve mathematics problems. What does a person need to know to be proficient in mathematics? To answer this question, this chapter examines research on the cognitive processes involved in mathematical problem solving. I begin with an introduction that includes definitions of key terms and a summary of four cognitive processes in mathematical problem solving—translating, integrating, planning, and executing. Then, for each cognitive process, I provide examples and explore exemplary research. Finally, the chapter ends with a conclusion in which I suggest some future directions for research on the cognitive psychology of mathematical problem solving.

Mathematical Cognition, pages 69–92

INTRODUCTION

Purpose

Everyone can and should become proficient in mathematics. When faced with basic mathematics problems, everyone can and should be able to solve them. This is the major conclusion of a panel of experts empaneled by the National Research Council and presented in their report, *Adding It Up: Helping Children Learn Mathematics* (Kilpatrick, Swafford, & Findell, 2001). Furthermore, the experts posit that to become proficient in mathematics means to build several different—but intertwined—strands of mathematical proficiency (or kinds of mathematical knowledge) that can be used to solve mathematics problems.

What does a person need to know to be proficient in mathematics? To answer this question, this chapter examines research on the cognitive processes involved in mathematical problem solving. I begin with an introduction that includes definitions of key terms and a summary of four cognitive processes in mathematical problem solving—translating, integrating, planning, and executing. Then, for each cognitive process, I provide examples and explore exemplary research. Finally, the chapter ends with a conclusion in which I suggest some future directions for research on the cognitive psychology of mathematical problem solving.

Definitions

Let's begin by defining some key terms—mathematics problem and mathematical problem solving. A *problem* exists when you have a goal but do not immediately know how to reach the goal (Mayer, 1992). Thus, a problem consists of three elements: a given state (i.e., the current state of the situation), a goal state (i.e., the desired state of the situation), and obstacles that block you from moving directly from the given state to the goal state.

A *mathematics problem* is a problem that involves mathematical content such as numbers, geometric shapes, or algebraic relations. The defining feature of mathematics problems is that they require mathematical reasoning—such as reasoning based on the rules of number systems, geometry, or algebra. It is important to note that in this definition, whether a situation is a problem depends on the problem solver. Schoenfeld (1985, p. 74) observed: "Problem solving is relative. The same tasks that call for significant efforts from some students may well be routine exercises for others.... Thus, being a problem is not a property inherent in a mathematical task. Rather, it is the particular relationship between the individual and the task that makes the task a problem for that person." Thus, the task, "2 + 4 = ___ " is not a problem for most adults because they can retrieve the answer without any obstacles; however, it may be a problem for some 5-year-olds who reason, "I can take one from the 4 and give it to the 2, so now I have 3 + 3, and the answer is 6."

Problem solving occurs when a problem solver determines how to solve a problem, that is, how to accomplish the goal (Mayer, 1992). Thus, the definition of problem solving includes three features: (a) cognitive—problem solving occurs internally in one's cognitive system (but must be inferred indirectly through behavior), (b) process—problem solving involves mental computation in which a mental operation is applied to a mental representation, and (c) directed—problem solving is based on one's goal and results in activity intended to solve a problem. Thus, problem solving is directed cognitive processing. Thinking refers to all forms of cognitive processing—including directed and non-directed (such as daydreaming).

Mathematical problem solving is problem solving for problems that contain mathematical content. This definition is consistent with Polya's (1965, p. ix) classic definition: "'Solving a problem means finding a way out of a difficulty, a way around an obstacle, attaining an aim which was not immediately attainable.'"

Types of Problems

It is useful to distinguish routine versus non-routine problems, well-defined versus ill-defined problems, and problems that require computation versus problems that require understanding (Mayer, 1992; Mayer & Hegarty, 1996). A *routine problem* (or exercise) is a problem for which the problem solver immediately knows a solution procedure. For example, 234 × 567 is a routine problem for most adults because they know the procedure for three-column multiplication. According to our definition of problem, routine problems are not problems at all because there is no obstacle. In contrast, a *non-routine problem* is a problem for which the problem solver does not immediately know a solution procedure. For example, Maier and Burke's (1967, p. 307) horse-trading problem is a non-routine problem for most people: "A man bought a horse for $60 and sold it later for $70. Then he bought it back for $80 and sold it for $90. How much did he make in the horse-trading business?" To correctly solve this problem, students must see it as two transactions (making $10 on the first buying and selling, and making $10 on the second buying and selling, yielding an answer of $20). According to Maier and Burke, some students incorrectly interpret the problem as having three transactions so a common solution is to subtract 60 from 70 to get 10, 80 from 70 to get −10, and 80 from 90 to get 10, and then add the results to yield an answer of 10. Although these students may compute correctly, they do not understand the problem (i.e., they misunderstand how many transactions took place).

A *well-defined problem* has a clearly specified initial state, goal state, and set of operators. For example, "3X + 2 = 8, Solve for X" is a well-defined problem because it has a clearly specified initial state (i.e., as presented), a clearly specified goal state (i.e., finding the value of X), and clearly specified set of operators (i.e., the operations allowed in algebra and arithmetic). In an *ill-defined problem*, the initial state, goal state, and/or set of operators is not clearly specified. For example, "How can a newly married couple get enough money to buy a new house?" is an ill-defined problem because "enough money" is not specified and the allowable operators are not specified (such as asking family for help or winning the lottery).

Not all well-defined problems are routine and not all ill-defined problems are non-routine. For example, the following problem from Sternberg and Davidson (1982) is well-defined but non-routine: "Water lilies double in area every 24 hours. At the beginning of the summer, there is one water lily on the lake. It takes 60 days for the lake to be covered with water lilies. On what day is the lake half covered?" According to Sternberg and Davidson, a common wrong answer is to divide 60 by 2 and get 30 as the answer. Although the computation is correct, the problem solver is using an inappropriate solution procedure. Thus, this problem is non-routine because the way to solve the problem is not immediately obvious to the problem solver. The problem is well-defined, however, because the initial state and goal state are clear, and the operators are the rules of arithmetic.

Finally, some mathematics problems require computation, such as "604 − 207 = ___" and some mathematics problems require understanding in addition to (or instead of) computation such as, "Christine borrowed $850 for one year from the Friendly Finance Company. If she paid 12% simple interest on the loan, what was the total amount she repaid?" (Dossey, Mullins, Lindquist, & Chambers, 1988). For computation problems, students must carry out basic mathematical procedures but for understanding problems, students must build a mental representation of the problem situation. Assessments of mathematical performance show that students in the United States perform adequately on computation but poorly on understanding problems (Dossey et al., 1988; Mayer & Hegarty, 1996). However, surveys of U.S. mathematics textbooks show that most space is devoted to computation rather than understanding problems (Mayer, Sims, & Tajika, 1995).

Cognitive Processes in Mathematical Problem Solving

Consider the following problem (Hegarty, Mayer, & Green, 1992; Hegarty, Mayer, & Monk, 1995):

> At Lucky, butter costs 65 cents per stick.
> This is 2 cents less per stick than butter at Vons.
> If you need to buy 4 sticks of butter,
> how much will you pay at Vons?

What does a problem solver need to know in order to solve this problem? The major thesis of this chapter is that mathematical problem solving depends on four intertwined cognitive processes—translating, integrating, planning, and executing (Mayer, 1992, 1999). Table 3.1 summarizes the definition, example, and knowledge involved for each cognitive process. I refer to this model as the componential theory of mathematical problem solving.

Translating occurs when a problem solver takes a problem sentence such as "At Lucky, butter costs 65 cents per stick" and converts it into a mental representation such as "LUCKY BUTTER = .65." The process of translating depends on the problem solver's storehouse of *semantic knowledge* (such as knowing that there are one hundred cents in a dollar) and linguistic knowledge (such as knowing the English language).

Table 3.1. Four Cognitive Processes In Mathematical Problem Solving

Process problem	Definition	Knowledge	Example from butter
Translating	Converting sentence into mental representation	Semantic & linguistic	"a stick of butter costs 65 cents at Lucky" is represented as "LUCKY BUTTER = .65"
Integrating	Building a mental model of the problem situation	Schematic	Butter problem seen as "total cost = (LUCKY BUTTER + 2) × 4"
Planning	Devising a plan for how to solve the problem	Strategic	First, add 2 cents to 65 cents. Then, multiply the result by 4.
Executing	Carrying out the plan	Procedural	65 + 2 = 67. 67 × 4 = $2.68

Integrating occurs when a problem solver builds a mental model of the situation described in the problem or what can be called a *situation model* or *problem model* (Kintsch & Greeno, 1985; Mayer & Hegarty, 1996). For example, in the butter problem the problem solver must mentally select relevant information and organize it into a coherent mental representation such as a mental number line with Lucky at 65 and Vons two steps to the right. The process of integrating depends on *schematic knowledge* (such as knowing that this problems fits the problem type, "total cost = unit cost × number of units").

Planning occurs when a problem solver devises a solution plan, such as first determining the price of a stick of butter at Vons by adding 2 to 65, and then determining the total cost of 4 sticks of butter by multiplying the result by 4. The process of planning requires *strategic knowledge* (such as knowing how to break a solution plan into component steps). In addition to planning, *monitoring* involves keeping track of the effectiveness of the solution plan, and *reflecting* involves looking back over the cognitive processing involved in producing a completed problem solution.

Executing occurs when a problem solver carries out a solution plan, such as adding 2 to 65 to get 67 and multiplying 4 times 67 to get $2.68. The process of executing requires *procedural knowledge* (such as how to carry out arithmetic computations).

It is customary in cognitive theories of problem solving to break problem solving into two interrelated stages—*problem representation* in which the problem solver builds a mental representation of the problem and *problem solution* in which the problem solver devises and carries out a solution plan. As you can see, translating and integrating are components in problem representation whereas planning and executing are components in problem solution. Although the cognitive processes can be listed in linear order, solving most problems involves many iterations among the cognitive processes so the processes of problem representation sometimes can occur after the processes of problem solution. In addition, although this chapter focuses only on cognitive processing, many scholars have pointed to the role of affective, motivational, and attitudinal processes in problem solving (Kilpatrick et al., 2001; Schoenfeld, 1985, 1992).

I focus on research on mathematics word problems because word problems are most often associated with problem solving in the mathematics curriculum (Reed, 1999). Verschaffel, Greer, and de Corte (2000, p. ix) define word problems as "verbal descriptions of problem situations wherein one or more questions are raised the answer to which can be obtained by the application of mathematical operations to numerical data available in the problem statement." The butter problem matches this definition because the problem solver must carry out arithmetic operations on numbers in the problem statement—adding 2 to 67 and multiplying the result by 4.

According to the componential theory of mathematical problem solving, mathematical problem solving requires each of these four cognitive processes applied in a coordinated and intertwined way. In the remainder of this chapter, I explore exemplary research concerning each of these cognitive processes involved in mathematical problem solving.

TRANSLATING

What Is Translating?

Translating occurs when a problem solver reads or hears a sentence from a problem (e.g., "At Lucky, butter costs 65 cents per stick") and constructs a mental representation corresponding to the sentence. The mental representation may be in verbal form (e.g., "a stick of butter is 65 cents at Lucky"), symbolic form (e.g., "LUCKY BUTTER = .65"), pictorial form (e.g., an image of a number line with Lucky at the 65 spot), or some other form. In any problem, there may be several sentences, and thus several representations that must be constructed. When sentences are long and contain many individual facts, translating involves representing each portion of the sentence. Translating is a key component in problem representation.

To accomplish the process of translating, a problem solver needs a vast storehouse of semantic and linguistic knowledge. Semantic knowledge refers to knowledge of facts about objects and events such as knowing that butter can come in sticks or that there are 100 cents in a dollar. Linguistic knowledge refers to knowledge of the language that is used to present the problem such as knowing that "65 cents per stick" means that each stick costs 65 cents.

Research on Translating

Although comprehending the sentences in a word problem may seem like a simple task, there is ample research evidence that many students experience serious difficulties. For example, the *structural hypothesis* posits that assignment sentence structures in which a value is assigned to a variable (such as "At Lucky, butter costs 65 cents per stick") are more psychologically basic than relational sentence structures, which express a quantitative relation between two variables (such as, "This [butter at Lucky] is 2 cents less per stick than at Vons"). Thus, students may have particular difficulty in representing relational sentences—showing a deficiency in the linguistic knowledge needed to support the process of translating.

In an early demonstration study, Soloway, Lochhead, and Clement (1982) asked college students to translate relational sentences into equations. For example, one task was to write an equation for "There are six times as many students as professors at this university" using S for students and P for professors. A common error was to write "6S = P," which can be called a *reversal error.* Across a set of several different relational sentences, college students produced reversal errors about one-third of the time.

In a more recent study, Hegarty et al. (1995) asked college students to solve a set of 12 problems and later gave a recognition test on several problems that contained relational sentences such as the butter problem described previously. Students failed to recognize the correct wording of the relational sentence (e.g., "This is 2 cents less per stick than butter at Vons") on more than one-third of the items. Interestingly, successful problem solvers tended to make literal errors by recognizing a problem containing a relational sentence that had the same meaning as the original (e.g., "Butter at Vons cost 2 cents more per stick than at Lucky") whereas unsuccessful problem solvers tended to make semantic errors by recognizing problems containing a relational sentence that had a different meaning from the original (e.g., "This is 2 cents more per sick than butter at Vons"). Complementary results were obtained by Lewis and Mayer (1987), in which students were far more likely to make errors in remembering relational sentences than in remembering assignment sentences.

Mayer (1982) asked college students to listen to a list of 8 word problems and then to recall them. Students made errors on 29% of the relational statements such as changing a relational statement from the problem ("The steamer's engine drives in still water at a rate of 12 miles per hour more than the rate of the current") into an assignment statement in the recall protocol ("Its engines push the boat 12 mph in still water").

Riley, Greeno, and Heller (1983) reported a similar result with children who were asked to listen to a word problem and then repeat it. When the problem contained a relational statement such as, "Tom has 5 more marbles than Joe," children frequently made errors in recall such as, "Tom has 5 marbles."

What happens when we reword relational sentences? To investigate this issue, Hudson (1983) found that only 17% of nursery school children correctly solved a simple word problem: "There are 5 birds and 3 worms. How many more birds are there than worms?" However, the solution rate soared to 83% when the relational sentence was reworded: "There are 5 birds and 3 worms. How many birds won't get a worm?"

Overall, these results provide consistent evidence that students have difficulty in processing relational sentences. These results provide support for the structural hypothesis, and point to the role of linguistic knowledge in mathematical problem solving.

Instructional Implications of Research on Translating

How can we help students become more effective problem solvers? One implication of research on translating is that some students may benefit from training in how to mentally represent problem sentences. In particular, many scholars have called for giving students practice with translating across multiple representations—such as being able to translate mathematical information among verbal, pictorial, and symbolic forms (Brenner, Mayer, Moseley, Barr, Duran, Reed, & Webb, 1997; Moreno & Mayer, 1999; van Someren, Reimann, Boshuizen, & de Jong, 1998).

For example, Lewis (1989) developed a 2-session translation training program for college students who were having difficulty in solving word problems. Students learned how to distinguish relational sentences and assignment sentences in word problems, and how to translate a sentence (verbal form) into a mark on a number line (pictorial form). On a typical work sheet, students first translate an assignment sentence (e.g., "Megan has saved $420 for vacation") into a mark on a number line (e.g., "Megan" written at the "420" point on the line). Then, students translate a relational sentence (e.g., "She saved one-fifth as much as James saved") by placing a mark for "James" either to the left or right or "Megan" on the number line. Students receive feedback and must justify their translation of the relational sentence. This process is intended to help students overcome what Schoenfeld (1991, p. 316) calls "suspension of sense-making—suspending the requirement that the way the problems are stated makes sense."

Does translation training affect mathematical problem solving? To answer this question, Lewis (1989) gave pretests and posttest containing word problems to students who received the training (trained group) and to equivalent students who did not (control group). The error rate fell greatly for the trained group but not for the control group, providing strong evidence for the effectiveness of teaching students how to translate sentences into pictorial representations.

More recently, Brenner et al. (1997) incorporated multiple representation training into a 4-week unit on functions in a junior high school pre-algebra course. For example, students learned how to draw a graph that corresponded to an equation or how to write a sentence to describe a functional relation in a table. Students who received instruction in how to translate among sentences, graphs, tables, and equations showed substantial pretest-to-posttest gains in solving algebra word problems as compared to equivalent students who received conventional instruction.

Overall, these training studies offer encouraging demonstrations that students can learn to become better mathematical problem solvers when then hone their problem translation skills. Learning to translate the sentences of a problem into another representation—such as a paraphrase, an equation, or a graphic—is a useful component in mathematical problem solving.

INTEGRATING

What Is Integrating?

The foregoing section shows that comprehending each sentence (i.e., translating each sentence into a mental representation) is an important component in understanding a word problem (i.e., problem representation). However, problem representation also involves building a mental model of the problem situation—which I call the process of integrating. A mental model consists of all relevant information organized into a coherent structure. In the butter problem, a mental model could be represented as an equation such as "total cost = (cost at Vons + 2) × 4," as a picture such as a number line with Vons at 65 and Lucky located 2 steps to the right, or some other form of representation. The construction of a mental model—also called a situation model or problem model (Kintsch & Greeno, 1985; Mayer & Hegarty, 1996; Nathan, Kintsch, & Young, 1992; Verschaffel et al., 2000)—is an act of sense making which requires that the problem solver apply relevant prior knowledge.

According to the componential theory of mathematical problem solving, integrating relies on schematic knowledge, that is, knowledge of problem situations. For example, a person's everyday knowledge about buying products in a supermarket includes the problem situation type that is relevant for the butter problem: "total cost = unit cost × number of units." The butter problem makes sense to a problem solver who interprets it as a situation in which total cost equals unit cost times number of items. Thus, problem solvers need a storehouse of knowledge about problem situations and need to know how to adapt that knowledge to understanding a problem statement.

Research on Integrating

There are numerous examples of students failing to see mathematical problem solving as a sense-making activity. Schoenfeld (1991, p. 316) posits that "suspension of sense-making develops in school as a result of schooling." For example, 13 year olds were asked to solve the following problem as part of the National Assessment of Educational Progress: "An army bus holds 36 soldiers. If 1128 soldiers are being bussed to their training site, how many busses are needed?" Carpenter, Linquist, Mathews, and Silver (1983) reported that most of students correctly divided 36 into 1128 to obtain a quotient of 31 remainder 12. However, less than one-fourth of the students went on to give the correct answer that 32 busses were needed. Instead, they often gave incorrect answers such as "31" or "31 remainder

12." Similar results were obtained when Silver, Shapiro, and Deutsch (1993) asked middle school students to solve the following problem: "The Clearview Little League is going to a Pirates game. There are 540 people including players, coaches, and parents. They will travel by bus, and each bus holds 40 people. How many buses will they need to get to the game?" Apparently, students failed to interpret the bus problem as a meaningful situation and instead engaged mainly in manipulating symbols.

Nesher (1980) asked fifth-graders to solve the following problem: "What will be the temperature of water in a container if you pour 1 jug of water at 80 degrees F and 1 jug at 40 degrees F into it?" The students knew that when you mix warm and cool water, you get lukewarm water; yet, many students gave "120 degrees F" as their answer. Rather than trying to understand the situation presented in the problem, they seem to have used a school-taught rule that when you put two things together you add the numbers.

Even when the problem contains internal contradictions, some students may focus on computing with the numbers rather than understanding the presented situation. For example, Paige and Simon (1966) asked students to solve the following problem: "The number of quarters a man has is seven times the number of dimes he has. The value of the dimes exceeds the value of the quarters by $2.50. How many of each coin does he have?" Only about one-third of the students recognized that the value of the dimes cannot exceed the value the quarters if the man has more quarters than dimes. Instead, many students correctly translated the sentences into equations, such as, "$Q = 7D$" and "$D(.10) = 2.50 + Q(.25)$," and then computed a numerical answer by solving the equations. For example, some students concluded that there would be a negative number of dimes.

Taken together, these results point to the difficulties that students have in building mental models from word problems. Verschaffel et al. (2000) have reviewed research studies documenting students' failures in making sense of word problems. According to the *suspension of sense-making hypothesis*, many errors in mathematical problem solving can be attributed to students failure to engage in the process of mental model building—that is, a failure to use their prior knowledge about problem situations to make sense of a current problem.

Hinsley, Hayes, and Simon (1977) demonstrated that high school students possess a rich storehouse of schematic knowledge concerning problem situations typically described in word problems. When they asked the students to sort a collection of word problems into categories, the students were able to do so easily and with high agreement. In all, 18 categories were constructed by the students such as work problems, time-rate-distance problems, river current problems, interest problems, mixture problems and so on.

In an analysis of word problems used in California secondary school mathematics textbooks, Mayer (1981) identified 20 basic problem situations, with each involving several different variations. In a follow-up study, students read and recalled a list of word problems selected for those appearing in the textbooks. Students tended to make errors in recall by changing a low-frequency version of a problem situation into a high-frequency version (Mayer, 1982).

In a related study, Riley et al. (1983) asked children in grades K through 3 to use objects to represent word problems. Problems involving a change situation—in which you begin with a set and add to (or subtract from) it—were the easiest for children to model, such as "Joe has 3 marbles. Then Tom gave him 5 more marbles. How many does he have now?" Problems involving a compare situation—in which you have two sets and a difference between them—were the most difficult, such as, "Joe has 3 marbles. Tom has 5 more marbles than Joe. How many marbles does Tom have?" There was a developmental trend in which the youngest children tended to represent all problems as change problems, but older students recognized a wider variety of problem situations. Even though the arithmetic computations were equivalent across problem types, students experienced difficulty when they were confronted with an unfamiliar problem situation. More recently, Marshall (1995) has found complimentary evidence for the role of schemas in problem solving.

Overall, research on integrating points to the need for students to build mental models of problem situations, that is, to engage in sense making rather than blind symbol manipulation. Mathematical problem solving depends on the construction of a coherent mental representation of the problem situation, and this activity is supported by having and using a storehouse of knowledge about familiar problem situations—what can be called schematic knowledge.

Instructional Implications of Research on Integrating

Can students learn to improve their integrating skills? Low, Over, Doolan, and Mitchell (1994) developed an 80-minute training problem in which low-ability students were given 27 word problems that contained sufficient, irrelevant, or missing information. For each problem, students in the trained group learned to recognize irrelevant information and underline it, to recognize that information was needed and specify what the missing information was, and to recognize when a problem contained the numbers needed to solve it. For example, the problem, "The length of a rectangular park is 6 meters more than its width. A walkway 3 meters wide surrounds the park. Find the dimensions of the park if it has an area of 432 square meters," contains irrelevant information about the 3-meter wide walkway. The problem, "The lengths of the sides of a blackboard are on a 2:3 ratio. What is the perimeter (in meters) of the blackboard?", lacks essential information such as the length of one of the sides. The problem, "The rectangular lawn is 12 meters long and 5 meters wide. Calculate the area of a path 1.75 meters wide around the lawn," contains sufficient information. Other students received no training (control group) or received 80 minutes of practice solving problems like those given to the trained group (conventional group).

Students in the trained group showed a large pretest-to-posttest gain in their ability to solve word problems whereas the other groups did not. These results are consistent with previous results showing a strong correlation between performance on recognizing problems with sufficient, irrelevant, and missing information and performance on solving word problems (Low & Over, 1989). When students learn how to recognize relevant and irrelevant information in a word problem, they are learning how to build a coherent mental model of the problem situation. Thus, improvements in model building skills lead to improvements in mathematical problem solving.

Schwartz, Nathan, and Resnick (1996) report another attempt to teach students how to build coherent mental models of word problems. Students learned how to use a computer program called ANIMATE, which created a visual representation of the problem that could be run as an animation. For example, one of the problems students learned to represent was the following: "A huge ant is terrorizing San Francisco. It travels east toward Detroit, which is 2400 miles away, at 400 miles per hour. The Army learns of this one hour later and sends a helicopter west from Detroit at 600 miles per hour to intercept the ant. If the ant left at 2 p.m., what time will the helicopter and ant collide (ignoring any time changes)?" (Nathan et al., 1992).

On a pretest most students failed to solve this problem, but conventional training on how to solve time-rate-distance problems did not result in much improvement on solving word problems. However, allowing students to use the ANIMATE problem to create and test various concrete representations of the problem resulted in huge pretest-to-posttest gains in solving new word problems. Thus, the ANIMATE training was successful in honing students' model building skills, which ultimately resulted in improvements in mathematical problem solving.

Taken together, these exemplary training studies encourage the idea that integrating skills can be taught. Further, the results are consistent with the idea that integrating skills are a key component in mathematical problem solving. Rather than seeing word problems as vehicles for symbol manipulation, students need practice in understanding the situation being described in the problem.

PLANNING

What Is Planning?

Planning occurs when a problem solver devises a plan for how to solve a problem. For example, in the butter problem, a problem solver may devise a two-step plan—first, find the cost of one stick of butter at Vons by adding 2 cents to 65 cents; and second, find the total cost of four sticks of butter at Vons by multiplying the result by 4. Planning is a key component in solution execution.

In devising a plan, a problem solver relies on strategic knowledge—that is, strategies for what to do when no plan is obvious. One of the most effective problem-solving strategies is to find a related problem that you know how to solve. Polya (1965, p. 3) states the strategy (or heuristic) as follows: "If you cannot solve the proposed problem, look around for an appropriate related problem." For example, Polya (p. 2) presents the following problem: "Find the volume F of the frustrum of a right pyramid with square base, given the altitude h of the frustrum, the length a of a side of its upper base, and the length b of a side of its lower base." If you do not know how to solve this problem, one strategy is to think of a problem you can solve. Suppose you know how to find the volume of right pyramid. Then, you must restate the presented problem in a slightly different way that is more consistent with the problem you can solve—such as seeing the volume of the frustrum as what is left over when you subtract the volume of the smaller pyramid from the volume of the larger pyramid. Thus, the problem is changed into a task you know how to do, namely, finding the volume of two pyramids and subtracting the smaller from the larger.

Monitoring and reflecting are metacognitive processes related to planning. In monitoring, during the course of problem solving you determine whether the plan is working and change it if it is not working. In reflecting, after the problem is solved you look back over what you have done in order to glean strategies for planning solutions in the future. In this section, I focus on planning strategies aimed at helping students find a related problem.

Research on Planning

The find-a-related-problem strategy relies on the idea that planning a problem solution involves analogical thinking. When presented with a word problem that does not seem to suggest an obvious solution procedure (called the *target problem*) the problem solver must think of related problem that he or she knows how to solve (called the *base problem*). According to the *analogical reasoning hypothesis*, three steps are involved in devising a solution plan: (a) *recognizing*, in which you find a base problem that is related to the target problem, (b) *abstracting*, in which you identify a general solution method or principle from the base problem, and (c) *mapping*, in which you adapt the solution method or principle to the target problem. A major challenge is that problem solvers may find a related problem on the basis of *surface similarity*—such as finding a base problem that has the same cover story as the target problem—rather than *structural similarity*—such as finding a base problem that has a solution method that is needed in the target problem.

There is overwhelming evidence that students often have difficulty in recognizing structural similarity between word problems (Reed, 1999). For example, Reed (1987) provided students with a detailed description of how to solve the nurse problem: "A nurse mixes 6% boric acid solution with a 12% boric acid solution. How many pints of each are needed to make 4.5 pints of an 8% boric acid solution?" Then, when students were asked to solve problems that were structurally identical ("A grocer mixes peanuts worth \$1.65 a pound and almonds worth \$2.10 a pound. How many pounds of each are needed to make 30 pounds of a mixture worth \$1.83 a pound?") and structurally similar to the nurse problem ("One alloy of copper is 20% pure copper and another is 12 pure copper. How much of each alloy must be melted together to obtain 60 pounds of alloy containing 10.4 pounds of copper?"), they performed poorly indicating that they did not recognize how to apply the solution method in the nurse problem to the new problems. As you can see, the new problems have the same or similar structure as the nurse problem but not the surface characteristics (i.e., not the same cover story). Thus, remembering a structurally related base problem is difficult when it does not share surface features with the target problem.

As another example, Bassok (1997) reports that physics students learned how to solve the following problem in the context of a physics lesson: "The speed of a car increases at a constant rate during a period of 10 seconds from 5 m/s to 25 m/s. What distance, in meters, will the car travel during the 10-second period?" Shortly, afterwards the student was given the following problem as a pretest to an algebra lesson: "Over the last 6 years, Juanita's salary increased every year by a constant amount, from \$21,000 in the first year to \$24,000 in the seventh year. How much money did she earn during this 6-year period?" Even though the problems are structurally equivalent—that is, they are based on the same mathematical solution method—almost all of the students failed to see that the problems were related. Bassok (1997) has shown that transfer of a solution method from one problem to another depends on several features, including the surface features of the problems.

Ross (1987) asked students to read a text on probability that contained several worked-out statistics problems and then take a test on new problems. Students performed well on test problems that had the same structural and surface features as a worked-out example, but poorly on problems that had the same structural with different surface features as a worked-out example. As with Reed's results, Ross's study shows that students have difficulty remembering a related problem when it does not share surface features with the target problem.

There is also consistent evidence that skilled problem solvers are more likely than beginners to recognize structural similarities among word problems. For example, Silver (1981) asked students to sort word problems into groups that were mathematically related and to solve the problems. Students who were successful in problem solving tended to sort the problems based on structural similarity—putting together problems that required the solution method—whereas unsuccessful problem solvers tended to sort the problems on the basis of surface similarity—putting together problems that had the same cover story.

Chi, Glaser, and Rees (1982) reported similar results. When novices in physics were asked to sort physics word problems into categories, the categories tended to share common objects such as inclined planes or springs (i.e., surface similarity). In contrast, experts in physics were more likely to sort the problems on the basis of physics principles such as putting all conservation-of-energy problems together or all Newton's-second-law problems together.

In a within-learner study, Quilici and Mayer (2002) asked students to sort statistics word problems before and after they took their first statistics course. Students were more likely to sort problems based on surface characteristics on the pretest and on the basis of structural characteristics on the posttest. Apparently, as students gain more experience, they are better able to find related problems that share compatible solution methods.

Instructional Implications of Research on Planning

Can students be taught to do a better a job at finding a related problem? A growing research base encourages the idea that such strategies can be taught successfully. For example, Quilici and Mayer (2002) taught students how to recognize structural similarities among statistic word problems. Students learned through direct instruction that t-test problems always involved two groups and a quantitative measure (using the form, Is group A different from group B on measure C?), chi-square problems always involved two groups and a categorical measure (using the form, Is group A more likely than group B to have characteristic C?), and correlation problems always involved one group and quantitative measures (using the form, Is measure A related to measure B for group C?). As a posttest, students were asked to sort a set of statistics word problems into groups based on similarities. Students who had received no training tended to sort the problems based on their surface characteristics (i.e., putting together problems with the same cover story), whereas students who received training tended to sort the problems based on their structural characteristics (i.e., putting t-test problems together, chi-square problems together, and correlation problems together). When asked to generate a similar problem for each grouping, the trained students were much more likely than the untrained students to produce a problem that was structurally similar. These results and related findings (Quilici & Mayer, 1996) suggest that it is possible to help students search for related problems on the basis of structural characteristics rather than surface characteristics.

Complementary results were obtained by Cummins (1992) using algebra word problems and by Dufresne, Gerace, Hardiman, and Mestre (1992) using physics word problems. For example, Cummins found that students who practiced on identifying corresponding variables in pairs of algebra word problems were subsequently more able to sort problems on the basis of structural similarity than were students who received practice in answering factual questions about the problems. Similarly, Dufresne et al. found that students who learned to systematically analyze the structural components of physics word problems were better able to sort problems based on structural characteristics than were control students who practiced on solving the problems. Overall, there is encouraging evidence that the strategy of finding a structurally related problem can be taught.

EXECUTING

What is Executing?

Executing occurs when the problem solver carries out mathematical operations, such as arithmetic computations or algebraic transformations. When the problem solver executes a solution plan, the problem solver engages in activity that changes the problem state. For example, in the butter problem the problem solver adds 2 cents to 65 cents using the rules of arithmetic and comes up with the answer, 67 cents; then the problem solver multiplies 67 cents by 4 using the rules of arithmetic, yielding an answer of $2.68.

The process of executing is supported by procedural knowledge, that is, knowledge of algorithms (or procedures) in which an operator is applied to a representation and results in the creation of a new representation. Algorithms specify a sequence of operations, resulting in a sequence of transformations of a mathematical representation. Thus, the procedure for addition or multiplication is an example of procedural knowledge. A procedure is different from a strategy because a procedure always produces the same output given the same input whereas a strategy is a general approach to a problem that does not guarantee solution.

Research on Executing

Although problem solving and computation are sometimes portrayed as competing goals in mathematics learning, cognitive research points to the role of computational fluency as an aid to mathematical problem solving (Kilpatrick et al., 2001; Mayer, 1999, 2002). When computations can be carried out without much conscious mental effort, students can devote more of their limited cognitive resources to other components of mathematical problem solving.

How do students develop computational fluency—the ability to carry out computations without much mental effort? Fuson (1992) has reviewed research showing that students may progress through four stages as they develop computational fluency for simple addition: counting-all, counting-on, derived facts, and known facts. In the counting-all method, students turn an addition problem such as $3 + 5 = $ ___ into a counting problem by counting out the first number (such as saying "1, 2, 3") and counting out the second number (such as saying "4, 5, 6, 7, 8"). In counting-on, students begin with the first number and increment it by the second, such as saying "3, [pause] 4, 5, 6, 7, 8." Groen and Parkman (1972) were the first to provide response-time data showing that many first graders used a version of the counting-on approach to simple addition. In the derived-facts method students change an unknown problem into a known problem, such as saying: "I can take 1 from the 5 and give it to the 3. Four plus 4 is 8." In the derived-facts method, the students have memorized answers for each addition fact, so they can say, "Five plus 3 is 8." Using intensive interviews and observations, Siegler and Jenkins (1989) found that primary grade students alternate among using each of these methods, sometimes solving one problem in one way and another in another way. Eventually, adults reach automaticity in which they effortlessly "look up" answers in their memory (Ashcraft & Stazyk, 1981).

Why do students make errors in carrying out computational procedures? To help answer this question, Brown and Burton (1978) asked primary grade children to solve a collection of three-column subtraction problems such as 564 − 472 = ___. Examining the pattern of errors showed that students often made errors by correctly applying a procedure that had one or more incorrect steps in it, analogous to running a program that had a few bugs in it. For example, in the *smaller-from-larger bug* a student always subtracts the smaller number from the larger one in each column, e.g., 564 − 472 = 112. Thus, learning a computational procedure involves repairing bugs that can be pinpointed by careful error analyses.

Instructional Implications of Research on Executing

Overall, the path to computational fluency requires focused practice with feedback. Practice means that the student solves many problems; feedback means that the student receives guidance on his or her performance; and focused means that the practice is on tasks that the student needs to learn. Thorndike (1922) was an early proponent of drill and practice as the preferred method for teaching arithmetic. Anderson (2000; Anderson, Corbett, Koedinger, & Pelletier, 1995) has shown how mathematical problem solving can be described as a collection of specific knowledge units, which he calls *productions*—of the form, IF a certain condition is met THEN carry out a certain action. Computer-based tutoring systems can provide focused practice with feedback that insure that students learn all the productions needed for a topic in a high school mathematics course (Anderson, Corbett et al., 1995). With practice, the productions become automatic, allowing for the construction of strategies for creative problem solving.

Some instructional techniques seek to help students embed their knowledge of computational procedures within their existing knowledge. For example, Brownell and Moser (1949) conducted a classic study in which students learned how to carry out two-column subtraction in the conventional way (i.e., focusing on the procedure for symbol manipulation) or using concrete manipulatives such as bundles of sticks. Although both groups performed similarly on two-column subtraction, the students who learned with manipulatives—intended to help them see the connection with their prior knowledge—performed better on transfer problems such as three column subtraction problems.

More recently, similar results were obtained by Moreno and Mayer (1999) in which elementary school children learned a mathematical procedure in the context of a computer game. Some students learned by translating symbol statements such as "3 − −2 = ___" into pictorial form such a bunny moving along a number line (multiple representation group) whereas other students learned only by using symbols (single representation group). The multiple representation group showed a greater decrease in computational errors and conceptual bugs than did the single representation group. Overall, research on teaching of computational skill points to the importance of focused practice with feedback and to the need for students to connect symbol-based procedures with more familiar representations.

CONCLUSION

In summary, the thesis of this chapter is that mathematical problem solving involves several intertwined processes that I have labeled translating, integrating, planning, and executing. In recent years, there have been important advances in the cognitive psychology of mathematical cognition (Campbell, 1992; English, 1997; Grouws, 1992; Sternberg & Ben-Zeev, 1996). Thus, the study of mathematical cognition continues both as a useful venue for research in cognitive science and as a test bed for educational reform (Kilpatrick et al., 2001; Reed, 1999). The growing research base in mathematical cognition is consistent with Reed's (1999, p. 12) proposal that "curriculum changes should be guided by research."

From my vantage point overlooking the current state of the literature on the psychology of mathematical cognition, I foresee a multifaceted research agenda. First, in the area of basic research, there is a need to continue focused theory-based experimental studies that have already served to make the study of mathematics learning one of the most advanced psychologies of subject matter (Mayer, 1999). Second, in the area of basic research, there is a need for longitudinal microgenic studies of mathematics learning in real students over an extended time period, including intensive interviews and observations. Third, in the area of applied research, there is a need for well-controlled classroom studies of instructional interventions so that it is possible to document improvements in mathematics learning attributable to specific instructional manipulations. Fourth, the study of mathematical cognition needs to be expanded beyond *cold cognition* to account for motivational, affective, cultural, social, and developmental factors (e.g., Nunes, Schliemann, & Carraher, 1993). Finally, it would be useful to clarify the implications of research on mathematical cognition for teacher education (e.g., Ma, 1999) and assessment (Anderson et al., 2001).

AUTHOR NOTE

Correspondence should be sent to: Richard E. Mayer, Department of Psychology, University of California, Santa Barbara, CA 93106. The author's email address is: mayer@psych.ucsb.edu.

REFERENCES

Anderson, J.R. (2000). *Learning and memory.* New York: Wiley.

Anderson, J.R., Corbett, A.T., Koedinger, K., & Pelletier, R. (1995). Cognitive tutors: Lessons learned. *Journal of the Learning Sciences, 4,* 167–207.

Anderson, L.W., Krathwohl, D.R., Airasian, P., Cruikshank, K.A., Mayer, R.E., Pintrich, P.R., Raths, J., & Wittrock, M.C. (2001). *A taxonomy for teaching, learning, and assessing: A revision of Bloom's taxonomy of educational objectives.* New York: Longman.

Ashcraft, M.H., & Stazyk, E.H. (1981). Mental addition: A test of three verification models. *Memory and Cognition, 9,* 135–196.

Bassok, M. (1997). Two types of reliance on correlations between content and structure in reasoning about word problems. In L.D. English (Ed.), *Mathematical reasoning: Analogies, metaphors, and images* (pp. 221–246). Mahwah, NJ: Erlbaum.

Brenner, M.E., Mayer, R.E., Moseley, B., Barr, T., Duran, R., Reed, B.S., & Webb, D. (1997). Learning by understanding: The role of multiple representations in learning algebra. *American Educational Research Journal, 34,* 663–689.

Brown, J.S., & Burton, R.R. (1978). Diagnostic models for procedural bugs in basic arithmetic skills. *Cognitive Science, 2,* 155–192.

Brownell, W.A., & Moser, H.E. (1949). Meaningful versus mechanical learning: A study on grade 3 subtraction. In *Duke University Research Studies in Education,* No. 8. Durham, NC: Duke University Press.

Campbell, J.I.D. (1992). (Ed.), *The nature and origins of mathematical skills.* Amsterdam: Elsevier.

Carpenter, T.P., Lindquist, M.M., Mathews, W., & Silver, E.A. (1983). Results of the third NAEP mathematics assessment: Secondary school. *Mathematics Teacher, 76,* 652–659.

Chi, M.T.H., Glaser, R., & Rees, E. (1982). Expertise in problem solving. In R.J. Sternberg (Ed.), *Advances in the psychology of intelligence* (Vol. 1, pp. 7–76). Hillsdale, NJ: Erlbaum.

Cummins, D.D. (1992). Role of analogical reasoning in the induction of problem categories. *Journal of Experimental Psychology: Learning, Memory, and Cognition, 15,* 153–166.

Dossey, J.A., Mullis, I.V.S., Lindquist, M.M., & Chambers, D.L. (1988). *The mathematics report card: Are we measuring up?* Princeton, NJ: Educational Testing Service.

Dufresne, R.J. , Gerace, W.J., Hardiman, P.T., & Mestre, J.P. (1992). Constraining novices to perform expertlike problem analyses: Effects on schema acquisition. *Journal of the Learning Sciences, 2,* 307–331.

English, L.D. (Ed.). (1997). *Mathematical reasoning.* Mahwah. NJ: Erlbaum.

Fuson, K.C. (1992). Research on whole number addition and subtraction. In D.A. Grouws (Ed.), *Handbook of research on mathematics teaching and learning* (pp. 243–275). New York: Macmillan.

Groen, G.J., & Parkman, J.M. (1972). A chronometric analysis of simple addition. *Psychological Review, 97,* 329–343.

Hegarty, M., Mayer, R.E., & Green, C. (1992). Comprehension of arithmetic word problems: Evidence from students' eye fixations. *Journal of Educational Psychology, 84,* 76–84.

Hegarty, M., Mayer, R.E., & Monk, C.A. (1995). Comprehension of arithmetic word problems: A comparison of successful and unsuccessful problem solvers. *Journal of Educational Psychology, 87,* 18–32.

Hinsley, D., Hayes, J.R., & Simon, H.A. (1977). From words to equations. In P. Carpenter & M. Just (Eds.), *Cognitive process in comprehension* (pp. 89–106). Hillsdale, NJ: Erlbaum.

Hudson, T. (1983). Correspondences and numerical differences between disjoint sets. *Child Development, 54,* 84–90.

Kilpatrick, J., Swafford, J., & Findell, B. (Eds.). (2001). *Adding it up: Helping children learn mathematics.* Washington, DC: National Academy Press.

Kintsch, W., & Greeno, J.G. (1985). Understanding and solving word problems. *Psychological Review, 92,* 109–129.

Lewis, A.B. (1989). Training students to represent arithmetic word problems. *Journal of Educational Psychology, 79,* 521–531.

Lewis, A.B., & Mayer, R.E. (1987). Students' miscomprehension of relational statements in arithmetic word problems. *Journal of Educational Psychology, 79,* 363–371.

Low, R., & Over, R. (1989). Detection of missing and irrelevant information within algebraic story problems. *British Journal of Educational Psychology, 59,* 296–305.

Low, R., Over, R., Doolan, L., & Mitchell, S. (1994). Solution of algebraic word problems following training in identifying necessary and sufficient information within problems. *American Journal of Psychology, 107,* 423–439.

Ma, L. (1999). *Knowing and teaching elementary mathematics.* Mahwah, NJ: Erlbaum.

Maier, N.R.F., & Burke, R.J. (1967). Response availability as a factor in problem-solving performance in males and females. *Journal of Personality and Social Psychology, 5,* 304–310.

Marshall, S.P. (1995). *Schemas in problem solving.* New York: Cambridge University Press.

Mayer, R.E. (1981). Frequency norms and structural analysis of algebra story problems into families, categories, and templates. *Instructional Science, 10,* 135–175.

Mayer, R.E. (1982). Memory for algebra story problems. *Journal of Educational Psychology, 74,* 199–216.

Mayer, R.E. (1992). *Thinking, problem solving, cognition* (2nd ed). New York: Freeman.

Mayer, R.E. (1999). *The promise of educational psychology: Volume 1, Learning in the content areas.* Upper Saddle River, NJ: Merrill/Prentice-Hall.

Mayer, R.E. (2002). *The promise of educational psychology: Volume 2, Teaching for meaningful learning.* Upper Saddle River, NJ: Merrill/Prentice-Hall.

Mayer, R.E. & Hegarty, M. (1996). The process of understanding mathematics problems. In R.J. Sternberg & T. Ben-Zeev (Eds.), *The nature of mathematical thinking* (pp. 29–53). Hillsdale, NJ: Erlbaum.

Mayer, R.E., Sims, V., & Tajika, H. (1995). A comparison of how textbooks teach mathematical problem solving in Japan and the United States. *American Educational Research Journal, 32,* 443–460.

Moreno, R., & Mayer, R.E. (1999). Multimedia-supported metaphors for meaning making in mathematics. *Cognition and Instruction, 17,* 215–248.

Nathan, M.J., Kintsch, W., & Young, E. (1992). A theory of algebra word problem comprehension and its implications for the design of learning environments. *Cognition and Instruction, 9,* 329–389.

Nesher, P. (1980). The stereotyped nature of school word problems. *For the Learning of Mathematics, 1*(1), 41–48.

Nunes, T., Schliemann, A.D., & Carraher, D.W. (1993). *Street mathematics and school mathematics.* New York: Cambridge University Press.

Paige, J.M., & Simon, H.A. (1966). Cognitive processes in solving algebra word problems. In B. Kleinmuntz (Ed.), *Problem solving: research, method, and theory.* New York: Wiley.

Polya, G. (1965). *Mathematical discovery, Volume II: On understanding, learning, and teaching problem solving.* New York: Wiley.

Quilici, J.H., & Mayer, R.E. (2002). Teaching students to recognize structural similarities between statistics word problems. *Applied Cognitive Psychology, 16,* 325–342.

Quilici, J.L. & Mayer, R.E. (1996). Role of examples in how students learn to categorize statistics word problems. *Journal of Educational Psychology, 88,* 144–161.

Reed, S.K. (1987). A structure-mapping model for word problems. *Journal of Experimental Psychology: Learning, Memory, and Cognition, 13,* 124–139.

Reed, S.K. (1999). *Word problems.* Mahwah, NJ: Erlbaum.

Riley, M., Greeno, J.G., & Heller, J. (1982). The development of children's problem solving ability in arithmetic. In H. Ginsburg (Ed.), *The development of mathematical thinking* (pp. 153–200). New York: Academic Press.

Ross, B.H. (1987). This is like that: The use of earlier problems and the separation of similarity effects. *Journal of Experimental Psychology: Learning, Memory, and Cognition, 13,* 629–639.

Schoenfeld, A.H. (1985). *Mathematical problem solving.* San Diego: Academic Press.

Schoenfeld, A.H. (1991). On mathematics as sense making: An informal attack on the unfortunate divorce of formal and informal mathematics. In J.F. Voss, D.N. Perkins, & J.W. Segal (Eds.), *Informal reasoning and education* (pp. 311–343). Hillsdale, NJ: Erlbaum.

Schoenfeld, A.H. (1992). Learning to think mathematically: Problem solving, metacognition, and sense making in mathematics. In D.A. Grouws (Ed.), *Handbook of research on mathematical teaching and learning* (pp. 334–370). New York: Macmillan.

Schwartz, B.B., Nathan, M.J., & Resnick, L.B. (1996). Acquisition of meaning for arithmetic structures with Planner. In S. Vosniadou, E. De Corte, R. Glaser, & H. Mandl (Eds.), *International perspectives on the design of technology-supported learning environments* (pp. 61–80). Hillsdale, NJ: Erlbaum.

Siegler, R.S., & Jenkins, E. (1989). *How children discover new strategies.* Hillsdale, NJ: Erlbaum.

Silver, E.A. (1981). Recall of mathematical problem information: Solving related problems. *Journal of Research in Mathematics Education, 12,* 54–64.

Silver, E.A., Shapiro, L.J., & Deutsch, A. (1993). Sense making and the solution of division problems involving remainders: An examination of middle school students' solution processes and their interpretations of solutions. *Journal for Research in Mathematics Education, 24,* 117–135.

Soloway, E., Lochhead, J., & Clement, J. (1982). Does computer programming enhance problem solving ability? In R.J. Seidel, R.E. Anderson, & B. Hunter (Eds.), *Computer literacy* (pp. 171–186). New York: Academic Press.

Someren, M.W. van, Reimann, P., Boshuizen, P.A., & de Jong, T. (Eds.). (1998). *Learning with multiple representations.* Amsterdam: Pergamon/Elsevier.

Sternberg, R.J., & Ben-Zeev, T. (1996). (Eds.), *The nature of mathematical thinking.* Hillsdale, NJ: Erlbaum.

Sternberg, R.J., & Davidson, J.E. (1982). The mind of the puzzler. *Psychology Today, 16,* 37–44.

Thorndike, E.L. (1922). *The psychology of arithmetic.* New York: Macmillan.

Verschaffel, L., Greer, B., & De Corte, E. (2000). *Making sense of word problems.* Lisse: Swets & Zeitlinger.

CHAPTER 4

LEARNING DISABILITIES IN BASIC MATHEMATICS

Deficits in Memory and Cognition

David C. Geary and Mary K. Hoard

ABSTRACT

Recent findings regarding the understanding of number concepts and counting principles, and the simple arithmetic competencies of normal and mathematically disabled (MD) children are reviewed. Differences across these groups are evident in the understanding of counting concepts and for several features of arithmetic skill development. In comparison to normal children, many children with MD show a developmental delay in the understanding of counting concepts, and use immature counting-based procedures and commit more procedural errors during the solving of arithmetic problems. Unlike normal children, children with MD do not transition as easily from use of counting-based procedures to memory-based processes, such as arithmetic fact retrieval. Use of immature counting procedures to solve arithmetic problems may be due to their poor understanding of counting concepts or poor skill at detecting and correcting counting-based errors. Deficits in arithmetic fact retrieval may be due to difficulties in lexical access

Mathematical Cognition, pages 93–115

(and storage) and/or inability to inhibit irrelevant associations from entering working memory during problem solving.

INTRODUCTION

During the past 30 years, considerable progress has been made in identifying the genetic, neural, and cognitive mechanisms that contribute to reading disability (RD), and in the ability to diagnose and remediate this form of learning disorder (LD; Lyon, Alexander, Yaffe, 1997; Morris et al., 1998; Smith, Kelley, & Brower, 1998; Torgesen, Wagner, Rashotte, Alexander, & Conway, 1997). Research on learning disabilities in mathematics (MD) has progressed more slowly than has research on RD, in part because of the complexity of the field of mathematics. In theory, MD can result from deficits in the ability to represent or process information used in one or all of the many areas of mathematics (e.g., arithmetic, geometry), or in one or a set of individual domains (e.g., theorems vs. graphing) within each of these areas (Geary, 1993; Russell & Ginsburg, 1984). To make the study of MD tractable, scientists have focused primarily on mathematical domains for which competency development in academically-normal children is well understood (Geary, Hamson, & Hoard, 2000; Jordan & Montani, 1997; Ostad, 1998a, 2000). These domains include number, counting, and arithmetic (e.g., Fuson, 1988; Geary, 1994; Gelman & Gallistel, 1978). The second section below provides an overview of normal development in these domains and the performance characteristics of children with MD. The section closes with an overview of research on the memory and cognitive deficits that contribute to these performance characteristics (McLean & Hitch, 1999). The first section provides the requisite background information on the etiology and prevalence of MD.

BACKGROUND CHARACTERISTICS OF CHILDREN WITH MD

Diagnosis

Measures that are specifically designed to diagnose MD are not available. As a result, most researchers rely on standardized achievement tests, often in combination with measures of intelligence (IQ). A score lower than the 20th or 25th percentile on a mathematics achievement test combined with a low average or higher IQ score are typical criteria for diagnosing MD (e.g., Geary et al., 2000; Gross-Tsur, Manor, & Shalev, 1996). However, lower than expected performance (based on IQ) on a mathematics achievement test does not, in and of itself, indicate the presence of MD.

Many children who score poorly on achievement tests one academic year score average or better during successive academic years. These children do not appear to have any of the underlying memory and (or) cognitive deficits described in the next section, and thus they should not be diagnosed as having MD (Geary, 1990; Geary, Brown, & Samaranayake, 1991; Geary et al., 2000). Children who have lower than expected achievement scores across successive academic years, in contrast, often have some form of memory and (or) cognitive deficit and thus a diagnosis of MD is often warranted.

It should also be noted that the cutoff of the 25th percentile on a mathematics achievement test does not fit with the estimation, described below, that between 5% and 8% of children have some form of MD. The discrepancy results from the nature of standardized achievement tests and the often rather specific memory and (or) cognitive deficits of children with MD. Standardized achievement tests sample a broad range of arithmetical and mathematical topics, whereas children with MD often have severe deficits in some of these areas and average or better competencies in others. The result of averaging across these topics is a level of performance (e.g., at the 20th percentile) that overestimates the competencies of children with MD in some areas and underestimates them in others.

Prevalence and Etiology

Measures that are more sensitive to MD than are standard achievement tests have been administered to samples of more than 300 children from well-defined populations (e.g., all fourth graders in an urban school district) in the United States (Badian, 1983), Europe (Kosc, 1974; Ostad, 1998b), and Israel (Gross-Tsur et al., 1996; Shalev, Manor, Kerem, Ayali, Badichi, Friedlander, & Gross-Tsur, 2001). These measures have largely assessed competencies in number and arithmetic and have been informed by neuropsychological studies of mathematical deficits following brain injury, that is, dyscalculia (for a discussion see Geary & Hoard, 2001; Shalev, Manor, & Gross-Tsur, 1993). Performance that deviates from age-related norms and is similar to that associated with dyscalculia is often considered an indication of MD. The use of these methods suggests that 5% to 8% of school-age children exhibit some form of MD.

As with other forms of LD, twin and familial studies suggest both genetic and environmental contributions to MD (Light & DeFries, 1995; Shalev et al., 2001). For instance, Shalev and her colleagues studied familial patterns of MD, specifically learning disabilities in number and arithmetic. The results showed that family members (e.g., parents and siblings) of children with MD are 10 times more likely to be diagnosed with MD than are members of the general population.

MODELS OF MATHEMATICAL DEVELOPMENT AND DISABILITIES

One framework for systematically approaching the study of MD involves applying the models and methods used to study mathematical development in academically-normal children to the study of children with poor mathematics achievement (e.g., Geary, 1990; Geary et al., 1991). As noted, this approach has been successfully followed in the areas of number, counting, and arithmetic, and has yielded many insights into the cognitive strengths and weaknesses of children with MD (Ackerman & Dykman, 1995; Barrouillet, Fayol, & Lathulière, 1997; Bull & Johnston, 1997; Bull, Johnston, & Roy, 1999; Garnett, & Fleischner, 1983; Geary, 1990, 1993; Geary & Brown, 1991; Geary, Widaman, Little, & Cormier, 1987; Hanich, Jordan, Kaplan, & Dick, 2001; Jordan, Levine, & Huttenlocher, 1995; Jordan & Montani, 1997; Ostad, 1997, 1998a, 2000; Räsänen, & Ahonen, 1995; Rourke, 1993; Russell, & Ginsburg, 1984; Svenson & Broquist, 1975). The sections below provide a brief overview of theoretical models of normal development in these areas, along with patterns that have been found with the comparison of children with MD and their academically-normal peers. Unless otherwise noted, MD refers to children with low achievement scores—relative to IQ in many of the studies—in mathematics. When studies have only focused on children with low mathematics achievement scores but average or better reading achievement scores, they will be referred to as children with MD only. Similarly, if the study assessed children with low achievement in mathematics and reading, they will be identified as children with MD/RD.

Number

The comprehension and production of numerical information require that children learn to process verbal (e.g., "three hundred forty-two") and Arabic representations (e.g., "342") of numbers and to transcode, or translate, these numerals from one representation to another (e.g., "three hundred forty-two" to "342"; Dehaene, 1992; McCloskey & Macaruso, 1995; Seron & Fayol, 1994). Equally important, children must come to understand the relation between the numerical representation and the quantity it represents, as well as related concepts, such as more than/less than, the base-10 structure of the Arabic number system, and so forth (see Fuson, 1988; Gallistel & Gelman, 1992; Geary, 1994).

Number production and comprehension in children with MD. Geary and colleagues found that first- and second-grade children with MD/RD or MD only showed normal competencies in comprehending, producing, and transcoding small-valued numerals (< 20; Geary, Hoard, & Hamson, 1999; Geary et al., 2000). The one exception was for the children with MD/RD, as these children had difficulties discriminating visually presented digits that were adjacent in magnitude (e.g., 8 9). In first grade, many of these children were unable to determine which numeral represented a larger number for small-valued (e.g., 2 3) or large-valued (e.g., 8 9) pairs. By second grade, most of the children knew that "3" represented more than "2" but still did not know that "9" represented more than "8." At both grade levels, IQ was used as a covariate and thus the performance of the children with MD/RD could not be attributed to intelligence.

These results suggest that the development of associations between Arabic numerals and the abstract representation of the associated magnitudes may develop more slowly in children with MD/RD than in other children. However, studies of older children with MD/RD or MD only suggest that they do eventually develop normal number production and comprehension skills, at least for the processing of simple numbers (Badian, 1983; Geary, 1993; Gross-Tsur et al., 1996). At the same time, much less is known about the ability of children with MD/RD or MD only to produce, comprehend, and transcode more complex numerals (e.g., 354) or understand larger-valued numbers (e.g., determining which represents more, 289 or 412). In one related study, Jordan and her colleagues found that second-grade children with MD/RD did not perform as well as other children on tasks that assessed knowledge of the base-10 system. The results of this study are difficult to interpret, however, given that the academically-normal children also performed poorly on the base-10 tasks, albeit not as poorly as the children with MD/RD (Hanich et al., 2001; Jordan & Hanich, 2000; see also Russell & Ginsburg, 1984).

Counting

It appears that children's counting knowledge emerges from a combination of inherent constraints and counting experience (Briars & Siegler, 1984; Geary, 1995; Gelman & Gallistel, 1978). Early inherent constraints on children's counting knowledge and counting behavior can be represented by Gelman and Gallistel's five implicit principles, described in Table 4.1. The principles of one-one correspondence, stable order, and cardinality define the "how to count" rules, which, in turn, provide constraints on the nature of preschool children's counting behavior and provide the skeletal structure for children's emerging knowledge of counting (Gelman & Meck, 1983).

In addition to inherent constraints, children also appear to make inductions about the basic characteristics of counting by observing standard counting behavior and the associated outcomes (Briars & Siegler, 1984; Fuson, 1988). These inductions likely elaborate Gelman and Gallistel's counting rules (1978), and result in a belief that certain unessential features of counting are essential, as noted in Table 4.1 (Briars & Siegler, 1984). In particular, young children often induce that the unessential features of adjacency and start at an end are in fact essential. The latter beliefs indicate that young children's conceptual understanding of counting is rather rigid and immature and influenced by the observation of standard counting procedures.

Counting knowledge in children with MD. Using the procedures developed by Gelman and Meck (1983) and Briars and Siegler (1984), Geary, Bow-Thomas, and Yao (1992) contrasted the counting knowledge of first grade children with MD/RD with that of their academically-normal peers. The procedure involves asking children to help a puppet learn how to count. The child watches the puppet count a series of objects. The puppet sometimes counts correctly and sometimes violates one of Gelman and Gallistel's (1978) counting principles or Briars and Siegler's unessential features of counting. The child's task is to determine if the puppet's count was "OK" or "not OK and wrong." In this way, the puppet performs the pro-

Table 4.1.   Implicit Counting Principles and Unessential Features of Counting

Implicit Principle	Description
One-one correspondence	One and only one word tag (e.g., "one," "two") is assigned to each counted object
Stable order	Order of the word tags must be invariant across counted sets
Cardinality	The value of the final word tag represents the quantity of items in the counted set
Abstraction	Objects of any kind can be collected together and counted
Order-irrelevance	Items within a given set can be tagged in any sequence
Unessential Feature	*Description*
Standard direction	Counting proceeds from left to right
Adjacency	Consecutive count of contiguous objects
Pointing	Counted objects are typically pointed at but only once
Start at an end	Counting starts at one of the end points of an array of objects

cedural aspect of counting (i.e., pointing at and tagging items with a number word), leaving the child's responses to be based on their conceptual understanding of counting.

In this study (i.e., Geary et al., 1992), the children were individually administered items that assessed all of Gelman and Gallistel's (1978) basic principles, as well as items that assessed most of Briars and Siegler's (1984) unessential features of counting. The results revealed that children with MD/RD and their academically-normal peers differed on only two types of counting trials, pseudo error and error. Pseudo error trials involved the puppet counting, for instance, the first, third, fifth, and seventh items and then returning to the left-hand side of the array and counting the second, fourth and sixth items. Technically the count is correct, but violates the adjacency rule. Labeling these counts as incorrect suggests that the children do not understand Gelman and Gallistel's (1978) order-irrelevance principle, and believe that adjacency is an essential feature of counting. Error trials involved double counting either the first or the last item. Children with MD/RD correctly identified these counts as errors when the last item was double counted, suggesting that they understand the one-one correspondence principle. Double counts were often labeled as correct when the first item was counted, suggesting that many children with MD/RD have difficulties holding information in working memory—in this case noting that the first item was double counted—while monitoring the act of counting (see also Hitch & McAuley, 1991).

In a more recent study, children with IQ scores in the 80–120 range were administered a series of experimental and achievement tests in first and second grade (Geary et al., 1999; Geary et al., 2000). Children who showed lower than expected (based on IQ) achievement scores in both grades were considered LD. The three resulting LD groups included children with MD/RD, MD only, and RD only. One of the experimental tasks consisted of a subset of the counting items that discriminated children with MD/RD and their academically-normal peers (Geary et al., 1992). Consistent with the results of Geary et al. (1992), children with MD/RD and MD only differed from the children with RD only and normal children on pseudo error trials in first and second grade and on error trials (double counting the first item in a series) in first grade. Table 4.2 shows mean scores for pseudo error and error trials; performance for filler items (i.e., correct counting and right-to-left counting) was greater than 84% correct identifications for all groups. The overall pattern suggests that even in second grade, many children with MD/RD and MD only do not fully understand counting concepts, and in first grade may have difficulty holding an error notation in working memory while monitoring the counting process (see also Hoard, Geary, & Hamson, 1999). In contrast, children with RD only performed as well as the academically-normal children on these items. The replication is also of interest, because IQ was used as a covariate in all analyses.

Table 4.2.   Mean Percentage of Correct Identifications for Pseudo Error and Error Counting Trials

Group	Pseudo Error Trials	Error Trials
Grade 1		
MD/RD	30	67
MD only	42	64
RD only	65	95
Normal	71	96
Grade 2		
MD/RD	30	88
MD only	16	86
RD only	73	95
Normal	63	90

In summary, many children with MD, independent of their reading achievement levels or IQ, have a poor conceptual understanding of some aspects of counting. These children understand most of the inherent counting rules identified by Gelman and Gallistel (1978), such as stable order and cardinality, but consistently err on tasks that assess order-irrelevance or adjacency from Briars and Siegler's (1984) perspective. It is not currently known whether the poor counting knowledge of children with MD/RD or MD only extends beyond the second grade. In any case, the poor counting knowledge of these children appears to contribute to their delayed procedural competencies (i.e., their delayed use of min counting) described in the next section, and may result in poor skill at detecting and thus correcting counting-procedure errors (Ohlsson & Rees, 1991).

Arithmetic

Developmental and schooling-based improvements in basic arithmetical competencies are reflected in changes in the distribution of procedures, or strategies, used in problem solving and in advances in children's conceptual understanding of arithmetic and related domains, such as counting (e.g., Ashcraft, 1982; Carpenter & Moser, 1984; Geary, 1994; Siegler, 1996; Siegler & Shrager, 1984). During the initial learning of addition, for instance, children typically count the addends to solve simple problems (e.g., 5+3). These counting procedures are sometimes executed with the aid of fingers—the finger counting strategy—and sometimes without them—the verbal counting strategy (Siegler & Shrager, 1984). The two most commonly used counting procedures, whether children use their fingers or not, are termed min, or counting-on, and sum, or counting-all (Fuson, 1982; Groen & Parkman, 1972). The min procedure involves stating the larger valued addend and then counting a number of times equal to the value of the smaller addend, such as counting 5, 6, 7, 8 to solve 5+3. The sum procedure involves counting both addends starting from 1. Occasionally, children will state the value of the smaller addend and then count the larger addend, which is termed the max procedure. The development of procedural competencies is related, in part, to improvements in children's conceptual understanding of counting and is reflected in a gradual shift from frequent use of the sum and max procedures to frequent use of min counting (Geary et al., 1992; Siegler, 1987).

At the same time, the use of counting procedures appears to result in the development of memory representations of basic facts (Siegler & Shrager, 1984). These memory representations support the use of memory-based problem-solving processes, specifically direct retrieval of arithmetic facts, decomposition, and fingers. With direct retrieval, children state an answer that is associated in long-term memory with the presented problem, such as stating "/eyt/" (i.e., eight) when asked to solve 5+3. Decomposition involves reconstructing the answer based on the retrieval of a partial sum. For instance, the problem 6+7 might be solved by retrieving the answer to 6+6 (i.e., 12) and then adding 1 to this partial sum. With the fingers strategy, children uplift a number of fingers corresponding to the addends and then state an answer without counting their fingers. The uplifted fingers appear to prompt retrieval of the answer. The use of retrieval-based processes is moderated by a confidence criterion. The confidence criterion represents an internal standard against which the child gauges confidence in the correctness of the retrieved answer. Children with a rigorous criterion only state answers that they are certain are correct, whereas children with a lenient criterion state any retrieved answer, correct or not (Siegler, 1988).

Figure 1 is a graphical summary of the expected direction of normal strategy development, as related to observational and reaction time studies and the amount of working memory resources required for strategy use. As the strategy mix matures, children solve problems more quickly because they use more efficient strategies and because, with practice, it takes less time to execute each strategy (Delaney, Reder, Staszewski, & Ritter, 1998; Geary, Bow-Thomas, Liu, & Siegler, 1996; Lemaire & Siegler, 1995). The transition to memory-based processes results in the quick solution of individual problems and in reductions in the working memory demands associ-

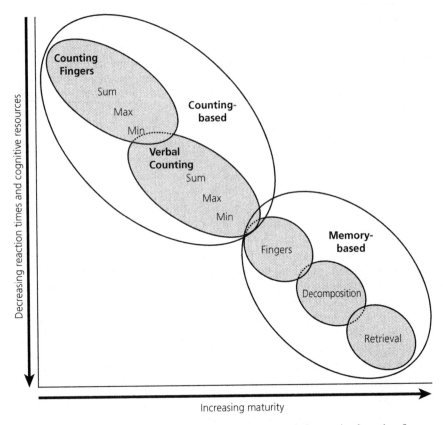

Figure 4.1.   Graphical representation of developmental change in the mix of strategies used to solve simple arithmetic problems.

ated with solving these problems. The eventual automatic retrieval of basic facts and the accompanying reduction in working memory demands, in turn, appear to make the solving of more complex problems in which the simple problems are embedded (e.g., word problems) less error prone (e.g., Geary, Liu, Chen, Saults, & Hoard, 1999; Geary & Widaman, 1992).

Arithmetic development in children with MD.   Studies conducted in the United States, Europe, and Israel have found consistent differences in the procedural and memory-based processes used by children with MD/RD and MD only and their academically-normal peers to solve simple arithmetic problems (e.g., Barrouillet et al., 1997; Geary, 1990; Geary & Brown, 1991; Gross-Tsur et al., 1996; Hanich et al., 2001; Jordan & Montani, 1997; Ostad, 1997, 2000; Svenson, & Broquist, 1975).

With respect to procedural differences, most of the research on children with MD/RD or MD only has focused on their ability to use counting procedures to solve simple arithmetic problems (e.g., 6–2, 4+8) and simple word problems (Geary, 1990; Hanich et al., 2001; Jordan et al., 1995; Jordan & Montani, 1997; Ostad, 1997, 1998a, 2000). During the solving of basic problems (e.g., 3+5) and word problems, children with MD/RD or MD only commit more procedural errors than do their academically-normal peers, although the differences are often more pronounced for children with MD/RD than MD only (Geary et al., 2000; Jordan & Montani, 1997). As a group, children with MD/RD and MD only also rely on finger counting and use the sum procedure for many more years than do academically-normal children (Geary et al., 1991; Geary et al., 2000; Ostad, 2000). However, many, but not all, of these children show more normal procedural skills by the middle of the elementary school years, at least when solving simple arithmetic problems (basic and word problems).

As an example, Geary et al. (1999, 2000) found consistent differences comparing the approaches used to solve simple addition problems of across groups of MR/RD, MD only, and RD only children, and as contrasted with academically-normal children (see also Jordan & Montani, 1997). In first and second grade, children with MD only and especially children with MD/RD committed more counting-procedure errors and used the developmentally immature sum procedure more frequently than did the children in these other groups. Moreover, in keeping with models of normal arithmetical development (see Figure 1), the children in the RD only and academically-normal groups showed a shift, from first to second grade, from heavy reliance on finger counting to verbal counting and retrieval. The children in the MD/RD and MD only groups, in contrast, did not show this shift, but instead relied heavily on finger counting in both grades. These patterns replicated previous studies of children with MD/RD and demonstrated that many of the same deficits, although to a lesser degree, are evident for children with MD only (e.g., Geary et al., 1991; Jordan & Montani, 1997; Ostad, 1998a). Again, it is noteworthy that children with RD only did not differ from the academically-normal children in the strategies used to solve simple addition problems or in the accuracy of strategy use, indicating that these procedural deficits are restricted to children with MD, independent of their reading competencies.

As noted, children with MD/RD or MD only consistently differ from their academically-normal peers in the ability to use retrieval-based processes to solve simple arithmetic and simple word problems (e.g., Barrouillet et al., 1997; Garnett, & Fleischner, 1983; Geary, 1990, 1993; Hanich, et al., 2001; Jordan & Montani, 1997; Ostad, 1997, 2000). Unlike their procedural competencies, it appears that the ability to retrieve basic facts does not substantively improve across the elementary-school years for most children with MD/RD and MD only. When these children do retrieve arithmetic facts from long-term memory, they commit many more errors and often show error and reaction time (RT) patterns that differ from those found with younger, academically-normal children. Moreover, these patterns are similar to the patterns found with children who have suffered from an early (before age 8 years) lesion to the left-hemisphere or associated subcortical regions (Ashcraft, Yamashita, & Aram, 1992; Barrouillet et al., 1997; Fayol, Barrouillet, & Marinthe, 1998; Geary, 1990; Geary & Brown, 1991; Räsänen & Ahonen, 1995). These patterns suggest that the memory retrieval deficits of children with MD/RD or MD only reflect a cognitive disability, and not, for instance, a lack of exposure to arithmetic problems, poor motivation, a low confidence criterion, or low IQ (Geary et al., 2000).

In summary, research on the problem-solving strategies used by young children to solve simple arithmetic and word problems have consistently revealed differences in the procedural and memory-based processes used by children with MD/RD or MD only and their academically-normal or RD only peers (e.g., Barrouillet et al., 1997; Geary, 1990; Geary et al., 1987; Gross-Tsur et al., 1996; Jordan & Montani, 1997; Ostad, 1997, 1998a; Svenson, & Broquist, 1975). As a group, children with MD/RD or MD only commit more procedural errors and use developmentally immature procedures (e.g., sum rather than min counting) more frequently and for more years than do their academically-normal peers. The differences are especially pronounced for children with MD/RD, as children with MD only appear to develop normal levels of procedural competency more quickly than do children with MD/RD (Geary et al., 2000; Jordan & Montani, 1997). At the same time, many children with MD/RD and MD only do not show the shift from procedural-based problem solving to memory-based problem solving that is commonly found in academically-normal children, suggesting difficulties in storing or accessing arithmetic facts in or from long-term memory (Garnett & Fleischner, 1983; Geary et al., 1991; Jordan & Montani, 1997; Ostad, 1997, 1998a).

DEFICITS IN MEMORY AND COGNITION

It has been hypothesized that the problem-solving characteristics of children with MD/RD or MD only are related, in part, to deficits in the supporting memory and cognitive systems (Geary, 1993; Rourke, 1993). The systems that have been most consistently associated with MD in general are spatial abilities, long-term memory, and working memory.

Spatial abilities. In theory, visuospatial deficits should affect performance in some mathematical domains, such as certain areas of geometry and the solving of complex word problems, but not other domains, such as fact retrieval or knowledge of geometric theorems (e.g., Dehaene, Spelke,

Pinel, Stanescu, & Tsivkin, 1999; Geary, 1993). Many children with MD/RD or MD only do not appear to differ from other children in basic visuospatial competencies (Geary et al., 2000; Morris et al., 1998). There is, however, evidence that some children with MD who show broader performance deficits in mathematics may have a deficit in visuospatial competencies (McLean & Hitch, 1999; Wilson & Swanson, 2001).

McLean and Hitch (1999) found that children with MD only showed a performance deficit on a spatial working memory task, although it is not clear if the difference resulted from an actual spatial deficit or from a deficit in executive functions (e.g., the ability to maintain attention on the spatial task). Hanich and her colleagues found that children with MD/RD differed from their academically-normal peers on an estimation task and in the ability to solve complex word problems (Hanich et al., 2001). Although performance on both of these tasks is supported by spatial abilities (Dehaene et al., 1999; Geary, Saults, Liu, & Hoard, 2000), it is not clear if the results of Hanich et al. were due to a spatial deficit in children with MD/RD. In any case, any such visuospatial deficit does not appear to contribute to the above described counting and arithmetic performance characteristics of children with MD/RD or MD only.

Long-term memory.   Geary (1993) suggested that the difficulties that children with MD/RD have in representing or retrieving arithmetic facts from long-term memory reflect a more general deficit in the ability to represent and retrieve information in phonetic and semantic memory, that is, difficulties in lexical access. It was argued further that the comorbidity of MD and RD in many children (i.e., children with MD/RD but not MD only) results from the same phonetic/semantic memory deficit, as such a deficit would result in difficulties retrieving words and arithmetic facts from long-memory. Barrouillet et al. (1997), in contrast, suggested that the retrieval deficit of children with MD/RD or MD only is the result of difficulties in inhibiting irrelevant associations from entering working memory (see Conway & Engle, 1994). These irrelevant associations compete with the actual answer for expression, which, in turn, results in more retrieval errors and less systematic retrieval times.

One difficulty in testing these alternative hypotheses and in assessing retrieval competencies in general is that most children will resort to counting if they cannot readily retrieve an answer. To circumvent this confound, Jordan and Montani used a retrieval only task—where children are instructed to solve arithmetic problems only by means of retrieval—to assess the retrieval competencies of third-grade children with MD/RD and MD only. Children in both the MD/RD and MD only groups committed more retrieval errors than did their academically-normal peers, suggesting that the retrieval characteristics of children with MD/RD or MD only were likely to be caused by a real retrieval deficit, as contrasted, for instance, with a low confidence criterion. More recently, Geary et al. (2000) administered a similar retrieval-only task to groups of children with MD/RD, MD only, RD only, as well as to a group of academically-normal children. Table 4.3 shows that the children in all of the groups followed these instructions and retrieved on the majority of trials. The children with MD/RD, and, to a lesser degree the children with MD only or RD only, committed more retrieval errors that did the academically-normal children, confirming the results of Jordan and Montani.

Table 4.3.   Addition Performance on Retrieval-only Trial

Group	% retrieval trials	% retrieval errors	Counting-string associates	
			% retrieval trials	% retrieval errors
MD/RD	88	81	23	29
MD only	79	55	9	17
RD only	90	39	8	21
Variable	81	31	2	5
Normal	83	23	1	4

The most important and interesting finding was with respect to the pattern of retrieval errors. Across groups, the most common error was a counting-string associate of one of the addends: For instance, retrieving 4 to the problem 6+3, or 8 to the problem 7+2 (4 is the counting-string associate of 3, and 8 is the counting-string associate of 7). Siegler and Shrager (1984) showed that counting-string associations form as children are learning the standard counting sequence, that is, "one, two, three,..." These associations aid in the counting process, but in the context of retrieving answers to simple addition problems they represent intrusions or a failure to inhibit irrelevant associations from entering into working memory during problem solving. The results confirm the position of Barrouillet et al. (1997) for children with MD/RD or MD only, and Gernsbacher's (1993) finding that poor readers often have difficulty inhibiting irrelevant word associations. Hanich and her colleagues found a similar pattern for children with MD/RD, MD only, or RD only (8%, 8%, and 2% respectively of retrieval errors were counting-string associates; Hanich et al., 2001), but the proportion of retrieval errors that were counting-string associates was lower than that found by Geary et al. (2000).

Geary et al. (2000) found evidence that difficulties in lexical access might also contribute to the fact retrieval deficits of children with MD/RD and to a lesser degree children with RD only. The method used to assess the ease of lexical access, that is, accessing information from phonetic long-term memory, involved comparing the different groups on tasks that involve articulating familiar words (e.g., numbers) and unfamiliar non-words (Denckla & Rudel, 1976; Fawcett & Nicolson, 1994; Gathercole & Adams, 1994). By definition, familiar words are represented in long-term memory, and access to these representations appears to facilitate the speed with which these words can be articulated. Nonwords, in contrast, are not represented in long-term memory and thus there are no direct long-term memory advantages for encoding or articulating these words (see Gathercole & Adams, 1994, for further discussion). As a result, differences in the speed of articulating familiar words and unfamiliar nonwords provides a useful means of assessing the ease of lexical access (Gathercole & Adams, 1994; Gathercole & Baddeley, 1989, 1990).

If difficulties in lexical access contribute to the retrieval (fact and word) deficits of MD/RD and RD only children, then these children should show slower articulation speeds for familiar words, relative to academically-normal peers, but not for unfamiliar words. This is exactly the pattern found by Geary et al. (2000) in both first- and second-grade. Once IQ and nonword articulation speeds were statistically controlled, the results showed slower familiar-word articulation speeds for the children in the MD/RD and RD only groups relative to the children in the MD only and academically-normal groups. In contrast, the groups did not differ in speed of articulating unfamiliar words. Further analyses revealed that familiar-word articulation speeds did not differ comparing children in the MD only and academically-normal groups.

These results are consistent with the view that RD is associated with disrupted phonetic processing (e.g., Morrison et al., 1998), specifically, poor activation of phonetic representations of familiar information. Furthermore, the finding of significant group differences even after controlling for nonword articulation speeds suggests that speed of word articulation per se is not the source of the slow familiar-word articulation speeds of the children with MD/RD or RD only. Rather, the pattern is consistent with difficulties in lexical access, that is poor phonetic activation of the problem addends when these are encoded into working memory, and poor activation of the associated answer. Equally important, the finding that the children with MD only did not show the same familiar-word articulation speed disadvantage found with the children with MD/RD and RD only suggests that the processes associated with the above described counting-string errors (i.e., inhibition) and those involved in the articulation tasks differ.

In summary, children with MD/RD or RD only had slower articulation speeds for familiar but not for unfamiliar words than did children with MD only or their academically-normal peers. The pattern indicates that children with RD, independent of their mathematics achievement scores, are slower at or have more difficulties in accessing familiar information in long-term memory, in keeping with findings that the phonetic system is disrupted in most children with RD (e.g., Morrison et al., 1998). In particular, it appears that the encoding of auditory information in phonetic working memory, such as number words, does not result in the same level of activation of the associated long-term memory representations for children with MD/RD or RD only as it does with other children. Poor activation of long-term memory representations should, in theory, result in the word retrieval difficulties that often accompany RD and the fact retrieval difficulties that often accompany MD/RD (Geary, 1993). At the same time, children with MD/RD, RD only, or MD only all showed difficulties in inhibiting irrelevant associations when retrieving answers to simple addition problems. The pattern suggests that both lexical access and inhibitory mechanisms can contribute to the memory retrieval deficits of LD children and that children with different forms of LD might show retrieval deficits for different reasons, that is, lexical access (MD/RD and RD only), inhibition (MD only), or both (MD/RD and RD only). Whatever the mechanisms, they appear to be more severely disrupted in children with MD/RD than in children with MD only or RD only (Geary et al., 2000; Hanich et al., 2001; Jordan & Montani, 1997).

Working memory. Working memory supports a variety of numerical and arithmetical processes and has been implicated as one factor contributing to the poor mathematical competencies of children with MD/RD or MD only (Bull et al., 1999; Bull & Johnston, 1997; Geary, 1990, 1993; Hitch, 1978; Hitch & McAuley, 1991; Ostad, 1998a; Siegel & Ryan, 1989; Swanson, 1993; Wilson & Swanson, 2001). In theory, working memory deficits can result from difficulties in representing information a phonetic or visuospatial memory store, or in the executive processes that control attention to and the manipulation of information represented in these stores (Baddeley & Hitch, 1974). On the basis of Siegler's strategy choice model, solving arithmetic problems by means of counting should eventually result in associations forming between problems and generated answers (Siegler, 1996; Siegler & Shrager, 1984). Because counting typically engages phonetic working memory, any disruption in the ability to represent or retrieve information from the phonetic store should, in theory, result in difficulties in forming problem/answer associations during counting and result in retrieval deficits (Geary, 1993).

In other words, the above described retrieval deficit that appears to result from poor activation of arithmetic facts is understandable in terms of the working-memory model proposed by Baddeley and Hitch (1974; Baddeley, 1986). When number words are encoded into the phonetic working-memory system, as the initial step in problem solving, poor activation of information stored in phonetic long-term memory (e.g., number words and arithmetic facts) should result in difficulties in fact retrieval. Difficulties in the second form of retrieval deficit, that is, intrusion of irrelevant associations, is also interpretable using this framework. However, the mechanism is not phonetic memory but rather the central executive: In addition to monitoring and attentional control, the central executive supports inhibitory mechanisms. Poor executive functions might also contribute to the tendency of children with MD/RD or MD only to rely heavily on finger counting to solve simple arithmetic problems (Geary, 1990). This is because fingers appear to serve as a working memory aid, specifically aiding in monitoring the counting processes, that is keeping tracking of which items have been counted and which remain to be counted.

In this view, children with MD/RD and MD only should perform poorly on working memory tasks, and they do (Bull et al., 1999; Geary et al., 2000; Hitch & McAuley, 1991; McLean & Hitch, 1999; Siegel & Ryan, 1989; Swanson, 1993; Wilson & Swanson, 2001). Siegel and Ryan showed that children with MD only exhibited deficits on span tasks that involved counting but not those involving other forms of language. Hitch and McAuley confirmed these findings and went on to show that average-IQ children with MD only showed slow counting speeds—and thus more decay of information in phonetic memory while counting—and difficulties in retaining numbers in working memory during the act of counting. More recently, McLean and Hitch assessed children with MD only and two groups of academically-normal peers, one age-matched and one ability matched. The children were administered a series of working memory tasks that assessed the ability to hold information in the phonetic and visuospatial stores, as well as executive functions. The results suggested that the primary working memory deficit of children with MD only involved executive functions.

Research on the working memory deficits of children with MD/RD or MD only is still in preliminary stages, but suggests the following: The primary deficit of children with MD only may involve the central executive. When solving simple arithmetic problems, the result is retrieval deficits due to the intrusion of irrelevant associations and poor skill at using counting procedures during problem solving, presumably due to difficulties in monitoring the act of counting. Children with MD/RD appear to have similar deficits in executive functions but these appear to be more severe than those evident in children with MD only or RD only. Children with MD/RD also appear to have more specific deficits in phonetic memory, specifically low activation of the associated long-term memory representations when phonetic information, such as number words, is encoded into working memory. Children with RD only also appear to have deficits in phonetic processing but these do not appear to be as severe as those found in children with MD/RD (Wilson & Swanson, 2001), and do not appear to greatly disrupt procedural competencies in arithmetic.

SUMMARY

Research conducted during the past 10 to 12 years has substantively expanded our understanding of the performance characteristics and potential deficits in memory and (or) cognition in children with learning disabilities in mathematics, especially in the areas of counting and arithmetic. Table 4.4 provides a summary of the functional deficits of children MD/RD or MD only and potential underlying causes. When first learning to problem solve in arithmetic, all children use counting procedures to solve basic (e.g., 3+5) and word problems (Geary, 1994; Siegler & Shrager, 1984). Children with MD/RD or MD only are no different, but differ from their academically-normal peers in the developmental maturity of the counting procedures used in problem solving, specifically they rely on sum counting more frequently than do other children (Geary, 1990; Jordan & Montani, 1997; Ostad, 1998a, 2000). The developmental delay in the use of min counting, in turn, appears to be related to a developmental delay in their understanding of counting concepts (Geary et al., 1992).

Table 4.4. Summary of MD Children's Cognitive Deficits in Elementary Mathematics

Functional deficits	Potential Deficits in Supporting Systems
Use of immature counting procedures to solve simple arithmetic problems	Immature conceptual understanding of counting (Geary et al., 1992)
Frequent counting procedure errors	Immature conceptual understanding of counting, and poor working memory (Hitch & McAuley, 1990; Geary, 1990; Siegel & Ryan, 1989)
Arithmetic fact retrieval deficits	Difficulties in lexical access (Geary, 1993) and/or difficulties in inhibiting irrelevant associations (Barrouillet et al., 1997; Conway & Engle, 1994)

Children with MD/RD and to a lesser extent children with MD only commit more errors during the execution of counting procedures and rely on finger counting more frequently than do other children. Their poor conceptual understanding of counting may contribute to these counting errors, in that poor conceptual knowledge appears to make the detection and therefore correction of errors difficult. Counting-procedure errors also appear to be related to deficits in working memory, as does heavy reliance on finger counting. In particular it appears that children with MD/RD or MD only have difficulty monitoring the counting process and use their fingers to aid monitoring and concretely representing this process (Geary, 1990). Finally, children with MD/RD or MD only have difficulties retrieving arithmetic facts from long-term memory. This performance characteristic has been known since the early work of Svenson and Broquist (1975) and Garnett and Fleischner (1983), but the mechanisms underlying this deficit have come to light only with more recent work. At this point, it appears that the fact retrieval deficits of children with MD/RD are related to difficulties in accessing information from long-term memory (Geary, 1993) and in inhibiting irrelevant associations from entering working memory (Barrouillet et al., 1997), whereas those of children with MD only are only related to the latter deficit (Geary et al., 2000).

AUTHOR NOTE

Preparation of the chapter was supported by grant R01 HD38283 from the National Institute of Child Health and Human Development.

REFERENCES

Ackerman, P.T., & Dykman, R.A. (1995). Reading-disabled students with and without comorbid arithmetic disability. *Developmental Neuropsychology, 11,* 351–371.

Ashcraft, M.H. (1982). The development of mental arithmetic: A chronometric approach. *Developmental Review, 2,* 213–236.

Ashcraft, M.H., Yamashita, T.S., & Aram, D.M. (1992). Mathematics performance in left and right brain-lesioned children. *Brain and Cognition, 19,* 208–252.

Baddeley, A.D. (1986). *Working memory.* Oxford: Oxford University Press.

Baddeley, A.D., & Hitch, G. (1974). Working memory. In G. H. Bower (Ed.), *The psychology of learning and motivation* (Vol. 8, pp. 47–90). New York: Academic Press.

Badian, N.A. (1983). Dyscalculia and nonverbal disorders of learning. In H.R. Myklebust (Ed.), *Progress in learning disabilities* (Vol. 5, pp. 235–264). New York: Stratton.

Barrouillet, P., Fayol, M., & Lathulière, E. (1997). Selecting between competitors in multiplication tasks: An explanation of the errors produced by adolescents with learning disabilities. *International Journal of Behavioral Development, 21,* 253–275.

Briars, D., & Siegler, R.S. (1984). A featural analysis of preschoolers' counting knowledge. *Developmental Psychology, 20,* 607–618.

Bull, R., & Johnston, R.S. (1997). Children's arithmetical difficulties: Contributions from processing speed, item identification, and short-term memory. *Journal of Experimental Child Psychology, 65,* 1–24.

Bull, R., Johnston, R.S., & Roy, J.A. (1999). Exploring the roles of the visual-spatial sketch pad and central executive in children's arithmetical skills: Views from cognition and developmental neuropsychology. *Developmental Neuropsychology 15,* 421–442.

Carpenter, T.P., & Moser, J.M. (1984). The acquisition of addition and subtraction concepts in grades one through three. *Journal for Research in Mathematics Education, 15*, 179–202.

Conway, A.R.A., & Engle, R.W. (1994). Working memory and retrieval: A resource-dependent inhibition model. *Journal of Experimental Psychology: General, 123*, 354–373.

Dehaene, S. (1992). Varieties of numerical abilities. *Cognition, 44*, 1–42.

Dehaene, S., Spelke, E., Pinel, P., Stanescu, R., & Tsivkin, S. (1999). Sources of mathematical thinking: Behavioral and brain-imaging evidence. *Science, 284*, 970–974.

Delaney, P.F., Reder, L.M., Staszewski, J.J., & Ritter, F.E. (1998). The strategy-specific nature of improvement: The power law applies by strategy within task. *Psychological Science, 9*, 1–7.

Denckla, M.B., & Rudel, R.G. (1976). Rapid 'automatized' naming (R.A.N.): Dyslexia differentiated from other learning disabilities. *Neuropsychologia, 14*, 471–479.

Fawcett, A.J., & Nicolson, R.I. (1994). Naming speed in children with dyslexia. *Journal of Learning Disabilities, 27*, 641–646.

Fayol, M., Barrouillet, P., & Marinthe, C. (1998). Predicting arithmetical achievement from neuro-psychological performance: A longitudinal study. *Cognition, 68*, B63-B70.

Fuson, K.C. (1982). An analysis of the counting-on solution procedure in addition. In T.P. Carpenter, J.M. Moser, & T.A. Romberg (Eds.), *Addition and subtraction: A cognitive perspective* (pp. 67–81). Hillsdale, NJ: Erlbaum.

Fuson, K.C. (1988). *Children's counting and concepts of number.* New York: Springer-Verlag.

Gallistel, C.R., & Gelman, R. (1992). Preverbal and verbal counting and computation. *Cognition, 44*, 43–74.

Garnett, K., & Fleischner, J.E. (1983). Automatization and basic fact performance of normal and learning disabled children. *Learning Disabilities Quarterly, 6*, 223–230.

Gathercole, S.E., & Adams, A.-M. (1994). Children's phonological working memory: Contributions of long-term knowledge and rehearsal. *Journal of Memory and Language, 33*, 672–688.

Gathercole, S.E., & Baddeley, A.D. (1989). Evaluation of the role of phonological STM in the development of vocabulary in children: A longitudinal study. *Journal of Memory and Language, 28*, 200–213.

Gathercole, S.E., & Baddeley, A.D. (1990). Phonological memory deficits in language disordered children: Is there a causal connection? *Journal of Memory and Language, 29*, 336–360.

Geary, D.C. (1990). A componential analysis of an early learning deficit in mathematics. *Journal of Experimental Child Psychology, 49*, 363–383.

Geary, D.C. (1993). Mathematical disabilities: Cognitive, neuropsychological, and genetic components. *Psychological Bulletin, 114*, 345–362.

Geary, D.C. (1994). *Children's mathematical development: Research and practical applications.* Washington, DC: American Psychological Association.

Geary, D.C. (1995). Reflections of evolution and culture in children's cognition: Implications for mathematical development and instruction. *American Psychologist, 50,* 24–37.

Geary, D.C., Bow-Thomas, C.C., Liu, F., & Siegler, R.S. (1996). Development of arithmetical competencies in Chinese and American children: Influence of age, language, and schooling. *Child Development, 67,* 2022–2044.

Geary, D.C., Bow-Thomas, C.C., & Yao, Y. (1992). Counting knowledge and skill in cognitive addition: A comparison of normal and mathematically disabled children. *Journal of Experimental Child Psychology, 54,* 372–391.

Geary, D.C., & Brown, S.C (1991). Cognitive addition: Strategy choice and speed-of-processing differences in gifted, normal, and mathematically disabled children. *Developmental Psychology, 27,* 398–406.

Geary, D.C., Brown, S.C., & Samaranayake, V.A. (1991). Cognitive addition: A short longitudinal study of strategy choice and speed-of-processing differences in normal and mathematically disabled children. *Developmental Psychology, 27,* 787–797.

Geary, D.C., Hamson, C.O., & Hoard, M.K. (2000). Numerical and arithmetical cognition: A longitudinal study of process and concept deficits in children with learning disability. *Journal of Experimental Child Psychology, 77,* 236–263.

Geary, D.C., & Hoard, M. K. (2001). Numerical and arithmetical deficits in learning-disabled children: Relation to dyscalculia and dyslexia. *Aphasiology, 15,* 635–647.

Geary, D.C., Hoard, M.K., & Hamson, C.O. (1999). Numerical and arithmetical cognition: Patterns of functions and deficits in children at risk for a mathematical disability. *Journal of Experimental Child Psychology, 74,* 213–239.

Geary, D.C., Liu, F., Chen, G.-P., Saults, S.J., & Hoard, M.K. (1999). Contributions of computational fluency to cross-national differences in arithmetical reasoning abilities. *Journal of Educational Psychology, 91,* 716–719.

Geary, D.C., Saults, S.J., Liu, F., & Hoard, M.K. (2000). Sex differences in spatial cognition, computational fluency, and arithmetical reasoning. *Journal of Experimental Child Psychology, 77,* 337–353.

Geary, D.C., & Widaman, K.F. (1992). Numerical cognition: On the convergence of componential and psychometric models. *Intelligence, 16,* 47–80.

Geary, D.C., Widaman, K.F., Little, T.D., & Cormier, P. (1987). Cognitive addition: Comparison of learning disabled and academically normal elementary school children. *Cognitive Development, 2,* 249–269.

Gelman, R., & Gallistel, C. R. (1978). *The child's understanding of number.* Cambridge, MA: Harvard University Press.

Gelman, R., & Meck, E. (1983). Preschooler's counting: Principles before skill. *Cognition, 13,* 343–359.

Gernsbacher, M.A. (1993). Less skilled readers have less efficient suppression mechanisms. *Psychological Science, 4,* 294–298.

Groen, G.J., & Parkman, J.M. (1972). A chronometric analysis of simple addition. *Psychological Review, 79,* 329–343.

Gross-Tsur, V., Manor, O., & Shalev, R.S. (1996). Developmental dyscalculia: Prevalence and demographic features. *Developmental Medicine and Child Neurology, 38,* 25–33.

Hanich, L.B., Jordan, N.C., Kaplan, D., & Dick, J. (2001). Performance across different areas of mathematical cognition in children with learning difficulties. *Journal of Educational Psychology, 93,* 615–626.

Hitch, G.J. (1978). The role of short-term working memory in mental arithmetic. *Cognitive Psychology, 10,* 302–323.

Hitch, G.J., & McAuley, E. (1991). Working memory in children with specific arithmetical learning disabilities. *British Journal of Psychology, 82,* 375–386.

Hoard, M.K., Geary, D.C., & Hamson, C.O. (1999). Numerical and arithmetical cognition: Performance of low- and average-IQ children. *Mathematical Cognition, 5,* 65–91.

Jordan, N.C., & Hanich, L.B. (2000). Mathematical thinking in second-grade children with different forms of LD. *Journal of Learning Disabilities, 33,* 567–578.

Jordan, N.C., Levine, S.C., & Huttenlocher, J. (1995). Calculation abilities in young children with different patterns of cognitive functioning. *Journal of Learning Disabilities, 28,* 53–64.

Jordan, N.C., & Montani, T.O. (1997). Cognitive arithmetic and problem solving: A comparison of children with specific and general mathematics difficulties. *Journal of Learning Disabilities, 30,* 624–634.

Kosc, L. (1974). Developmental dyscalculia. *Journal of Learning Disabilities, 7,* 164–177.

Lemaire, P., & Siegler, R. S. (1995). Four aspects of strategic change: Contributions to children's learning of multiplication. *Journal of Experimental Psychology: General, 124,* 83–97.

Light, J.G., & DeFries, J.C. (1995). Comorbidity of reading and mathematics disabilities: Genetic and environmental etiologies. *Journal of Learning Disabilities, 28,* 96–106.

Lyon, G.R., Alexander, D., & Yaffe, S. (1997). Progress and promise in research in learning disabilities. *Learning Disabilities, 8,* 1–6.

McCloskey, M., & Macaruso, P. (1995). Representing and using numerical information. *American Psychologist, 50,* 351–363.

McLean, J.F., & Hitch, G.J. (1999). Working memory impairments in children with specific arithmetic learning difficulties. *Journal of Experimental Child Psychology, 74,* 240–260.

Morris, R.D., Stuebing, K.K., Fletcher, J.M., Shaywitz, S.E., Lyon, G.R., Shankweiler, D.P., Katz, L., Francis, D.J., & Shaywitz, B.A. (1998). Subtypes of reading disability: Variability around a phonological core. *Journal of Educational Psychology, 90,* 347–373.

Ohlsson, S., & Rees, E. (1991). The function of conceptual understanding in the learning of arithmetic procedures. *Cognition and Instruction, 8,* 103–179.

Ostad, S.A. (1997). Developmental differences in addition strategies: A comparison of mathematically disabled and mathematically normal children. *British Journal of Educational Psychology, 67,* 345–357.

Ostad, S.A. (1998a). Developmental differences in solving simple arithmetic word problems and simple number-fact problems: A comparison of mathematically normal and mathematically disabled children. *Mathematical Cognition, 4,* 1–19.

Ostad, S.A. (1998b). Comorbidity between mathematics and spelling difficulties. *Log Phon Vovol, 23,* 145–154.

Ostad, S.A. (2000). Cognitive subtraction in a developmental perspective: Accuracy, speed-of-processing and strategy-use differences in normal and mathematically disabled children. *Focus on Learning Problems in Mathematics, 22,* 18–31.

Räsänen, P., & Ahonen, T. (1995). Arithmetic disabilities with and without reading difficulties: A comparison of arithmetic errors. *Developmental Neuropsychology, 11,* 275–295.

Rourke, B.P. (1993). Arithmetic disabilities, specific and otherwise: A neuropsychological perspective. *Journal of Learning Disabilities, 26,* 214–226.

Russell, R.L., & Ginsburg, H.P. (1984). Cognitive analysis of children's mathematical difficulties. *Cognition and Instruction, 1,* 217–244.

Seron, X., & Fayol, M. (1994). Number transcoding in children: A functional analysis. *British Journal of Developmental Psychology, 12,* 281–300.

Shalev, R.S., Manor, O., & Gross-Tsur, V. (1993). The acquisition of arithmetic in normal children: Assessment by a cognitive model of dyscalculia. *Developmental Medicine and Child Neurology, 35,* 593–601.

Shalev, R.S., Manor, O., Kerem, B., Ayali, M., Badichi, N., Friedlander, Y., & Gross-Tsur, V. (2001). Developmental dyscalculia is a familial learning disability. *Journal of Learning Disabilities, 34,* 59–65.

Siegel, L.S., & Ryan, E.B. (1989). The development of working memory in normally achieving and subtypes of learning disabled children. *Child Development, 60,* 973–980.

Siegler, R.S. (1987). The perils of averaging data over strategies: An example from children's addition. *Journal of Experimental Psychology: General, 116,* 250–264.

Siegler, R.S. (1988). Strategy choice procedures and the development of multiplication skill. *Journal of Experimental Psychology: General, 117,* 258–275.

Siegler, R.S. (1996). *Emerging minds: The process of change in children's thinking.* New York: Oxford University Press.

Siegler, R.S., & Shrager, J. (1984). Strategy choice in addition and subtraction: How do children know what to do? In C. Sophian (Ed.), *Origins of cognitive skills* (pp. 229–293). Hillsdale, NJ: Erlbaum.

Smith, S.D., Kelley, P.M., & Brower, A.M. (1998). Molecular approaches to the genetic analysis of specific reading disabilities. *Human Biology, 70,* 239–256.

Svenson, O., & Broquist, S. (1975). Strategies for solving simple addition problems: A comparison of normal and subnormal children. *Scandinavian Journal of Psychology, 16,* 143–151.

Swanson, H.L. (1993). Working memory in learning disability subgroups. *Journal of Experimental Child Psychology, 56,* 87–114.

Torgesen, J.K., Wagner, R.K., Rashotte, C.A., Alexander, A.W., & Conway, T. (1997). Preventive and remedial interventions for children with severe reading disabilities. *Learning Disabilities, 8,* 51–61.

Wilson, K.M., & Swanson, H.L. (2001). Are mathematical disabilities due to a domain-general or domain-specific working memory deficit? *Journal of Learning Disabilities, 34,* 237–248.

CHAPTER 5

RELATIONSHIPS AMONG BASIC COMPUTATIONAL AUTOMATICITY, WORKING MEMORY, AND COMPLEX MATHEMATICAL PROBLEM SOLVING

What We Know and What We Need to Know

Loel N. Tronsky and James M. Royer

ABSTRACT

In this chapter we present a review of the literature that supports the relationship between the development of basic computational automaticity and the development of complex mathematical problem solving skills. More specifically, we take the position that automaticity of lower level skills such as basic arithmetic results in the freeing up of cognitive resources (working memory) that can be used in complex problem solving contexts. The chapter begins with a review of arithmetic research that shows that fewer working

Mathematical Cognition, pages 117–146

memory resources are needed to solve arithmetic problems as automaticity develops. Section two is a review of studies showing that there is a strong relationship between computational fluency and complex problem solving ability, even when IQ and other important variables are taken into consideration. In our conclusion we outline future research that will help to further specify the aforementioned relationship.

INTRODUCTION

Over the past 20 years the development of arithmetical competence and expertise has become an important topic for cognitive psychologists as well as educators (e.g., Ashcraft, 1995; Geary, 1994; Royer, Tronsky, Chan, Jackson, & Marchant, 1999). It has become even more of a focal point with the release of the new standards developed by the National Council of Teachers of Mathematics (NCTM, 2000). One important change from the 1989 standards to the more recent standards is a greater emphasis on the development of numerical reasoning (e.g., the development of estimation abilities and number sense) and making use of this number knowledge in more complex mathematical domains. The following pages will be dedicated to outlining why one aspect of number sense, namely being able to accurately and rapidly produce answers to basic number facts, is an important precursor to the development of more complex mathematical problem solving abilities. The theoretical position reviewed in this chapter is that developing basic arithmetic automaticity results in a reduction of working memory resource use, and it is this savings that is the key factor in being able to develop more complex problem solving abilities. Several groups of researchers have outlined similar positions (e.g., Geary, 1994; Hiebert, 1990; Kaye, 1986; Pellegrino & Goldman, 1987; Resnick & Ford, 1981; Silver, 1987); therefore this chapter will review what is currently known about the relationships among arithmetic proficiency, working memory, and the development of more complex mathematical skills and will discuss what evidence is still lacking in the aforementioned theoretical perspective and how some of this evidence can be garnered in the near future.

Essentially three pieces of evidence must be established and linked to support the claim that basic number fluency paves the way for the development of more complex mathematical skills via working memory savings. The first piece is to establish that before automatization of basic arithmetic facts working memory resources are needed, while after automatization working memory involvement is minimal or zero. The second piece is to establish that there is a significant relationship between automaticity and more complex mathematical problem solving. A final piece is to determine that the aforementioned relationship is a result of taking the working memory resource savings resulting from basic math fact automaticity and applying it toward acquiring more complex problem solving strategies/ abilities. This chapter will review the empirical evidence that supports the existence of each of these pieces of evidence, and the linkage among them.

WORKING MEMORY INVOLVEMENT IN SIMPLE MENTAL ARITHMETIC

A Theoretical Model of Working Memory

Working memory is usually defined as the ability to hold information in mind while transforming it, or other, information (e.g., Swanson, 1993). Working memory is limited both in its capacity and duration, and therefore one must work quickly and efficiently during problem solving for problem solving to be most effective. The theoretical reasons why working memory capacity might be related to math achievement test performance are best understood in the context of a description of mathematical reasoning. In her review of the Studies of Mathematically Precocious Youth research, Benbow (1988) suggested that mathematical talent (as measured by tests like the SAT) "...was best defined as the ability to handle long chains of reasoning." Completing long chains of reasoning makes heavy demands on conscious reasoning capacity, and conscious reasoning is conducted using a limited capacity working memory system. To make this relationship more explicit, we will examine a specific theory of working memory, and the evidence that working memory activity is connected to mathematical performance.

Baddeley's Model of Working Memory

Baddeley's model of working memory has been used successfully to examine several cognitive domains including the processes involved in counting and arithmetic (e.g., Baddeley, 1986, 1992a, 1992b, 1996; Baddeley & Hitch, 1994; Healey & Nairne, 1985; Lemaire, Abdi, & Fayol, 1996; Logie & Baddeley, 1987; Logie, Gilhooly, & Wynn, 1994; Seitz & Schumann-Hengsteler, 2000), and due to this (and other reasons) is the model of choice for the current review. According to Baddeley's model, there are three components in the working memory system, the central executive and two slave systems, the phonological loop and the visuo-spatial sketchpad. Although the functions of the central executive at this point are still not totally clear, among its responsibilities are thought to be things such as initiating and directing processing, selecting strategies, coordinating the slave systems and the resources allocated to them, and retrieving information (especially information that requires effortful or conscious retrieval) from long-term memory (e.g., Ashcraft, 1995; Baddeley, 1992b, 1996). Visual material and the spatial orientation of that material is stored and manipulated in the visuo-spatial sketchpad while speech-based information (e.g., mental counting) is stored and manipulated in the phonological loop.

Experiments employing dual task methodologies have been used to try to delineate the components of this tripartite model as well as the components' functions. For example, in one such experiment (Logie, Zucco, & Baddeley, 1990) participants were given a primary task that required them to concurrently perform either a verbal task (adding) or an imaging task with another task that was supposed to tax the verbal or visuo-spatial system of working memory. In this experiment the concurrent tasks were given through different modalities. The results showed a double dissociation between performance in the different dual task conditions. When the concurrent tasks both required visuo-spatial working memory or verbal working memory, performance on the two measures dropped dramatically; when concurrent tasks taxed different proposed systems, performance dropped minimally. This and other studies like it lend support to the multiple resource model, one resource for visuo-spatial and one for verbal material. Other cognitive and neuropsychological research using similar methodologies has further delineated Baddeley's model and the involvement of working memory in simple arithmetic. We now turn to the latter subject.

Arithmetic/Working Memory Studies Using Baddeley's Model

The most common method of assessing arithmetic ability and automaticity has been computer-administered tasks where accuracy and response times are recorded. One such computer-administered task is the production task. In this task participants are presented with arithmetic problems (in some research with a trailing equal sign and in other research without), and participants are instructed to state the correct answer to the problem into a microphone connected to the computer as quickly as they can while still being accurate (e.g., Geary, 1996a; Lefevre & Liu, 1997; Lefevre, Sadesky, & Bisanz, 1996; Royer et al., 1999).

Other researchers have opted to use a verification task. In verification tasks participants are presented with arithmetic problems, an equal sign, and either the correct answer or an incorrect answer for the given problem (e.g., $6 \times 7 = 42$ or $6 \times 7 = 48$). The participant's task is to determine whether the answer stated in the problem is correct or not, and a response is made by pressing one of two predetermined keys on a keyboard or buttons on a response box. Initially it was thought that this task was simply an extension of the production task. That is, it was assumed that participants were calculating the answers to the given arithmetic problem, were comparing that answer to the given answer, and were then pressing the appropriate button. This assumption made interpretation of verification task response times straightforward. Response time for any verification problem was the response time for producing the answer to the problem, plus the response time associated with comparing the calculated/retrieved answer and the answer presented on the screen, plus the time associated with determining the proper button to press. A number of studies have demonstrated that the simple production plus comparison process assumption is unfounded as participants have other methods of choosing an answer that obviate the need for producing a numerical answer to the given problem (e.g., Campbell & Tarling, 1996; Krueger, 1986; Lemaire & Fayol, 1995; Lemaire & Reder, 1999; Lochy, Seron, Delazer, & Butterworth, 2000; Zbrodoff & Logan, 1990). Due to the aforementioned findings, researchers have chosen to examine working memory involvement in simple mental arithmetic using both verification and production tasks as the nature of the underlying processes may have implications for working memory involvement. Therefore, we will review the results of verification and production studies in separate sections.

Findings Using Verification Task Methodologies

One of the first arithmetic/working memory studies to use the verification technique and a dual task paradigm was conducted by Ashcraft, Donley, Halas, and Vakali (1992). Participants were given 20 simple addition and 20 complex addition problems to verify. Because the present review is concerned with simple fact automatization, only the method and results related to simple facts will be reported (in addition to Ashcraft et al., 1992; see also Adams & Hitch, 1997, 1998; Fürst & Hitch, 2000; Hitch, 1978a, 1978b; Logie et al., 1994; Seitz & Schumann-Hengsteler, 2000; Tronsky, submitted-b, for discussions of multi-digit arithmetic and working memory). Participants solved the set of simple and complex problems in each of three dual task conditions. In the control condition participants saw a letter repeated on the screen four times and were instructed to repeat the letter throughout the entire trial (repeat condition). In the word generation condition participants saw the same letter as in the repeat condition and had to retrieve and say out loud words that began with that letter. The final condition was the alphabetization condition where subjects saw four different consonants before the arithmetic trial and were required to name the four letters out loud in their correct alphabetic order while solving the arithmetic problem. The control condition is an example of a task that should require phonological loop involvement but no central executive involvement. The two other secondary tasks should have involved both the phonological loop as well as central executive resources as these tasks required production of verbal material as well as simultaneous monitoring and carrying out of additional operations (e.g., retrieval and ordering of stimuli). If central executive resources are required in simple mental arithmetic, then there should be an increase in RT and/or errors in arithmetic verification when performed simultaneously with the word generation or alphabetization dual task conditions.

Ashcraft et al. conducted analyses with the dependent variables arithmetic error rate and RT's. In addition to the three level dual task independent variable, a problem difficulty variable (low, medium, high) and veracity variable (true problem, false problem) were also included in the analyses. The problem difficulty variable stems from research showing that participants are slower and more error prone at solving arithmetic problems that have larger sums or products (e.g., Ashcraft, 1992, 1995; Geary, 1996a; Hecht, 1999; Koshmider & Ashcraft, 1991; Manly & Spoehr, 1999; Tronsky, in preparation-a). Error percentage analysis yielded only a marginally significant difficulty effect while RT analysis yielded significant main effects for veracity, problem difficulty, and working memory condition. The most important finding for the present discussion is that the RT's in the control (repeat) condition were significantly faster than those in the conditions that required the central executive.

Lemaire et al. (1996) sought to improve the methods and therefore extend the results of Ashcraft et al. (1992). To do this, Lemaire et al. used a similar methodology with a few modifications. Participants were tested in each one of the following conditions: arithmetic verification with no concurrent task, arithmetic verification with articulatory suppression (repeating the word "the"), arithmetic verification with canonical letters (repeating the letters "abcdef,") and arithmetic verification with random letters (generating a random series of letters from a list of five letters). Arithmetic verification consisted of blocks of addition and blocks of multiplication problems. Lemaire et al., like Ashcraft et al. (1992), looked at a problem size/difficulty variable as well.

Participants in the random letter generation condition had higher RT's and error rates than subjects in the three other conditions, and there were no other differences among conditions. There was also a marginally significant difficulty by working memory load interaction for response times with the largest difference noted between the control and random letter generation conditions. Planned comparisons also showed that significant problem difficulty effects were obtained in each one of the memory load conditions. Conducting these analyses on the data from Experiment 2 yielded the same results. Lemaire et al. also found that there was a difference between the true and false problems: both phonological and central executive working memory resources were needed for true problems and only central executive resources were needed for false problems.

To further our understanding of working memory resource use in simple arithmetic verification, De Rammelaere et al. (2001) altered Lemaire et al.'s (1996) design to eliminate some methodological shortcomings. De Rammelaere et al. made addition (Experiment 1) and multiplication (Experiment 2) stimuli using a wider range of problems, a larger group of subjects, and a slightly different set of dual tasks. The control task and articulatory suppression task were used again and the random letter generation task was replaced with a random time interval generation task. The random time interval generation task required participants to tap an unpredictable rhythm on the zero key of the numeric keypad. Previous research has determined that this task requires central executive resources but does not involve the phonological loop (e.g., Vandierendonck, De Vooght, & Van Der Goten, 1998). This allowed De Rammelaere to test phonological loop and central executive involvement separately. Analyses revealed that the main variable of interest, concurrent task, was significant. Participants in the random interval generation condition had significantly longer response times for both true and false problems when compared to the control condition while articulatory suppression did not significantly affect response times. In summary, the results of this study (in conjunction with those from De Rammelaere et al., 1999) show that central executive resources are used in arithmetic verification while phonological resources most likely are not.

One issue that was not addressed in the studies outlined so far is the effect that strategy use has on working memory resource involvement in mental arithmetic. Hecht (2002) sought to address this issue by administering addition verification alone, with an articulatory suppression task (repeating a letter of the alphabet from the a-f set), or with a random letter generation task. The major difference in this experiment was in the control condition where participants' solution strategies (retrieval vs. non-retrieval) were recorded on a problem by problem basis. This enabled Hecht to determine whether non-retrieval strategies such as counting or decomposition (e.g., recasting 9 + 7 as the problem 9 + 6 + 1) use working memory resources while retrieval strategies use less or no working memory resources.

The most interesting results from this study were when problems were analyzed separately based on whether retrieval or counting strategies were used to solve them. This was done through two sets of regression analyses. Analysis of retrieval only trials revealed that a variable that indexed speed of retrieval had equal slopes across the dual task conditions while analysis of counting trials showed that counting processes were slowed as working memory load increased. In addition, when Hecht examined degree of secondary task adherence he found no interaction with retrieval trials but a significant interaction with counting trials. This indicated that when working memory resources are taxed the result is often decrements in both primary and secondary task performance. Taken together these results suggest that arithmetic fact retrieval is virtually working memory load independent while arithmetic fact computation (use of a counting procedure) is working memory load dependent.

Findings Using Production Task Methodologies

Only a few production task studies of working memory involvement in arithmetic have been conducted, most likely the result of the nature of the secondary tasks that have been used in previous research. The secondary tasks used often require subjects to produce verbal responses, something which is at odds with participants verbalizing answers to the arithmetic problems in a typical production task design. Nevertheless, a few researchers have attempted to modify typical methodologies to study working memory processes in a simple arithmetic production task (e.g., De Rammelaere & Vandierendonck, in press; Seitz & Schumann-Hengsteler, 2000; Tronsky, submitted-a). Seitz and Schumann-Hengsteler (2000), for instance, conducted two experiments to examine working memory resource use in simple and complex multiplication using a production task (again, we will only report methods and results related to simple multiplication). In Experiment 1 participants solved the aforementioned problems while performing one of the following secondary tasks: neutral tapping (presumably tapping at a constant rate), articulatory suppression (repeating "lemonade" in German), irrelevant speech (listening to a female speak Armenian), and visuo-spatial tapping (tapping the figure 8 on a board, designed to overload the visual-spatial sketchpad). Participants were required to state the answers to the arithmetic problems out loud and one of the experimenters pressed a button to record response times. In Experiment 2 the same methods were used except the irrelevant speech task was replaced with the random letter generation task described previously.

Analysis of the results showed that none of the conditions in either experiment that had a secondary task that involved either slave system of Baddeley's working memory model (AS, irrelevant speech, visuo-spatial tapping) resulted in slower RT's or increased error rates in comparison to the neutral tapping condition. The random letter generation condition, however, led to a significant response time increase compared to neutral tapping, something the authors suggested was due to central executive involvement in simple multiplication production. One criticism of the above methodology involves response competition. In the random letter generation condition a participant was required to verbally produce a random pattern of letters and presumably had to switch to produce a verbal response to the arithmetic problem. If a participant had mentally solved a problem and was preparing the answer for spoken production while at the same time preparing or carrying out another verbal response, competition at this output stage may be responsible for the increase in response time rather than the arithmetic processing.

De Rammelaere and Vandierendonck (in press) also examined what effect overloading the central executive might have in an arithmetic production task. As in the verification example above (De Rammelaere et al., 2001) a random interval generation task was used to tax the central executive while participants solved either addition or multiplication problems. They found, like Seitz and Schumann-Hengsteller (2000), that response times did increase in the dual task compared to single task condition.

We have examined working memory resource use in a mental arithmetic production task in our own lab (Tronsky, submitted-a). In this research participants solved multiplication problems in both verification and production formats. For both formats participants completed three sets of tasks. The dual task conditions required that participants solve a multiplication production or verification problem while trying to keep in mind a meaningless six letter consonant string. One drawback to this method is that it did not involve multiple dual task conditions to examine working memory effects related to the different systems in Baddeley's model. It is hypothesized, however, that holding a six letter consonant string in working memory while solving arithmetic problems most likely uses both the phonological loop and central executive and is therefore most like the random letter generation tasks mentioned previously.

Results revealed that response times were significantly slower in the dual task condition for both multiplication formats, and letter recall was significantly poorer in the dual task condition for the production format but just missed reaching conventional significance for the verification format. The above results indicate that multiplication performance suffers due to working memory overload, regardless of presentation format. One question does linger, and that is whether the use of non-retrieval strategies (one could define this as level of arithmetic skill or expertise) is largely responsible for the working memory involvement found. Therefore a second component of the Tronsky (submitted-a) investigation involved analyzing the performance of participants that were highly practiced in basic mental multiplication.

Working Memory Resource Use in Mental Arithmetic as a Function of Practice/Development

In Tronsky (submitted-a) participants were trained for four hours on a subset of the 2 through 12 operand mulitplication problems. A group of "expert" calculators with simple arithmetic response times that were 700 ms or less were also selected. Both the post-training and expert groups were given the production and verification working memory tasks outlined above. Analyses at the group level indicated that multiplication practice significantly reduced the response time gap in dual vs. single task performance for both the production and verification formats and reduced the letter recall gap for both formats as well. While dual vs. single task gaps in letter recall were reduced to zero at post-practice for both arithmetic formats, response time differences were still significantly greater than zero for both formats indicating working memory resource use even after practice. Analyses of the expert group's performance largely mirrored those of the post-practice group. Individual analyses were planned from the outset to determine if post-practice and expert differences on the dual vs. single task conditions held for most or all individuals. These analyses revealed that several individuals evidenced no effects of the dual task conditions; response time and letter recall were equal across the memory load conditions for these participants.

Another training study was conducted by Klapp et al. (1991) that involved extended practice and automaticity (defined as the reliance on direct retrieval as opposed to algorithmic solution strategies). Klapp et al. (1991) wanted to determine if there were any benefits to practice after automaticity had been achieved and did so via a series of five experiments. Participants were given alpha arithmetic problems to practice. An alpha arithmetic problem is a problem such as C + 4 = ? which is used to control for exposure effects. In the aforementioned example the person would count on four letters from C—D (1), E (2), F (3), G (4)—to arrive at the correct answer G. Participants also were required to perform these tasks with the secondary task of repeated month saying (January, January, January, etc.) and sequential month saying (saying January, February, March, etc.) while verifying the alpha addition problems. This dual task situation was presented before training (novice level), once problems could be solved by direct retrieval (automatic level), and after practice beyond the automatic level. The results revealed at the novice level both dual task conditions interfered significantly with arithmetic performance. At the automatic level, verification time was faster and was not affected by repetitive month saying but was still affected by sequential month saying. Finally, at the overtrained level overall verification RT was faster than at the previous level with no interference from either of the dual tasks.

A third study that falls under the development heading of this section is that of Kaye, de Winstanley, Chen, and Bonnefil (1989). These researchers selected 2nd, 4th, and 6th graders as well as college students to test what stages of addition verification were affected when a working memory load was imposed. They did this by giving participants arithmetic problems and then providing an incorrect or correct answer one second later for them to verify. Auditory probes were presented on half of the trials at various intervals and participants were required to press the space bar with their free hand as quickly as possible in response to these probes. Presenting the auditory probe at different intervals (both before and after presentation of the answer to be verified) allowed the researchers to determine what stage of problem solving was most resources demanding. That is, they were able to determine if early processing that reflected encoding of the problem and computing an answer, or late processing that reflected encoding of the given answer, comparing the given and computed answers and decision processes related to responding (deciding which button to press) were most resource demanding.

The results indicated that the second graders experienced great difficulty with the dual task situation and that both stages of processing were resource demanding. At fourth grade the encoding and computation stage was found to be more process demanding than the encode/compare/respond stage. Sixth graders showed decreasing processing demands compared to the fourth graders and the demands were equal at both stages. College students still showed some processing demands but these demands were concentrated at the post-computational processing stage. Overall these analyses revealed that processing demands initially are large across problem solving stages and these demands decrease with development and shift to being more prevalent at the encode answer/compare/respond stage. This is similar to one of Hecht's (2002) findings that verification of arithmetic facts requires processing resources, but that these resources may be due to decision processes in a verification task as opposed to arithmetic fact retrieval processes.

Summary of Working Memory Involvement in Arithmetic

Piecing together the information from the aforementioned studies warrants three general conclusions. First, people (children or adults) use working memory resources while solving simple arithmetic verification or production problems. Second, in regard to Baddeley's model of working memory, it appears that the central executive, and in certain instances the phonological loop, are taxed while the visuo-spatial sketchpad most likely is not. The central executive appears to be involved when non-retrieval strategies are invoked and when the compare/decision stage of processing of arithmetic verification is occurring; the phonological loop is also involved but only when counting strategies are used in arithmetic problem solving (Hecht, 2002). Because so few production task investigations have been completed, we are unsure whether the verification results will transfer; however, given the preliminary results of a few studies (e.g., De Rammelaere & Vandierendonck, in press; Seitz & Schuman-Hengsteler, 2001; Tronsky submitted-a, submitted-b) it appears that comparable results will be obtained. The final conclusion, which will take us into the next section, is that automated arithmetic skill developed via intense practice results in decreased working memory resource use. Given enough practice working memory involvement may be reduced to zero (e.g., Tronsky, submitted-a; Klapp et al., 1991). Let us now turn to the next question: does efficiency of computation have any implications for higher level mathematical problem solving?

THE RELATIONSHIP BETWEEN COMPUTATIONAL EFFICIENCY AND COMPLEX MATHEMATICAL PROBLEM SOLVING

Empirical Evidence for the Relationship

The number of studies that have examined the connection between basic math fact automaticity and higher level problem solving is large, and most of that research has found a significant relationship (e.g., Balow, 1964; Bull & Johnston, 1997; Bull, Johnston, & Roy, 1999; Cumming & Elkins, 1999; Dowker, 1998; Geary & Brown, 1991; Geary & Burlingham-Dubree, 1989; Geary, Liu, Chen, Saults, & Hoard, 1999; Geary, Saults, Liu, & Hoard, 2000; Geary & Widaman, 1992; Gray & Mulhern, 1995; Hecht, Torgesen, Wagner, & Rashotte, 2001; Kail & Hall, 1999; Kaye et al., 1989; Muth, 1984; Royer et al., 1999; 2001; Siegler, 1988; Suppes, Jerman, & Brian, 1968; Suppes & Morningstar, 1972; Whang & Hancock, 1997; Zentall, 1990), although a few studies have found null results (Hecht, 1998; Rabinowitz & Woolley, 1995; Swanson, Cooney, & Brock, 1993). Due to space constraints the current discussion of the aforementioned relationship will focus on a subset of studies that are indicative of the group of studies as a whole. We will begin by examining those that have used correlation, regression, and structural equation modeling methods to ascertain the computation/higher problem solving connection. In the second section we briefly will examine how the study of certain select samples, such as the mathematically disabled, the mathematically precocious, and cross-cultural samples has added to our understanding of the connection. Finally, we will entertain theoretical accounts of the aforementioned relationship and will discuss what future research might help to specify and constrain existing theoretical accounts further.

Correlation, Regression, and Structural Equation Modeling Studies

Studies of Elementary Students

The first series of studies we will review are studies of young children's strategy use while solving basic arithmetic problems. Siegler (1988) conducted a study (composed of two experiments) where first graders were given basic addition and subtraction problems to solve as well as individual words (taken from their textbooks) to read. Accuracies and RT's were recorded for each one of the three tasks as were strategies used on the three tasks such as retrieval, back-up counting (arithmetic), or sounding out (reading). Siegler (1988) performed a cluster analyses on the data using the percentage use of retrieval, percent correct on retrieval trials, and percent correct on back-up strategy trials on the three sets of tasks to categorize children into three groups: good students, not-so-good students, and perfectionists. The good students were better than the not-so-good students on all measures while the perfectionists were better than the not-so-good group on all measures except use of retrieval for the arithmetic tasks, and were equal or better than the good group on all measures except the use of retrieval. Siegler interpreted the perfectionists as having a higher confidence criterion for using retrieval as a strategy than the good students, meaning that the perfectionists were only willing to state a retrieved answer if they were very confident that it was correct (evidenced by a higher subtraction retrieval accuracy than the good group), otherwise a back-up counting strategy was used. Perfectionists and good students scored equally well, and both scored significantly better than the not-so-good students on the computational and problem solving sub-tests of the Metropolitan Achievement Test. This indicates that math fact skills, as evidenced by fast and accurate use of retrieval and/or back-up counting strategies, is predictive of more general problem solving abilities.

Geary and Burlingham-Dubree (1989) conducted a similar study with kindergartners. An addition test incorporating sums less than 10 was administered via computer that recorded RT and accuracy. Also, problem solving strategies were recorded by the experimenter as one of the following: (1) counting fingers—raising the number of fingers specified in the problem and then counting to reach the sum, (2) fingers—the same as counting fingers except children do not visibly count the raised fingers, (3) verbal counting—children would audibly count or move their lips, or (4) no visible strategy—most likely retrieval of the answer from memory. Two additional tests were also administered, the Arithmetic subtest of the Wide Range Achievement Test (the WRAT) and the Wechsler Preschool and Primary Scale of Intelligence (the WPPSI, composed of an arithmetic sub-test and nine other sub-tests). The WRAT sub-test samples items such as counting, number identification, and simple addition and subtraction. Problems from the arithmetic sub-test of the WPPSI were more comprehensive sampling counting, ordinality, and arithmetical word problems. Geary and Burlingham-Dubree used the strategy data to compute a strategy choice variable which indexed whether the kindergartners were making adaptive strategy choices (i.e., whether kindergarteners were using retrieval for smaller, less difficult problems and verbal or finger counting for larger or more difficult problems). Regression analyses revealed that individual differences on the strategy choice variable were related to individual differences on the WRAT sub-test while both strategy choice and speed of fact retrieval predicted performance on the broader WPPSI sub-test.

Additional studies using strategy choice data to predict mathematical problem solving abilities have been conducted by Geary and Brown (1991) and Geary et al. (1991). Geary and Brown (1991) conducted a study with a first grade sample of mathematically disabled and non-disabled students. Strategy use and speed of problem solution data while solving basic arithmetic problems were collected, and The Science Research Associates Survey (SRAS) of basic skills was administered as a measure of mathematical achievement. One other task of note was administered, a forward digit span task where students had to repeat back ordered lists of numbers of various lengths, a task that was used as an index of working memory. Collapsing the data across groups yielded a significant linear relationship between working memory and SRAS score and a significant quadratic relationship between frequency of correct memory retrieval and SRAS score. The quadratic relationship was a result of the highest scorers on the SRAS resorting to non-retrieval strategies more often than the middle scorers— similar to what Siegler (1988) found with his perfectionist and good groups. Another study by Geary et al. (1991) used groups of fourth grade mathematically disabled and non-disabled students and gifted third and fourth grade students were given the addition task and strategy classification methodology of Geary and Brown (1991). Frequency of correct retrieval trials was significantly different for all group comparisons with gifted students having the highest percentage and mathematically disabled students the lowest. Collapsing across groups, frequency of correct retrieval was a significant predictor of SRAS performance accounting for over 50% of the variance.

While the studies above show that there is a relationship between computational abilities and general mathematical abilities, there are limitations to the studies. First, they were limited to younger students where one might expect the relationship between computational skill and other mathematical problem solving might be highest. Second, due to the younger samples, the general mathematical ability measures were somewhat limited in their scope as elementary students have not been exposed to the type of material (in terms of breadth and depth) to which middle school and older students have been exposed. Finally, the studies described above used simple regression models with very few predictor variables. It may be that other variables such as working memory, reading ability, general processing ability, problem classification, memory for propositions in word problems, etc., explain more unique variance in complex mathematical problem solving domains.

Studies Using Older Students and Additional Predictor Variables

Muth (1984) and Tronsky (1997) both have examined the predictive abilities of computational and reading measures in middle school word problem solving. Muth sampled a large group of sixth graders using arithmetic and reading sub-scores on the Comprehensive Test of Basic Skills to predict performance on a word problem solving test adapted from the NAEP (1977). Multiple regression analyses revealed that the two predictor variables accounted for 54% of the variance in correct word problem solution with 14% and 8% of the variance uniquely attributable to reading and arithmetic, respectively. Tronsky (1997) collected arithmetic response times to simple arithmetic problems, reading scores using SVT test (see Royer, 1990; Royer, Carlo, & Cisero, 1993 for description of the SVT), and scores on a researcher generated word problem test modeled after the Iowa Test of Basic Skills for grades five through eight. Multiple regression analyses revealed that arithmetic response time, reading performance, and grade were all significant predictors of word problem solving performance accounting for a total of 55% of the variance.

Kail and Hall (1999, Experiment 2) examined the word problem solving performance of eight through 12-year-olds seeking to extend previous work by including information processing measures in addition to basic arithmetic and reading variables. The measures were general processing speed (a cross-out and visual matching task), short term memory (letter span), working memory (reading span), basic arithmetic fact knowledge, and reading skill (Reading Recognition Task of the Peabody Individual Achievement Test) in addition to an untimed word problem task with problems taken from Morales, Shute, and Pellegrino (1985). Hierarchical regression analyses revealed that basic arithmetic ability measures and general information processing measures were important predictors of word problem solving performance. The analyses also showed that processing speed and reading were more important predictors than the memory measures and that both arithmetic speed and accuracy were important predictors.

A more recent study by Hecht et al. (2001) is worth underscoring as well because it not only focused on the relationships among information processing, basic arithmetic computation, and higher level problem skills but used methodological and analysis techniques that allowed for determining what the most important predictors of the development of basic and more complex computational abilities are. Hecht et al. followed a random sample of more than 200 students from second through fifth grade. These students were given a large battery of tests including simple arithmetic, complex arithmetic, three reading tasks, three phonological memory tasks, five phonological tasks, six measures of processing speed, and a vocabulary-based measure of general intelligence. The simple arithmetic task was addition and subtraction problems presented via computer, and the complex arithmetic task was the calculation sub-test from the Woodcock-Johnson Psycho-Educational Battery which included some simple addition and subtraction problems, multidigit arithmetic, addition and subtraction of fractions, and algebraic equations with one unknown. It should also be noted that the working memory task was given only to second graders and the simple arithmetic task only to fourth and fifth graders.

Two findings are of major interest to the present review. First it was found that simple arithmetic efficiency (speed in this case) in fourth grade accounted for a small but significant proportion of variance in fifth grade complex arithmetic score even after controlling for verbal IQ, phonological variables, speed of processing, reading ability, and fourth grade complex arithmetic ability. The second interesting finding was that fourth grade complex arithmetic ability was predictive of fifth grade simple arithmetic efficiency even after controlling for all of the information processing variables and fourth grade simple arithmetic efficiency. These findings suggest that the relationship of simple arithmetic efficiency and the complex arithmetic problems measures in this study is bidirectional.

Structural Equation Modeling Studies

Several structural equation modeling studies have been conducted to determine the relationships among information processing variables and arithmetical reasoning or general mathematical reasoning abilities (e.g., Geary et al., 1992, 2000; Royer et al., in preparation; Whang & Hancock, 1997; Widaman, Little, Geary, & Cormier, 1992). Widaman et al. (1992) collected data from second, fourth, and sixth graders on a battery of tests including basic addition verification and eight sub-tests from the Stanford Achievement Test (three mathematics and five verbal comprehension/reading sub-tests). Regression models were fit to the students' verification response times to determine if each person's data were better fit by a variable that indexed retrieval (the product of the two addends in the addition problem) or a variable that indexed counting or computational strategies (the smaller, or minimum, addend of the problem). Widaman et al. then took those students whose data were better fit by the retrieval index and used them in the structural equation modeling analyses to be described. The measured variables of age and age squared were partialed from the latent variables Addition Efficiency, Speediness (processing speed as defined by intercept and time to encode digit estimates from the aforementioned regression analyses), Math Achievement, Verbal Comprehension, and Reading Skills. The results revealed that the Addition Efficiency latent variable was highly related to the Math Achievement latent variable showing that efficiency of basic fact retrieval is a significant predictor of computational, conceptual, and application skill in mathematics.

In another study Whang and Hancock (1997) selected a sample of Asian-American students from fourth, fifth, and sixth grade whose average scores on the mathematics portion of the Comprehensive Test of Basic Skills (CTBS) were at the 99th percentile. Six latent variables were estimated in this study including Processing Efficiency (as defined by processing speed and consistency), Working Memory Capacity, Arithmetic Production, Arithmetic Verification, Mathematics Achievement, and Reasoning Ability. Analyses revealed seven direct paths: from Processing Efficiency to Reasoning Ability and Arithmetic Verification Speed, from Working Memory Capacity to Arithmetic Production and Reasoning ability, from Reasoning Ability to Arithmetic Production and to Mathematics Achievement, and from Arithmetic Production to Mathematics Achievement. Four indirect paths to Mathematics Achievement were also significant originating from Working Memory Capacity and Processing Efficiency with three of the four significant indirect effects going through Reasoning Ability. The results show that arithmetic production is strongly related to mathematics achievement in an (elite) elementary/middle school sample even when controlling for general reasoning. Geary et al. (2000) found similar results with an older sample. Their structural model included the observed variable Sex and latent variables IQ, Arithmetical Reasoning, Spatial Cognition, and Arithmetical Computations. Even after partialing out the effects of IQ and Sex, Arithmetical Computations maintained a strong relationship with Arithmetical Reasoning. Royer et al.'s (in preparation) structural model (without an IQ latent variable) showed that Arithmetic response time is still strongly associated with SAT Math score when controlling for Spatial Rotation ability and SAT Verbal score. This last piece of research is key as it indicates that the arithmetic efficiency/problem solving connection is not limited to those problem solving measures that are dominated by arithmetical reasoning problems.

Evidence from Select Samples

In a chapter in this volume, Geary and Hoard review research that shows students with math disabilities (MD) evidence memory deficits. More specifically, it appears that students with MD alone have a working memory deficit specific to the central executive. This central executive dysfunction impacts these students' abilities to monitor the use of counting procedures during problem solving as well as their ability to inhibit the intrusion of irrelevant associations when they attempt to retrieve arithmetic facts from memory. Students who have MD and reading disability (RD) have more severe central executive deficits and also have deficits in phonetic memory thus making it more difficult for them to count accurately and to store and retrieve phonetic information (such as number words and problem-answer associations). These students' working memory deficits should impact their ability to master more complex mathematics in (at least) two ways. First, it is likely that their working memory deficits directly affect their ability to problem solve. An example would be when they have to keep a number of statements from a word problem in mind while simultaneously trying to represent the information in mathematical form and construct and carry out a solution. Second, these students' inability to automatize basic arithmetic means that computational answers have to be either consciously retrieved or computed, thereby consuming precious additional working memory resources that further impairs problem solving.

A second set of studies conducted by Dark and Benbow (1990, 1991, 1993, 1994) sought to determine the connection between working memory capacity and efficiency and mathematical precocity. Dark and Benbow concluded from their four studies that a specific ability, the ability to represent numerical material and a generally ability, the ability to manipulate information in working memory, is predictive of mathematical precocity (e.g., high SAT Math scores in 13 and 14-year-olds). Although it is unclear form this research whether there is a causal connection and what direction that connection runs, the results are intriguing. One interesting possibility is that math precocious students spend a great deal of time working with numbers and arithmetical stimuli, presumably automatizing basic arithmetic facts that they can quickly and effortlessly recall and manipulate in working memory to help them with more complex problem solving.

The final line of evidence comes from cross-cultural comparisons of arithmetic computation and mathematical problem solving abilities. It is a fairly well established finding that students from Asian countries outperform students from the U.S. in both basic arithmetic computation (e.g., Geary, 1996a; Geary, Bow-Thomas, Fan, & Siegler, 1993; Geary, Bow-Thomas, Liu, & Siegler, 1996; Geary et al., 1992; Geary, Salthouse, Chen, & Fan, 1996) and higher level problem solving in mathematics (e.g., Beaton, Mullis, Martin, Gonzalez, Kelly, & Smith, 1996; Geary, 1994; Stevenson,

Chen, & Lee, 1993; Stevenson, Lee, & Stigler, 1986). It appears that these differences are a recent phenomenon and result from a decline in mathematical skills in U.S. students coupled with an increase in skills in the Chinese students.

Several explanations have been offered for differences in mathematical reasoning across cultures. Included are differences in language, schooling, cultural valuation of mathematics, and basic computational abilities (e.g., Geary, 1994, 1996b; Geary et al., 1992, 1999; Miller, Smith, Zhu, & Zhang, 1995; Stevenson, et al. 1993; Towse & Saxton, 1998). To illustrate the role that basic computational abilities have in explaining cross cultural mathematical reasoning differences, Geary et al. (1999) had high school and college students from the United States and China complete IQ, arithmetical computation, arithmetical reasoning, and mental rotation tasks (only college students). The arithmetical computation tasks were paper and pencil tasks made up of three sub-tests, Simple Subtraction (SS, e.g., 9 – 4), Complex Addition (CA, e.g., 17 + 6 + 28), and Complex Subtraction (CS, e.g., 77 – 8), that each had two forms. Participants were also given two arithmetical reasoning tasks, the Necessary Arithmetic Operations (NAO) and Arithmetic Aptitude (AA) tasks. The former required students to represent and set up the solution procedure for word problems without actually carrying out the procedure to completion while the latter required students to set up and solve multi-step word problems.

Descriptive statistics revealed that after correcting for IQ the Chinese college students had large advantages over the U.S. students on all of the computational measures and both of the reasoning measures, but not on the Mental Rotation task. The same pattern of significant differences was found for the high school sample, although the differences were somewhat smaller. Regression analyses were then performed using the two mathematical reasoning tasks as criterion variables. IQ, computational abilities, and nation were partialed from the national difference on the NAO test and IQ, computational abilities, nation, and NAO performance were partialed from the national difference on the AA test. All of the predictors for both mathematical reasoning measures were significant and significantly reduced the cross-cultural mathematical reasoning differences. In addition, the cross national differences in AA performance dropped more when only IQ and computation were used versus when only IQ and NAO were used as predictors, suggesting that computation is more important in equalizing cross national mathematical reasoning abilities. The same pattern of results emerged from analysis of the high school students' data.

IMPLICATIONS FOR FUTURE RESEARCH

We have learned a great deal from the research that has been conducted to date involving mental arithmetic, working memory and the role of mental arithmetic automatization in more complex mathematical problem solving. These domains of mathematical development, however, are especially ripe for the introduction of new research designs and methods so that we may gain a finer grained and more complete understanding of the interaction of the aforementioned variables. In this concluding section we would like to summarize what we think are some interesting and much needed new avenues for future research. This will be done in two subsections, the first dedicated to future research concerning working memory involvement in mental arithmetic, and the second dedicated to further investigation of the arithmetic automatization/complex problem solving relationship.

Working Memory Involvement in Mental Arithmetic

First and foremost, the methods that have been used in adult research to study working memory involvement in arithmetic need to be applied directly or in modified forms to samples of children. Only a few studies have looked at working memory involvement in mental arithmetic in children, and these have either focused on general effects or the role that the phonological loop plays in early arithmetic processing (e.g., Adams & Hitch, 1997, 1998; Hitch, Cundick, Haughey, Pugh, & Wright, 1987; Kaye et al., 1989).

A second research area that needs further investigation is the impact that expertise and/or strategy use have on working memory involvement in mental arithmetic. Hecht (2002) demonstrated using a verification task that working memory resources are recruited only when non-retrieval strategies are being used to solve problems while retrieval of arithmetic facts from memory is virtually load-free. Klapp and Logan (1991) came to the same conclusion using an alpha arithmetic verification task, and Tronsky (submitted-a) has shown that working memory involvement is significantly reduced after extensive arithmetic practice and may be reduced essentially to zero for many individuals. It would be interesting to see if these results can be replicated using other methods such as De Rammelaere et al.'s (1999, 2001) random interval generation task.

Finally, it would be interesting to see if additional methodologies might be used that are more closely related to what students actually do in the classroom. For example, while the methods of De Rammelaere et al. (2001) have been important in assessing the involvement of different working memory systems in mental arithmetic, they are not high in ecological validity. That is, students in the classroom are never asked to randomly tap on a keyboard while solving arithmetic problems. The letter recall task used in Tronsky (submitted-a, submitted-b) might be a better approximation of what happens in a math class. Students often have to hold information in working memory while solving arithmetic problems and then need to recall that information and use it at a later point. Even this task, however, is still somewhat low on the ecological validity scale as the recall of meaningless consonant strings is not educationally relevant.

Future Research on the Arithmetic Automatization/Higher Problem Solving Relationship

It is apparent that what is most sorely needed is true experimental evidence that to date is almost nonexistent. To our knowledge only two sets of studies have tried to determine experimentally whether there is a relationship between computational abilities and higher mathematical problem solving (Rabinowitz & Woolley, 1995; Suppes et al., 1968; Suppes & Morningstar, 1972). The Stanford project conducted more than thirty years ago (Suppes et al. 1968; Suppes & Morningstar, 1972) had children practice complex computational problems via computer and determined that students gained on standardized measures of computational *and* conceptual knowledge in mathematics. Rabinowitz and Woolley's experiment (1995) involved having college students and sixth graders solve word problems. The researchers varied the difficulty of the word problems and the size of the numbers used in the problems. They predicted that if computational efficiency contributes to word problem solving performance, an interaction between difficulty of word problem and size of numbers (related to arithmetic difficulty) would occur such that problem solving accuracy and time would show the largest decrement in the high word problem and high arithmetic difficulty condition. Neither the college students' nor the sixth graders' data showed the interaction. This experiment suffers from a number of shortcomings, one of which is that the word problems may have been too easy for the two student samples thereby imposing only minimal working memory load. Improvement on and extension of Rabinowitz and Woolley's research is one of the many experimental avenues that needs to be explored. We would now like to delineate additional experimental paths that would be interesting and informative.

A simple research design would be to select one group of students and train them on the basic arithmetic facts to the point of automaticity and select another group to be the control. The students would then be followed longitudinally to determine whether the automatization group develops better complex problem solving skills and whether this group does so more quickly than the control group. A variation of the aforementioned design would be to take the same two groups and instead of "passively" following them longitudinally, give them instruction and have them practice problem solving in some higher math problem solving domain. Researchers could then compare the two groups to see if the automatization group learned the higher level problem solving skills better and/or faster than the control group.

A third possibility would be to use microgenetic methods (e.g., Rittle-Johnson & Siegler, 1998; Siegler & Crowley, 1991) that are characterized by repeatedly examining student knowledge over a substantial period of time. This allows for, among other things, the measuring of iterative development. This would be especially helpful in exploring the findings of Hecht et al. (2001) that there was a bidirectional relationship between basic arithmetic and more complex arithmetic. It could also be used to try to assess the role of computation in word problem solving. One might test students' ability to remember representations and solution procedures after calculating answers to word problems. Assessing this repeatedly as computational abilities develop or after specific training on arithmetic problems would give an indication of the impact of basic arithmetic. It has been shown with adults that even for arithmetic problems such as 39 + 16 that require algorithmic solutions, after solution the addends of the problem have decayed enough from working memory that people often cannot recall them (Thevenot, Barrouillet, & Fayol, 2001). An analogous situation may occur during word problem solution that causes word problem representations, solution procedures, and the connection of the two to decay in working memory.

Designs that allow for the testing of number sense, how it develops, and how it may be applied to more advanced problem solving situation is an intriguing avenue for future research. For example, Dowker (1998) has shown that those students who have mastered the basic arithmetic and subtraction facts know more derived addition and subtraction strategies that they can explain and apply to unknown arithmetical facts. She also found that students that have better calculation abilities are better at estimating. Similar relationships may exist between basic calculation abilities and strategy construction for multi-digit arithmetic. Several researchers have shown that having students construct their own solutions to multi-digit arithmetic problems is much more beneficial than teaching the standard algorithmic solution that has been demonstrated in textbooks for years (e.g., Fuson, 1998; Hiebert & Wearne, 1996). It may be that basic calculation automatization has a role in strategy construction for more complex arithmetic. Yet another example would be on the SAT that has a standard section that requires comparing two values to see if one is larger than another or if they are equivalent; these problems use both numerical and nonnumerical values. Students that have a strong interconnected knowledge of numbers and number combinations, presumably rooted in their strong basic calculation abilities, may be able to solve these and other types of SAT problems faster and more accurately.

A final area that could be investigated is how often students use non-traditional, numerical methods to solve reasoning problems. For example, in a recent class of the first author we were studying problem solving, and as an exercise students had to solve different problems so we could discuss the solution strategies they used. One problem was a problem that is typically solved by setting up two equations with two unknowns, normally solved using simultaneous equations. One student who had finished the problem very quickly shared his solution. Based on the numbers given in the problem he was able to estimate what values (for x and y using the equation method) should be close to the solution. His values yielded answers that came close to working and he was then able to quickly adjust his original values to get the answer to the problem. Perhaps those students who have a well-developed number sense (again presumably rooted in strong basic computational abilities) can use that knowledge to construct non-traditional (numerically based) solution procedures to solve mathematical reasoning problems.

CONCLUSION

Several important conclusions can be drawn based on the research that has been reviewed here. The first is that working memory resources are involved in basic mental arithmetic, these resources are greatly reduced over development and after training, and when retrieval is used and/or skill is high often working memory resource use can be reduced to zero. Another important conclusion is that almost all studies that have examined the connection between basic arithmetic automatization and higher level problem solving abilities in math have found a significant relationship. It is squarely on the shoulders of researchers to come up with sound, and in some cases, creative methodologies to experimentally determine the primary cause(s) of the relationship and to determine whether the cause(s) rely on the construct of working memory.

REFERENCES

Adams, J.W., & Hitch, G.J. (1998). Children's mental arithmetic and working memory. In C. Donlan (Ed.), *The development of mathematical skills* (pp. 153–173). East Sussex. UK: Psychology Press Limited.

Adams, J.W., & Hitch, G.J. (1997). Working memory and children's mental addition. *Journal of Experimental Child Psychology, 67,* 21–38.

Ashcraft, M.H. (1992). Cognitive arithmetic: A review of data and theory. *Cognition, 44,* 75–106.

Ashcraft, M.H. (1995). Cognitive psychology and simple arithmetic: A review and summary of new directions. *Mathematical Cognition, 1,* 3–34.

Ashcraft, M.H., Donley, R.D., Halas, M.A., & Vakali, M. (1992). Working memory, automaticity, and problem difficulty. In J.I.D. Campbell (Ed.), *The nature and origins of mathematical skills* (pp. 301–329). Amsterdam: Elsevier.

Baddeley, A.D. (1986). *Working memory.* Oxford: Clarendon Press.

Baddeley, A.D. (1992a). Working memory. *Science, 255,* 556–559.

Baddeley, A.D. (1992b). Is working memory working? The fifteenth Bartlett Lecture. *The Quarterly Journal of Experimental Psychology, 44A,* 1–31.

Baddeley, A.D. (1996). Exploring the central executive. *The Quarterly Journal of Experimental Psychology, 49A,* 5–28.

Baddeley, A.D., & Hitch G.J. (1994). Developments in the concept of working memory. *Neuropsychology, 8,* 485–493.

Balow, I.H. (1964). Reading and computation ability as determinants of problem solving. *The Arithmetic Teacher, 11,* 18–22.

Beaton, A.E., Mullis, I.V., Martin, M.O., Gonzalez, E.J., Kelly, D.L., Smith, T.A. (1996). *Mathematics achievement in the middle school years: IEA's third international mathematics and science study (TIMSS).* Chestnut Hill, MA: Boston College.

Bull, R., & Johnston, R.S. (1997). Children's arithmetical difficulties: Contributions from processing speed, item identification, and short-term memory. *Journal of Experimental Child Psychology, 65,* 1–24.

Bull, R., Johnston, R.S., & Roy, J.A. (1999). Exploring the roles of the visual-spatial sketch pad and central executive in children's arithmetical skills: Views from cognition and developmental neuropschology. *Developmental Neuropsychology, 15,* 421–442.

Campbell, J.I.D., & Tarling, D.P.M. (1996). Retrieval processes in arithmetic production and verification. *Memory & Cognition, 24,* 156–172.

Cumming, J.J., & Elkins, J. (1999). Lack of automaticity in the basic addition facts as a characteristic of arithmetic learning problems and instructional needs. *Mathematical Cognition, 5,* 149–180.

Dark, V.J., & Benbow, C.P. (1990). Enhanced problem translation and short-term memory: Components of mathematical talent. *Journal of Educational Psychology, 82,* 420–429.

Dark, V.J., & Benbow, C.P. (1991). Differential enhancement of working memory with mathematical versus verbal precocity. *Journal of Educational Psychology, 83,* 48–60.

Dark, V.J., & Benbow, C.P. (1993). Cognitive differences among the gifted: A review and new data. In D.K. Detterman (Ed.), *Current topics in human intelligence* (Vol. 3). Norwood, NJ: Ablex.

Dark, V.J., & Benbow, C.P. (1994). Type of stimulus mediates the relationship between working memory performance and type of precocity. *Intelligence, 19*, 337–357.

De Rammelaere, S., Stuyven, E. , & Vandierendonck, A. (1999). The contribution of working memory resources in the verification of simple mental arithmetic sums. *Psychological Research, 62*, 72–77.

De Rammelaere, S., Stuyven, E. , & Vandierendonck, A. (2001). Mental arithmetic and working memory. *Memory and Cognition, 29*, 267–273.

De Rammelaere, S., & Vandierendonck, A. (in press). Are executive processes used to solve simple mental arithmetic production tasks? *Current Psychology Letters: Behaviour, Brain, & Cognition.*

Dowker, A.D. (1998). Individual differences in normal arithmetic development. In C. Donlan (Ed.), *The develompent of mathematical skills* (pp. 275–302). East Sussex, UK: Psychology Press.

Fürst, A.J., & Hitch, G.J. (2000). Separate roles for executive and phonological components of working memory in mental arithmetic. *Memory & Cognition, 28*, 774–782.

Fuson, K.C. (1998). Pedagogical, mathematical, and real-world, conceptual-support nets: A model for building children's multidigit domain knowledge. *Mathematical Cognition, 4*, 147–186.

Geary, D.C. (1994). *Children's mathematical development*. Washington, DC: American Psychological Association.

Geary, D.C. (1996a). The problem-size effect in mental addition: Developmental and cross national trends. *Mathematical Cognition, 2*, 63–93.

Geary, D.C. (1996b). International differences in mathematical achievement: Their nature causes, and consequences. *Current Directions in Psychological Science, 5*, 133–137.

Geary, D.C., Bow-Thomas, C.C., Fan, L., & Siegler, R.S. (1993). Even before formal instruction, Chinese children outperform American children in mental addition. *Cognitive Development, 8*, 517–529.

Geary, D.C., Bow-Thomas, C.C., Liu, F., & Siegler, R.S. (1996). Development of arithmetical competencies in Chinese and American childres: Influence of age, language, and schooling. *Child Development, 67*, 2022–2044.

Geary, D.C., & Brown, S.C. (1991). Cognitive addition: Strategy choice and speed-of-processing differences in gifted, normal, and mathematically disabled children. *Developmental Psychology, 27*, 398–406.

Geary, D.C., Brown, S.C., & Samaranayake, V.A. (1991). Cognitive addition: A short longitudinal study of strategy choice and speed-of-processing differences in normal and mathematically disabled children. *Developmental Psychology, 27*, 787–797.

Geary, D.C., & Burlingham-Dubree, M. (1989). External validation of the strategy choice model for addition. *Journal of Experimental Child Psychology, 47*, 175–192.

Geary, D.C., Fan, L., Bow-Thomas, C.C. (1992). Numerical cognition: Loci of ability differences comparing children from China and the United States. *Psychological Science, 3*, 180–185.

Geary, D.C., Liu, F., Chen, G.P., Saults, S.J., & Hoard, M.K. (1999). Contributions of computational fluency to cross-national differences in arithmetical reasoning abilities. *Journal of Educational Psychology, 91*, 716–719.

Geary, D.C., Salthouse, T.A., Chen, G.P., & Liu, F. (1996). Are east Asian versus American differences in arithmetical ability a recent phenomenon? *Developmental Psychology, 32*, 254–262.

Geary, D.C., Saults, S.J., Liu, F., & Hoard, M.K. (2000). Sex differences in spatial cognition, computational fluency, and arithmetical reasoning. *Journal of Experimental Child Psychology, 77*, 337–353.

Geary, D.C., & Widaman, K.F. (1992). Numerical cognition: On the convergence of componential and psychometric models. *Intelligence, 16*, 47–80.

Gray, C., & Mulhern, G. (1995). Does children's memory for addition facts predict general mathematical ability? *Perceptual and Motor Skills, 81*, 163–167.

Hecht, S.A. (1998). Toward an information-processing account of individual differences in fraction skills. *Journal of Educational Psychology, 90*, 545–559.

Hecht, S.A. (1999). Individual solution processes while solving addition and multiplication math facts in adults. *Memory and Cognition, 27*, 1097–1107.

Hecht, S.A. (2002). Counting on working memory in simple arithmetic when counting is used for problem solving. *Memory & Cognition, 30*, 447–455.

Hecht, S.A., Torgeson, J.K., Wagner, R.K., & Rashotte, C.A. (2001). The relations between phonological processing abilities and emerging individual differences in mathematical computation skills: A longitudinal study from second to fifth grades. *Journal of Experimental Child Psychology, 79*, 192–227.

Hiebert, J. (1990). The role of routine procedures in the development of mathematical competence. In T.J. Cooney & C.R. Hirsch (Eds.), *Teaching and learning mathematics in the 90's*, (pp. 31–39). Reston, VA: The National Council of Teachers of Mathematics, Inc.

Hiebert, J., & Wearne, D. (1996). Instruction, understanding, and skill in multidigit addition and subtraction. *Cognition and Instruction, 14*, 251–283.

Hitch, G.J. (1978a). Mental arithmetic: Short-term storage and information processing in a cognitive skill. In A.M. Lesgold, J.W. Pellegrino, S.D. Fokkema, & R. Glaser (Eds.), *Cognitive psychology and instruction* (pp. 331–338). New York: Plenum.

Hitch, G.J. (1978b). The role of short-term working memory in mental arithmetic. *Cognitive Psychology, 10*, 302–323.

Hitch, G.J., Cundick, J., Haughey, M., Pugh, R., & Wright, H. (1987). Aspects of counting in children's arithmetic. In J. Sloboda & D. Rogers (Eds.), *Cognitive processes in mathematics* (pp. 26–41). Oxford: Oxford University Press.

Kail, R., & Hall, L.K. (1999). Sources of developmental change in children's word-problem performance. *Journal of Educational Psychology, 91*, 660–668.

Kaye, D.B. (1986). The development of mathematical cognition. *Cognitive Development, 1*, 157–170.

Kaye, D.B., de Winstanley, P., Chen, Q., & Bonnefil, V. (1989). Development of efficient arithmetic computation. *Journal of Educational Psychology, 81*, 467–480.

Klapp, S.T., Boches, C.A., Trabert, M.L., & Logan, G.D. (1991). Automatizing alphabet arithmetic: II. Are there practice effects after automaticity is achieved? *Journal of Experimental Psychology: Learning, Memory, and Cognition, 17,* 196–209.

Koshmider, J.W., & Ashcraft, M.H. (1991). The development of children's mental multiplication skill. *Journal of Experimental Child Psychology, 51,* 53–89.

Lefevre, J., & Liu, J. (1997). The role of experience in numerical skill: Multiplication performance in adults from China and Canada. *Mathematical Cognition, 3,* 31–62.

Lefevre, J., Sadesky, G.S., & Bisanz, J. (1996). Selection of procedures in mental addition: Reassessing the problem size effect in adults. *Journal of Experimental Psychology: Learning, Memory, and Cognition, 22,* 216–230.

Lemaire, P., Abdi, H., & Fayol, M. (1996). The role of working memory resources in simple cognitive arithmetic. *European Journal of Cognitive Psychology, 8,* 73–103.

Lemaire, P., & Fayol, M. (1995). When plausibility judgments supersede fact retrieval: The example of the odd-even effect on product verification. *Memory & Cognition, 23,* 34–48.

Lemaire, P., & Reder, L.M. (1999). What affects strategy selection in arithmetic? The example of parity and five effects on product verification. *Journal of Experimental Psychology: Learning, Memory, and Cognition,* 27, 364–382.

Lochy, A. , Seron, X., Delazer, M., & Butterworth, B. (2000). The odd/even effect in multiplication: Parity rule or familiarity with even numbers? *Cognition, 28,* 358–365.

Logie, R.H., & Baddeley, A.D. (1987). Cognitive processes in counting. *Journal of Experimental Psychology: Learning, Memory, and Cognition, 13,* 310–326.

Logie, R.H., Gilhooly, K.J., & Wynn, V. (1994). Counting on working memory in arithmetic problem solving. *Memory and Cognition, 22,* 395–410.

Logie, R.H., Zucco, G., & Baddeley, A.D. (1990). Interference with visual short term memory. *Acta Psychologica, 75,* 55–74.

Manly, C.F., & Spoehr, K.T. (1999). Mental multiplication: Nothing but the facts? *Memory & Cognition, 27,* 1087–1096.

Mercer, C.D. (1979). *Children and adolescents with learning disabilities.* Columbus, OH: Charles E. Merrill.

Miller, K.F., Smith, C.M., Zhu, J., & Zhang, H. (1995). Preschool origins of cross-national differences in mathematical competence: The role of number naming systems. *Psychological Science, 6,* 56–60.

Morales, R.V., Shute, V.J., & Pellegrino, J.W. (1985). Developmental differences in understanding and solving simple mathematics word problems. *Cognition and Instruction, 2,* 41–57.

Muth, K.D. (1984). Solving arithmetic word problems: Role of reading and computational skills. *Journal of Educational Psychology, 76,* 205–210.

Pellegrino, J.W., & Goldman, S.R. (1987). Information processing and elementary mathematics. *Journal of Learning Disabilities, 20,* 23–32.

Rabinowitz, M., & Woolley, K.E. (1995). Much ado about nothing: The relation among computational skill, arithmetic word problem comprehension, and limited attentional resources. *Cognition and Instruction, 13,* 51–71.

Resnick, L.B., & Ford, W.W. (1981). *The psychology of mathematics for instruction.* Hillsdale, NJ: Erlbaum.

Rittle-Johnson, B., & Siegler, R.S. (1998). Mathematical understanding and mathematical performance. In C. Donlan (Ed.), *The development of mathematical skills* (pp. 75–110). East Sussex, UK: Psychology Press.

Royer, J.M. (1990). The Sentence Verification Technique: A new direction in the assessment of reading comprehension. In S.M. Legg & J. Algina (Eds.), *Cognitive assessment of language and math outcomes.* Norwood, NJ: Ablex.

Royer, J.M., Carlo, M.S., & Cisero, C.A. (1992). School-based uses for the Sentence Verification Technique of measuring listening and reading comprehension. *Psychological Test Bulletin, 5,* 5–19.

Royer, J.M., Tronsky, L.N., Chan, Y., Jackson, S.G., & Marchant, H.G. (1999). Math fact retrieval as the cognitive mechanism underlying gender differences in math achievement test performance. *Contemporary Educational Psychology, 24,* 181–266.

Seitz, K., & Schumann-Hengsteler, R. (2000). Mental multiplication and working memory. *European Journal of Cognitive Psychology, 12,* 552–570.

Siegler, R.S. (1988). Individual differences in strategy choices: Good students, not-so-good students, and perfectionists. *Child Development, 59,* 833–851.

Siegler, R.S., & Crowley, K. (1991). The microgenetic method: A direct means for studying cognitive development. *American Psychologist, 46,* 606–620.

Silver, E.A. (1987). Foundations of cognitive theory and research for mathematics problem-solving. In A.H. Schoenfeld (Ed.), *Cognitive science and mathematics education* (pp. 33–60). Hillsdale, NJ: Erlbaum.

Stevenson, H.W., Chen, C., & Lee, S.Y. (1993). Mathematics achievement of Chinese, Japanese, and American children: Ten years later. *Science, 259,* 53–58.

Stevenson, H.W., Lee, S.Y., & Stigler, J.W. (1986). Mathematics achievement of Chinese, Japanese, and American children. *Science, 251,* 693–699.

Suppes, P., Jerman, M., & Brian, D. (1968). *Computer-assisted instruction: Stanford's 1965–66 arithmetic program.* New York: Academic Press.

Suppes, P., & Morningstar, M. (1972). *Computer-assisted instruction at Stanford, 1966–1968: Data, models, and evaluation of the arithmetic programs.* New York: Academic Press.

Swanson, H.L. (1993). Working memory in learning disability subgroups. *Journal of Experimental Child Psychology, 56,* 87–114.

Swanson, H.L., Cooney, J.B., & Brock, S. (1993). The influence of working memory and classification ability on children's word problem solution. *Journal of Experimental Child Psychology, 55,* 374–395.

Towse, J., & Saxton, M. (1998). Mathematics across national boundaries: Cultural and linguistic perspectives on numerical competence. In C. Donlan (Ed.), *The development of mathematical skills* (pp. 129–150). East Sussex: UK: Psychology Press.

Tronsky, L.N. (1997). *Mental arithmetic skill and its relation to complex mathematical problem solving ability.* Unpublished masters thesis.

Tronsky, L.N. (submitted-a). *Practice, problem size, and working memory resource use in mental arithmetic: Group and individual differences.*

Tronsky, L.N. (submitted-b). *Strategy use, problem size, and working memory resource use in complex multiplication before and after practice: An individual differences perspective.*

Vandierendonck, A., De Vooght, G., & Van Der Goten, K. (1998). Does random time interval generation interfere with working memory executive functions? *European Journal of Cognitive Psychology, 10,* 413–442.

Whang, P.A., & Hancock, G.R. (1997). Modeling the mathematics achievement of Asian-American elementary students. *Learning and Individual Differences, 9,* 63–88.

Widaman, K.F., Little, T.D., Geary, D.C., & Cormier, P. (1992). Individual differences in the development of skill in mental addition: Internal and external validation of chronometric models. *Learning and Individual Differences, 4,* 167–213.

Zbrodoff, N.J., & Logan, G.D. (1990). On the relation between production and verification tasks in the psychology of simple arithmetic. *Journal of Experimental Psychology: Learning, Memory, and Cognition, 16,* 83–97.

Zentall, S.S. (1990). Fact-retrieval automatization and math problem solving by learning disabled, attention disordered, and normal adolescents. *Journal of Educational Psychology, 82,* 856–865.

CHAPTER 6

MATHEMATICS INSTRUCTION

Cognitive, Affective,
and Existential Perspectives

Allan Feldman

ABSTRACT

The intent of this chapter is to explore why math teaching is out of line with the expectations of the mathematics education community as detailed in the NCTM standards. It begins by presenting two examples of research-based math teaching, one at the college level and the other at a middle school, to illustrate the NCTM vision in practice. This is followed with an analysis of the research on math teaching as a way to understand why research-based teaching is rarely seen. Included in this section are the multiple perspectives or meta-theories that are used to structure studies on teaching. This is followed by examples of frameworks developed from these perspectives. The chapter ends by suggesting a theoretical framework that uses an existential view to look at the interactions between teachers and students in classrooms. This perspective allows us to recognize that teaching and learning are part of a dialectical whole that includes the ways that teachers and students are in the educational situations that they create through the choices that they make.

Mathematical Cognition, pages 147–174

INTRODUCTION

We, as a nation, are concerned about how well our children learn mathematics. While this as a simple statement has little that one can fault, what it means to learn mathematics and what the teaching and learning of math should be like in schools has been fiercely debated by policymakers. However, in the mathematics education community there is a clear consensus of what it means to know mathematics.[1] This can be seen in "A Vision for School Mathematics" in the current NCTM standards (NCTM, 2000):

> Students confidently engage in complex mathematical tasks chosen carefully by teachers. They draw on knowledge from a wide variety of mathematical topics, sometimes approaching the same problem from different mathematical perspectives or representing the mathematics in different ways until they find methods that enable them to make progress. Teachers help students make, refine, and explore conjectures on the basis of evidence and use a variety of reasoning and proof techniques to confirm or disprove those conjectures. Students are flexible and resourceful problem solvers. Alone or in groups and with access to technology, they work productively and reflectively, with the skilled guidance of their teachers. Orally and in writing, students communicate their ideas and results effectively. They value mathematics and engage actively in learning it (p. 3).

Unfortunately, when one goes out to schools to observe what is taught and how, the NCTM's vision is nowhere in sight. What we see instead are mathematical concepts being taught in the ways that would be familiar to our parents and grandparents (Cuban, 1993).

My intent in this chapter is to explore why math teaching is so out of line with the expectations of the mathematics education community. I begin by presenting two examples of research-based math teaching, one at the college level and the other at a middle school, to illustrate the NCTM vision in practice. I then turn to the research on math teaching as a way to understand why research-based teaching, such as the examples in this chapter, is rarely seen. In this section I review the multiple perspectives or meta-theories that are used to structure studies on teaching. This is followed by examples of frameworks developed from these perspectives. I end the chapter by suggesting another way to look at teaching that takes an existential view of what happens between teachers and students in classrooms. This perspective allows us to recognize that teaching and learning are part of a dialectical whole that includes the ways that teachers and students are in the educational situations that they create through the choices that they make.

RESEARCH-BASED INSTRUCTION

The NCTM vision of student learning is tied to a constructivist theory of learning (Fosnot, 1989).

> Constructivism is a theory about knowledge and learning; it describes both what "knowing" is and how one "comes to know." Based on work in psychology, philosophy, and anthropology, the theory describes knowledge as temporary, developmental, nonobjective, internally constructed, and socially and culturally mediated. Learning from this perspective is viewed as a self-regulatory process of struggling with the conflict between existing personal models of the world and discrepant new insights, constructing new representations and models of reality as a human meaning-making venture with culturally developed tools and symbols, and further negotiating such meaning through cooperative social activity, discourse, and debate. (Fosnot, 1996, p. ix)

Fosnot defines constructivism as both a way to explain the generation of mathematics knowledge (i.e., a new mathematics theory) and a way to model how people come to understand mathematics knowledge (e.g., making sense of the mean value theorem means and learning how to use it). In this way she ties together the uses of the term *constructivism* in epistemology and psychology. There is also a third way that people use the term: it is used to describe a form of pedagogy. Putting aside the epistemological aspect of constructivism because it has little effect on theories of learning or pedagogy, constructivist math educators see students as people who come to math instruction with knowledge and beliefs about mathematics that have grown from their past experiences. Learning mathematics becomes a process of engaging in mathematical activities in ways that enable students to construct their understanding of mathematics concepts.

Constructivism as a learning theory has served as a framework for the numerous cognitive studies on math learning. These studies have provided researchers, curriculum developers, and teachers with detailed information about how people learn mathematical concepts. There are almost countless examples of this type of research, as can be seen in the nine chapters that review cognitive studies in the *Handbook of research on mathematics teaching and learning* (Grouws, 1992). These chapters deal with research on the learning of specific aspects of mathematics such as whole number addition and subtraction (Fuson, 1992), multiplication and division (Greer, 1992), and probability and statistics (Shaughnessy, 1992), to name a few.

The research literature also contains examples of instruction that has been shaped by research from these perspectives. For example, the book *How People Learn* (Bransford, Brown, & Cocking, 1999), developed by the National Research Council, presents three vignettes of math instruction that exemplify what has been learned from cognitive studies of math learning. Two of the vignettes are of university researchers, Magdalene Lampert and Deborah Ball, teaching math to young children. The third vignette is an example of cognitively guided instruction by Annie Keith, an early childhood teacher in Wisconsin.

Math Teaching in College

A detailed description of research-based instruction can be found in Cynthia Smith's action research study of her teaching of remedial mathematics at the State University of New York College at Fredonia (Smith, 1998). To Smith, her students' mathematics knowledge is constructed through the doing of mathematics as part of a community of learners. She refers to this as a social constructivist perspective and pays close attention to the way that she and her students talk about mathematics. Using this perspective, Smith characterizes her practice as continuous motion "within and among the roles of initiator, facilitator, and expert" (p. 749). It should be clear from this description of her practice, her method of inquiry (observation, journal keeping, and reflection), as well as the sources that Smith cites in her article, that she is aware of recent research in mathematics learning and that she uses it to guide her instruction.

The lesson that Smith describes is centered on a problem that she posed to her students (Figure 6.1). Smith presented the problem and asked the students to work on it in groups. They began by reading the problem and thinking about it individually. Smith struggled to keep from speaking and "breaking the silence." As she listened to the students argue with one

---

Two Hands Are Better Than One
(How much better?)

Darlene and John Edinger were looking for someone to paint their front porch. They received several estimates. The two best came from Michael and Tim. Michael said that he could do the job in 8 hours. Tim told the Edingers that he could complete the job in only 6 hours. Darlene and John wanted the porch painted as quickly as possible, so they decided to hire both men. Approximately how long should it take for Michael and Tim—working together—to complete the job?

Please provide written justification of your logic and reasoning.

Figure 6.1.   Smith's "two hands are better than one" problem (Smith, 1998).

another about the solution to the problem, she began to realize that all six groups had accepted the idea that the solution was obtained by averaging the two men's time and dividing by two.

At this point it would not have been unusual for an instructor to give the students the "correct" solution. Instead, Smith reflected on what had happened in her journal:

> Their solution is so close to the exact answer, 24/7, that it is going to be difficult to motivate further exploration. … Why does their faulty algorithm provide such a good estimate. (pp. 751–752)?

This led her to look at the mathematics of the problem. Smith found that the algorithm that the students had used to solve the problem is exact if and only if the two painters work at the same speed, and that the accuracy of the method decreases as the difference in rates of painting increases. As a result of her mathematical analysis of the classroom event she constructed a new problem, one in which the painters had a much larger difference rate of work. It was not until the students realized that their algorithm failed for this problem that Smith provided them with a mathematics concept to use in the suggestion that they consider each worker's rate.

Smith's description of her classroom resonates with the NCTM vision statement. She encourages her students to think deeply about the mathematics of the problem in order to construct a solution. When the class reached consensus on an incorrect solution, rather than marking them wrong, Smith presented them with another problem that challenged the understanding that they had developed from their attempts on the first. In this way she structured the class so that her students engaged in activities similar to that of mathematicians.

Middle School Mathematics

A second detailed view of research-based math teaching can be seen in Azita Manouchehri and Mary Enderson's study of "Ms. L" who is part of the Missouri Middle School Mathematics Project (Manouchehri & Enderson, 1999). This NSF-funded project has as its goal to "initiate and support the effective implementation of exemplary middle school mathematics curricula (*Mathematics in Context, Connected Mathematics, Seeing and Thinking Mathematically,* and *Six through Eight Mathematics*) in Missouri schools" (MMMP, undated).

Ms. L began her lesson by handing out a piece of paper to the students that had a number pyramid on it (Figure 6.2). She then said to the students, "OK everyone. Here is a situation; explore it" (Manouchehri & Enderson,

Figure 6.2.   Ms. L's number pyramid problem (Manouchehri & Enderson, 1999).

1999). The students knew what to do: They formed small groups and began to talk about the number pyramid. Ms. L walked around the room and spoke with students about what they were thinking about the situation. After 15 minutes of small group work, she got the class' attention and asked for a student from each group to share with the class the group's initial thoughts. From the description supplied by Manouchehri and Enderson, it appears that the students knew what the teacher expected from them. Each group presented some type of number pattern that they found in the pyramid. As the students presented, Ms. L asked other students to comment on the observations. She also suggested possibilities for further exploration based on the students' initial observations. Through the   remainder of the lesson Ms. L asked for students to give feedback to their peers. She also had the class vote as to whether they agreed or not with a group's analysis of the pattern.

Ms. L had taught the class how to engage in this inquiry type of lesson. They knew that the pyramid was a puzzle that they needed to figure out. Ms. L helped them to do so by guiding student discourse about the situation. Manouchehri and Enderson observed four different types of discourse interventions in Ms. L's teaching that were intended to:

- Facilitate the establishment of situations in which student had to share ideas and elaborate on their thinking...;
- Help students expand the boundary of their exploration...;
- Encourage students to make connections among different discoveries and develop a deeper understanding of the interrelationships among the patterns that the students identified...; and
- Invite multiple representations of ideas (Manouchehri & Enderson, 1999, p. 219).

In their analysis of the lesson, Manouchehri and Enderson refer to Cobb's work on social constructivism (Cobb & others, 1997) and Schoenfeld's focus on classroom culture (Schoenfeld, 1994). They use these theories to conclude that:

The teacher's reactions during the session were fundamental in emphasizing both the social and the sociomathematical norms of the classroom as she recognized the value of each individual, encouraged each member's participation and input, and expanded the domain of the class's mathematical investigation and communication as she asked for evaluations of ideas that were shared by others. (Manouchehri & Enderson, 1999, pp. 221–222)

In other words, Ms. L was using research-based instructional practices in a manner consonant with the NCTM vision.

RESEARCH ON TEACHING IN SCHOOLS

The examples from *How People Learn* and the two vignettes that I presented here are exemplars of the type of math instruction that is consonant with NCTM's vision for school mathematics. Although other examples of research-based practice can be found throughout the US, policy studies suggest that they are few and far between, especially at the middle school, high school, and college levels (Cohen, 1991; NISACA, undated; USDOE, 2000).

Before examining possible reasons for this lack of evidence of research-based teaching, I address a concern raised by David Klein in this volume that contrary to the findings of studies such as TIMSS, American teachers, especially in California, have implemented curriculum materials and instructional methods that are consonant with the NCTM Standards. Klein uses two pieces of evidence of the widespread use of NCTM style curriculum materials and methods in California. The first is that the California State Board of Education approved math curricular materials for grades K–8 aligned to the 1992 California Mathematics Framework, which was based on the NCTM Standards, and that consequently those curricular materials were purchased, with State funds, for use in classrooms (Klein, p. 25). The other is that 95% of teachers in the TIMSS study self-reported that they were aware of current ideas about mathematics teaching, and that 75% self-reported that their lessons were at least somewhat in accord with the NCTM vision. In addition, one-third of the teachers surveyed listed the NCTM standards documents as books they read to stay informed about current ideas in mathematics.

Unfortunately, neither of these types of evidence can be accepted uncritically. The purchase of curricular materials is not necessarily an indicator of their use. For example, although school districts throughout the US purchased materials to support the NSF-funded elementary science curricula such as SCIS the boxes languished on shelves collecting dust. Even when they were used, teachers frequently were not provided with funds to restock the expendable supplies. What we see in classrooms instead is the use of worksheets that were once mimeographed and now xeroxed. In understanding teachers' reliance on worksheets, it is important to acknowledge their use as a classroom management tool. Not only do they keep children busy, they are the primary task that students perform in classroom token economies (Feldman, Kropf, & Alibrandi, 1998).

Teachers' self-reporting is also suspect. David Cohen's now classic study of "Mrs. Oublier," done as part of the evaluation of California's 1985 curriculum framework, vividly illustrates this (Cohen, 1991). In this case, Cohen documents how Mrs. Oublier's teaching of mathematics was traditional even though she had attended workshops on new pedagogy, used research-based curriculum materials, and spoke the language of reform.

My reason for responding to Klein's comments is not to support the NCTM Standards but rather to question his assertion that there is widespread use of the types of curricular materials and instructional methods consonant with those standards. Instead, what we see is that there has been little effect of more than 50 years of reform efforts and more than 20 years of cognitive research on what happens in schools.

PERSPECTIVES ON TEACHING

Teaching and learning in classrooms is a result of negotiations that occur among the various participants in schooling, including teachers, students, administrators, parents, and policy makers (Clandinin & Connelly, 1992). Because of the complexities of schooling, we tend to develop perspectives or meta-theories that we use to understand what is going on in schools. Our perspectives on teaching, which we take on or develop new, are connected to our beliefs about what it means to know mathematics as well as ideological stances toward the purposes of schooling (Eisner, 1992). As a result, these perspectives are linked to the ways that mathematics teaching and learning is researched.

In their review of research on mathematics teaching practices, Mary Koehler and Douglas Grouws (Koehler & Grouws, 1992) argued that there is a clear link between the five research perspective that they identify and particular conceptions of teaching. In a constructivist approach (e.g., Fosnot, 1989) the goal of teaching is to "structure, monitor, and adjust" (p. 119) learning activities for students. When teachers engage in cognitively guided instruction, which is a model developed by Elizabeth Fennema and her colleagues (Fennema et al., 1993), teachers use their knowledge from cognitive science about how students learn to make decisions about what and how to teach. Expert-novice studies focus on the difference between what experienced teachers know and do compared to novice teachers. In the studies that follow on Lee Shulman's work on teacher knowledge (Shulman, 1986), teachers are seen as those who have particular subject matter knowledge, pedagogical knowledge, and pedagogical content knowledge, all of which can change and grow through a process of pedagogical reasoning on instruction.

The three perspectives mentioned in the previous section focus on what teachers know and can do. Koehler and Grouws also identified two perspectives that are based on researchers' conceptions of what it means to know mathematics. They attribute a sociological and epistemological view to Magdeline Lampert (1990), who believes that students construct their understanding of mathematics similar to the way that mathematicians construct new knowledge. From this perspective, math teaching is seen as the development of opportunities for students and teachers to engage in authentic mathematical reasoning. Finally, Koehler and Grouws identified a perspective on math teaching in which teachers use instructional sequences that have been developed to help students gain conceptual understanding of mathematical concepts (e.g., Hiebert & Wearne, 1988). This perspective tends to view mathematics teaching as the implementation of those instructional sequences.

There are two other research perspectives that influence our conceptions of math teaching that have gained in influence since the publication of the *Handbook* (Grouws, 1992). One is a social constructivist perspective. From this perspective the learning of mathematics is viewed as a social process that occurs among teachers and students as they talk and argue about math (Bowers, Cobb, & McClain, 1999; Brenner et al., 1997; Steele, 1999; Cobb et al., 1997). The social process perspective assumes that cognition is situated and that individuals construct their understandings as part of a community. From this perspective, math teachers are those who develop communities of learners who engage in discourse about authentic mathematical processes.

The other perspective uses feminist theory to understand math teaching and learning. Although issues of gender equity have been explored in math education for more than three decades (e.g., Fennema, 1974), feminist studies were not made explicit in Koehler and Grouw's (1992) review. For example, although they included the work of Fennema and her colleagues in their review, they failed to note the connection between cognitively guided instruction (CGI) and issues of gender equity. To Fennema, CGI was developed as a result of studies that indicated little difference in the ways that girls and boys reason mathematically. Fennema (1974) reasoned that if teachers were aware of the results of cognitive studies on mathematics, their best practices would be equally effective for both girls and boys. This hypothesis was confirmed by her research with Tom Carpenter (Carpenter & Fennema, 1992). Since then, Fennema has begun to explore the perspective of feminist standpoint theory:

> Instead of interpreting the challenges related to gender and mathematics as involving problems associated with females and mathematics, I begin to look

at how a male view of mathematics has been destructive to both males and females ... I am coming to believe that females have recognized that mathematics, as currently taught and learned, restricts their lives rather than enriches them (Fennema, 2000, p. 6).

As a result, she finds herself asking questions such as, "Would mathematics education, organized from a feminist perspective, be different from the mathematics education we currently have?" (p. 6).

Cognitive science research, as it identifies universals, would suggest that looking at the world through either feminine or masculine eyes does not make sense. Feminist perspectives suggest just the opposite: female/male differences permeate the entirety of life and must be considered whenever scholarship is planned (Fennema, 2000, p. 7).

Therefore, for those who study math teaching and learning from a feminist perspective, teachers must not only be aware of the findings from cognitive research, they must also be aware of the effects of gender on mathematics as a discipline, mathematics education, and the interactions that occur in their classrooms and in their students' lives.

Research findings from the perspectives identified by Koehler and Grouws, as well as the sociocultural and feminist perspectives, have had an effect on policy statements such as the NCTM standards and state curriculum frameworks, and publications for teachers like those available from NCTM, ASCD and ERIC. For example, Terese Herrera and Asli Ozgun-Koca (1999) provide this list of "promising practices" in their article in *The ERIC Review*.

1. Problem-solving approach;
2. Experimental approach;
3. Development of mathematical reasoning;
4. Cooperative/group learning;
5. Illustration of mathematical connections;
6. Use of technology;
7. Communication of mathematical ideas (Herrera & Ozgun-Koca, 1999).

Similar publications that link methods to research have been made available to teachers in other countries (e.g., Askew & Wiliam, 1995). More recently there has been a move to encourage teachers to incorporate formative assessment practices into their teaching (Black & Wiliam, 1998; McIntosh, 1997; Wilcox & Zielinski, 1997) that build upon the findings of cognitive studies.

In the remainder of this chapter I explore several possible explanations for this lack of effect. I begin with David Cohen and Deborah Ball's analysis derived from policy studies (Cohen & Ball, 1999). I then turn to Barbara Jaworkski's constructivist analysis of math teaching derived from research on practice (Jaworski, 1992). I argue that even though these models stress the importance of situated teacher-student interactions, they are incomplete because they do not acknowledge the existential concerns that teachers and students bring into schools. I end the chapter by suggesting another perspective on teaching, one that relies on existentialism as a theoretical framework. Building on the work of Barbara Stengel (Stengel, 1996), I have called the latter focus the teaching as a way of being perspective (Feldman, 1997). What makes way of being an existential concept is that it is not a teacher characteristic or resource (Cohen & Ball, 1999) such as teachers' knowledge or reasoning skills. It is the teacher being in a situation in a way that is defined and informed by what was and is for the teacher, and his or her intentions for what could be.

A Model of Instructional Capacity

David Cohen and Deborah Ball have been involved in policy studies of mathematics education for more than ten years. Their first large-scale study was of the effects of the implementation of the 1985 *California Mathematics Framework*. While this framework predated the first set of NCTM standards by several years (NCTM, 1989), it contained many of the same ideas about mathematics and mathematics education. In the study done by Cohen and Ball and their colleagues, which was published in a special edition of *Educational Evaluation and Policy Analysis*, they found that there was little evidence of the type of teaching called for in the Framework (e.g., Cohen, 1991). While a follow-up study showed that certain types of professional development practices could affect the instructional methods that teachers report that they use, there was evidence that most professional development activities do not have the characteristics that lead to sustained, effective change (Cohen & Ball, 1999; Cohen & Hill, 1998).

Cohen and Ball suggest two possible explanations for the lack of effect of education reform on student learning outcomes. First, they acknowledge that schools are complex social organizations that are located within the complex social systems that make up our lives. Second, they note that even when interventions are shown to be effective in small-scale implementations, adequate education and support for teachers is rarely provided when they are implemented on larger scales. Cohen and Ball continue their argument to suggest that instruction must be seen as an interactional relationship among teacher, student, and educational materials (see Figure 6.3).

Teachers bring intellectual and personal resources to the educational experiences that influence how they "apprehend, interpret, and respond to materials and students" (Cohen & Ball, 1999, p. 3). To Cohen and Ball, these resources include teachers'

- Conceptions of knowledge,
- Understanding of content,
- Flexibility of understanding,
- Acquaintance with students' knowledge
- Ability to relate to, interact with, and learn about students,
- Ways to represent and extend knowledge and to establish classroom environments (Cohen & Ball, 1999, p. 3).

Not unexpectedly, these resources are similar to the types of knowledge, including pedagogical content knowledge, that Lee Shulman described in the 1980s (Shulman, 1986).

Students are located at the second apex of the interactional triangle. Cohen and Ball tell us that "students' experiences, understandings, interests, commitments, and engagement are crucial to instructional capacity" (p. 3). How students respond to instruction shapes instruction, either through teachers' overt use of formative assessment to modify instruction

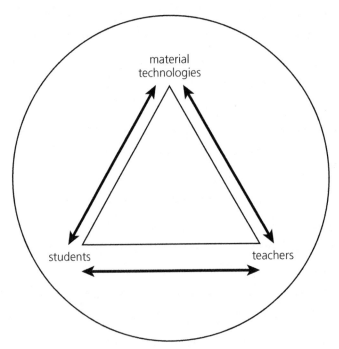

Figure 6.3.   The internal dynamics of instructional units (Cohen & Ball, 1999)

to help students learn, or through teachers' beliefs about what the students can and cannot accomplish. It is clear that Cohen and Ball's conception of *student* is constructivist. However, it is not clear whether their conception focuses on the cognitive construction or the social construction of students' understanding and beliefs about mathematics.

At the third apex are what Cohen and Ball call *material technologies*. By this they mean more than what is usually referred to as curriculum materials. Material technologies include:

> what students are engaged in, as presented in texts, and other media, as well as in problems, tasks, and questions posed to students.... They can be thought of as the material (as opposed to social) technologies of instruction, including print, video, and computer-based multimedia (p. 4).

Cohen and Ball's description of material technologies raises the question as to where the "social" technologies of instruction are located in their model. By social technologies they mean the ways that teachers organize and implement the material technologies.

When we look at the two examples of research-based instruction, we can see the ways in which teacher, students, and material technologies interact via social technologies. For example, Smith's roles as initiator, facilitator, and expert are ways that she referred to her techniques for implementing her social constructivist instruction methods in her class. In the same way we can think of Ms. L's small groups and mathematical situation posing as some of the social technologies that she uses to encourage mathematical discourse among her students. Both cases illustrate the importance of teachers' knowledge of these social technologies and their ability to implement them, in addition to their knowledge about research-based instructional materials and knowledge about their students.

It is important to note that Cohen and Ball focus on instructional *capacity* rather than on instruction. By capacity they mean the ability of a community or society to provide institutions such as schools with the instructional resources needed to provide students with quality education. As a result, they do not focus so much on methods of instruction as on the factors that affect its quality. Given this, they argue that capacity is dependent on "conceptions of professional knowledge and on the aims, content, and methods of instruction" (p. 5). In the development of their framework Cohen and Ball develop a set of continua that show the possible ranges of beliefs about professional knowledge, subject matter knowledge, student thinking, and discourse (Figure 6.4).

This framework is important for the purposes of this chapter because it allows us to see that method alone cannot be the only criterion for the evaluation of mathematics teaching. If we go back to the list of methods from

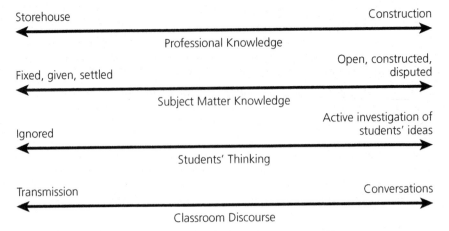

Figure 6.4.   Cohen and Ball's (1999) "conceptions of professional knowledge and on the aims, content, and methods of instruction."

Herrera and Ozgun-Koca (1991), it is possible to argue that each of their promising practices could be configured in a way so that it could fit anywhere on each of the four continua in Figure 6.4. Take for example the use of a problem-solving approach. One could imagine approaching the pedagogical knowledge needed to teach using this approach as being in a knowledge base for teaching that is delivered to teachers. Or one could see expertise in using a problem-based approach as something that a teacher develops as she reflects and inquires into her practice. Similarly, it is just as possible to transmit knowledge about problem solving to students as it is to encourage them to engage in conversations about problems.

A View of Math Teaching from Practice

Barbara Jaworski in her constructivist analysis of mathematics teaching (Jaworski, 1992) identified three elements of mathematics teaching:

1. Providing a supportive learning environment;
2. Offering appropriate mathematical challenge; and
3. Nurturing processes and strategies that foster learning (Jaworski, 1992, p. 8).

From this and her observations in the field, she developed the teaching triad as a synthesis of the three elements. The triad consists of three domains: the management of learning; mathematical challenge; and sensitivity to children. To Jaworski, the management of learning (ML) includes the organization of the classroom and decisions about what ought to be in the curriculum. It also involves the establishment of classroom values, expectations, and ways of working. In short, in managing learning, a teacher creates and modifies the environment in which learning takes place. Teachers mathematically challenge (MC) their students by providing them with stimulating mathematical thought and inquiry, and by motivating them to engage in mathematical thinking. Sensitivity to students (SS) goes beyond gaining knowledge of what students know. To be sensitive to one's students means to become aware of their individual characteristics and needs, and to work with students in a way that recognizes those needs (Jaworski, 1992, p. 8). Her representations of the teaching triad can be seen in Figure 6.5.

Jaworski's conception of the relationship among the three domains changed as she contemplated her data and theorized about it. At first (representation #1) she felt that the domains each had equal status. When she presented the idea of the teaching triad to another teacher, he responded with representation #2 in which the teaching is viewed as primarily the management of learning with sensitivity to students and mathematical challenge being aspects of management. Finally, she arrived at the conception of teaching as a three-dimensional space in which the three domains are represented as axes of that space.

Jaworski's struggle with finding a way to represent her model is indicative of the problematic nature of teachers' work. Where Cohen and Ball focused on the resources that are needed for research-based instruction to be implemented in the classroom, such as knowledgeable teachers and quality materials, Jaworski highlights what teachers ought to be able to do. Her terms *management of learning* and *mathematical challenge* are in some ways equivalent to the way that I used Cohen and Ball's concept of social technologies. Smith's roles can be seen as the personas that she uses to manage learning. She mathematically challenged her students by posing the initial problem and following that with extensions to the problem rather than telling them the "right answer." Ms. L, too, manages learning and challenges her students, using instructional methods that are in line with research findings.

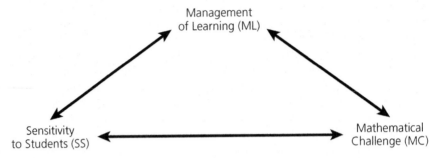

Figure 6.5a.   Jaworski's (1992) teaching triad.

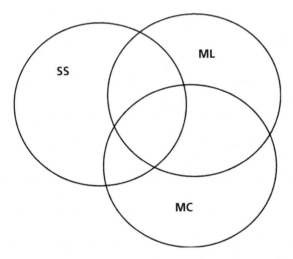

Figure 6.5b.   Jaworkski's teaching triad representation #1.

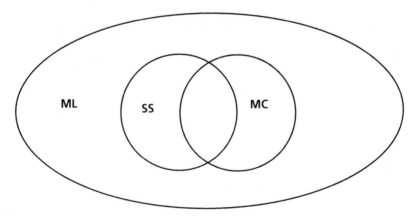

Figure 6.5c.   Jaworski's teaching triad representation #2.

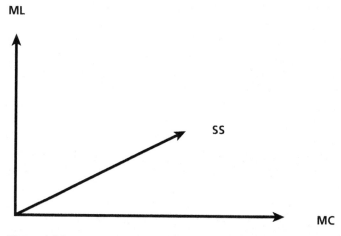

Figure 6.5d.   Jaworski's teaching triad representation #3.

Research on the Affective Domain

What Jaworski adds to the picture is sensitivity to students. One could argue that sensitivity to students is embedded in Cohen and Ball's teachers' "ability to relate to, interact with, and learn about students." For example, while both Smith and Ms. L listen to and respond to their students, it is not at all clear that they vignettes show what Jaworski means by sensitivity. One way to think about sensitivity to students is to distinguish between sensitivity to cognitive and affective aspects. For example, a teacher who subscribes to a constructivist teaching approach would try to assess her students' knowledge and conceptual understanding of mathematics prior to instruction and then shape materials and methods according to their cognitive needs. Much of the research on mathematics learning in the past two decades has both assumed the need for this type of sensitivity and the effectiveness of shaping instruction in response to it.

Less attention has been paid to sensitivity in the affective domain. Even so, it has long been clear that affective issues play a central role in the learning of mathematics (McLeod, 1992). What is not so clear is what is meant by affective issues. Douglas McLeod, in his review chapter, includes beliefs, attitudes and emotions within the affective domain for mathematics education. During the past two decades, researchers have also looked to affective domain to explain performance differences along racial, ethnic, and gender lines.

Although written as a critique of reform-based instruction in science, the review by Paul Pintrich and his colleagues at the University of Michigan

(Pintrich, Marx, & Boyle, 1993) argues for the importance of a sensitivity to affective issues. In particular they look at the motivational constructs of goals, values, self-efficacy and control beliefs. The effects on policy of differences in beliefs about the value of mathematics and the goals for mathematics education among educators, parents, and mathematicians was made abundantly clear by Klein in this volume. Pintrich and his colleagues ask us to consider the influence of students' goals and beliefs about mathematics on their learning. In addition, they remind us that their goals and values can be valid given the context of their lives. The strength of these beliefs is brought to life in James Gee's profiles of two high school students (Gee & Crawford, 1998), one who can be labeled as successful and the other at-risk. Emily is "oriented , in word and value, toward school ... She is connecting her everyday persona to the values and forms of life" (1998, p. 243) to public institutions such as schools. The other girl, Sandra, "does not connect with school... her everyday life is cut off from them, partly defined in opposition to them" (1998, p. 243). Clearly Sandra, whose "epistemological map is not convergent" with schooling, would have goals and values divergent from those of mathematics educators, as well as self-efficacy and control beliefs that could impede her doing mathematics in the way envisioned by NCTM. What is more surprising is that Gee and Crawford found that while Emily was highly successful in school, she lacked the type of affiliation with it that would enable her to work authentically in math class. Instead, she sees school as part of the trajectory that she needs to follow if she is to be successful in life (Gee & Crawford, 1998).

The difference between students' and instructors' beliefs about goals and values are a significant factor in the implementation of research-based instructional methods at all levels. If students see their math courses as hoops to jump through to reach their goal of a degree or certificate, they have little to feel good about when they are asked to do more than complete tasks for a satisfactory grade.

Teachers are generally aware of the differences between their goals and values and those of their students. Too often they become enshrined in what Tobin and McRobbie have called cultural myths (Tobin & McRobbie, 1996). Teachers' strong beliefs about what students want to and can do limit the instructional methods that they are willing to try out.

Pintrich and his colleagues also looked at the effect of students' self-efficacy and control beliefs on their participation in research-based instructional activities. Self-efficacy beliefs are beliefs that people have about what they can accomplish, while control beliefs concern external factors that may facilitate or impede their activities (Pintrich et al., 1993). Again, teachers' awareness of their students' beliefs in these domains can have an effect on their beliefs about they types of instruction that will work with their students.

Pintrich et al. argue persuasively that for instruction based on cognitive studies to be effective, students must choose to participate in those activities in the ways expected by researchers. Students' beliefs about the goals of mathematics courses, the value of knowing mathematics, and their beliefs about their own ability to know math and what controls their behavior can have a major impact on the ability of teachers to implement reform-based instructional methods. Gee's profile of Emily suggests that even successful students might not have values or goals consonant with those of researchers or teachers.

When we combine Cohen and Ball's framework with that of Jaworski, we see that teachers need to have the knowledge of mathematics and pedagogy that enables them to provide students with supportive learning environments in which they are mathematically challenged. Teachers must also be sensitive to the cognitive and affective needs of their students in order to support their learning and to challenge them appropriately. In addition, teachers must have educational materials that help them to do this. Although there has been great effort to modify pre-service and in-service teacher education to produce teachers with these capabilities and to acquaint them with research-based instructional materials, there is little evidence of their large-scale effect on classroom practice.

Teaching as a Way of Being: an Existential Perspective on Teachers and Teaching

So far in this chapter I have examined what is meant by instruction in mathematics, the origin of new practices, the low level of their implementation, and possible reasons for this. In addition, I have looked at two theoretical models for understanding the implementation of new practices. I now turn to the teacher as way of being perspective and its existential roots. So far in this chapter we have seen teachers defined as a sum of characteristics such as their knowledge, skills, beliefs and so on. The way of being perspective suggests that this is problematic because these characteristics do not add up to who the teacher is in the same way that the blind men's parts of the elephant (the trunk is like a snake, the tail like a piece of rope, the legs like tree trunks...) do not add to the elephant (Feldman, 1997). Instead, the way of being perspective begins with Heidegger's definition of who we are: "the beings who are aware of their own being (Heidegger, 1962)." Simply put, the way of being perspective begins by acknowledging that teachers, as human beings in the role of teacher, are conscious human beings. Therefore, a central tenet of existentialism is the idea of intentionality. John Searle, who is not an existentialist per se, has defined intentionality in the following way:

[Intentionality is] the feature by which our mental states are directed at, or about, or refer to, or are objects and states of affairs other than themselves (Searle, 1984).

He continues that intentionality refers not only to intentions, in the everyday sense of the word, but also to:

beliefs, desires, hopes, fears, love, hate, lust, disgust, shame, pride, irritation, amusement, and of those mental states (whether conscious or unconscious) that refer to, or are about, the world apart from the mind (1984, p. 16).

Our way of being in the world is constituted by our consciousness through its intentionality. What this suggests is that if we want teachers to teach in particular ways then we must affect their beliefs, desires, hopes, fears, and so on that constitute their intentional mental states. This has profound implications for pre- and in-service mathematics teacher education because it suggests that for teachers to change what they *do* means that they need to change who they *are*.

The application of existential thought to education has been a significant part of Maxine Greene's work as a philosopher of education. Greene has provided us with an explication of a set of concepts that underlie an existential perspective on teaching. Basing her work on that of Arendt, Dewey, Sartre and others, Greene suggests the following as characteristics of personhood (Greene, 1973):

1. The person is always situated. Everyone exists in a web of relationships that spread through time and space.
2. The self emerges through experience.
3. People are free to choose, but freedom is finite.

To existentialists situation is more than the context within which people act. To speak of context suggests a mechanical model in which people are separate entities, who are acted upon and on other people and things. Situation, on the other hand, suggests an immersion in the world. For example, to Dewey:

What is designated by the word 'situation' is not a single object or event or set of objects and events ... For we never experience nor form judgments about objects and events in isolation, but only in connection with a contextual whole ... In actual experience, there is never any such isolated single object or event; an object or event is always a special part, phase, or aspect, of an environing experienced world—a situation (Dewey, 1938, pp. 66–67).

As a result, people find themselves thrown into a situation constituted by all that has occurred in the past and from which they project themselves into the future (Heidegger, 1962).

The recognition that people exist as part of situations allows us to see that to teach is more than knowing and reasoning (Greene, 1973; Feldman, 1997). We become aware of what Greene calls the "existing being"— the person being in the situation with "all of its shifting moods, feelings, impulses, [and] fantasies" (Greene, 1967, p. 7). We also acknowledge that the teacher is more than the rational knower and reasoner in the classroom, and that almost everything that occurs in the teaching situation is affected by the teacher's past and present, presence, moods and gestures, expectations, intentions, the students with whom she is continually engaged, and the milieu of particular human "traditions, institutions, customs and the purposes and beliefs" (Greene, 1967, 1973; Dewey; 1938).

The existential characteristic that the self emerges through experience at first seems similar to the idea that we construct new knowledge by employing cognitive processes as we experience the world. However, the existential concept that "existence precedes essence" (Sartre, 1995) is focused on who we are rather than what we know, and includes the notion that we are not passive recipients of experiences but rather choose how we live our lives.

Choice is an integral part of the existential concept of freedom. To Greene, freedom "is the capacity to surpass the given and look at things as they could be otherwise" (Greene, 1988, p. 3). By doing so, a person can identify the possible choices within his or her situation. It is important to note that this is not necessarily freedom to take any action—it is freedom to choose even when there are real constraints on what one can do.

At this point in the chapter I begin to use the teacher as a way of being perspective to understand why teachers infrequently implement new teaching methods. In doing so, I will include myself and the readers of the chapter as teachers and will refer to teachers in the first person plural rather than as "they." I do this for two reasons. The first is that an existential perspective requires that we recognize that all people are human beings. To refer to teachers as "they" is to objectify them. The second is that the language of an existential analysis can be harsh and by referring to ourselves we accept the validity of the language.

Greene's existential characteristics of personhood can help us to understand why we as teachers so often do not implement the new instructional methods that we have learned about. It also accounts for the fact that we can be knowledgeable about the methods without using them. For example, existentialists, such as Sartre (1995), claim that the freedom to choose is an essential part of being human. However, what we see over and over again is that people, and in our case people who are teachers, act as if we have very limited choices or none at all. One way to understand this is to say that freedom puts a burden on people in that freedom to choose allows one to make wrong or bad choices. So when we hear ourselves and other teachers say things like "If it's not broken, why fix it?" in response to requests for us to change our practice, it may be due to our decisions that to use the new methods would be a bad choice for *our* students in *our* educational situation (Feldman & Kropf, 1999). This could be the case even when we as teachers have knowledge about research in math learning and are familiar with documents such as the NCTM Standards.

It is also possible that no choice is being made. Rather, we may see our practice as so constrained that we lack the freedom to choose. That there are constraints is incontrovertible. For example, here in Massachusetts as I write this, teachers are constrained by decisions made by local education authorities, and statewide by the policies of a government that has imposed high stakes examinations on children and teachers. At the same time, we teachers feel the constraints of cultural myths, such as those related to the need to transmit knowledge, content coverage, academic rigor, and the preparation of students to be successful in the next course (Tobin & McRobbie, 1996). These are just the types of constraints that we hear ourselves referring to when we are asked to change our instructional methods. While some of these constraints are real—students do need to pass a mathematics test in 10th grade in order to obtain a high school diploma in Massachusetts—others are like the urban myths that are told and retold uncritically.

Existentialist psychologists such as Irvin Yalom (1980) and Rollo May (1983) suggest that we accept structure and constraints rather than acknowledge that each one of us "is entirely responsible for ... his or her own world, life design, choices and actions" (Yalom, 1980, p. 9), and that freedom can be terrifying: "it means that beneath us there is no ground—nothing, a void, an abyss" (p. 9). The result is that individuals seek structure and constraints to ground themselves.

What this existentialist analysis suggests is that for many teachers to implement new teaching methods means to change who we are in the world so that we can distinguish between the real and the mythic to freely make choices about how and what to teach. To do this requires that we accept responsibility for our choices, even when our choice is not to change, and to be responsible for our students.

As with the other perspectives on teaching that I reviewed earlier in this chapter, the teacher as a way of being perspective is associated with a particular conception of teaching. It is one that underscores the humanness of both teacher and students. What this means is that both teacher and student (and I would add administrators, parents, and policy makers) acknowledge that each is an individual human being who is situated, whose self emerges through experience, and who has freedom to choose is the basis for an existential approach to education. Unfortunately, this occurs infrequently. We teachers are prone to objectify our students, and they often cannot imagine us having lives outside of schools. For teachers and students, the result is that we engage in an "I-It" relationship with our students rather than an "I-Thou" relationship (Buber, 1937).

An I-Thou relationship between our students and us can begin to emerge when we acknowledge and become involved with each student as an individual. To be involved means to take on the responsibility that we have for them as others. The way that we interact with each student can have a profound effect on how he or she sees himself or herself and what choices they make about who they are and what they are becoming.

This can be seen in the case of Janice DeLuca, a middle school teacher in an urban district, who learned the importance of focusing on her students as people as a result of an action research study. DeLuca's starting point was that she felt uncomfortable about the tracking that was occurring in her school and the effects that it had on her, her students, and their interactions. She was particularly concerned about the class she met at the end of each day in which "all of the low students and behavior problems" were "lumped together."[2] This tracking caused management problems for DeLuca, but she was also concerned about the way tracking leads to teachers having low expectations for their students.

> I know that I felt this way. These students came to me for the last period of the day. By then I was exhausted and so were they. I felt that I was cheating them. My level of expectations was not same for them as it was for other classes.

In response to an assignment in the action research course and after discussions with her peers in a collaborative action research group, she decided to do an interaction analysis in her last period class. To do this she arranged the classroom into five learning centers rather than her usual rows of seats facing the blackboard. As the students worked at the centers in small groups, DeLuca went from center to center asking and answering questions. As a result of the patterns of interaction seen by an observer in her class, another teacher, she decided that "it was necessary to talk to the kids." She did this informally during lunch, recess, or when they were working on in-class assignments.

> I learned many things about these children's personal lives as well as what they thought about school. I was amazed at how they continue to want to talk with me. I'm finding that by learning more about these kids and telling them things about me that some walls are breaking down. Stephen has begun to act "less tough" in my presence. He still acts out but when I talk to him about

it he acknowledges me and will say things like, "I forgot" or "okay." Our battles have become manageable and become less frequent.

Through her conversations with her students she began to see them more clearly as individual human beings. This can be seen in her report, in which her language shifts from referring to the students as "they" to referring to them individually be name. Most striking is the "epilogue" to her report, in which DeLuca gives a brief, poignant report on what happened to the children after they left her class.

As a result of this first part of her action research DeLuca concluded, "I feel that students' lives outside of school effect their behavior, attitude, and to some degree, their academic achievement. By trying to understand more about them, I may be able to break down some barriers and help them to develop a need and a want in learning."

Janice DeLuca continued to talk with the students individually and to shift her instruction so that the students took more responsibility for their learning. She also instituted time for students to meet with her before and after school for homework help. The conversations continued, she provided opportunities for students to take on more responsibility, and she accepted the responsibility of providing them with a safe, supportive place in which to learn. As a result, her students found her classroom to be a port in the storm of their lives, where they could attend to themselves and begin to accept the responsibility of who they are.

It appears that Janice DeLuca developed a new sensitivity of her students. But it is not a sensitivity that consists of an analysis of cognitive or affective needs. Instead, the students' and her horizons (Gadamer, 1992) shifted and merged as they lived in the world together and grew aware of each other's humanness. With the development of her I-Thou relationships with her students she began to make choices to do things like special homework help sessions. Where before she would have said that *these kids* would never show up for extra help, once the connection was made she chose to offer the sessions because she knew the students in ways that she never had before.

From the teaching as a way of being perspective we see that we, as teachers, need to become aware of our own being, our situatedness, and our freedom. This is not a trivial task. As Maxine Greene has reminded us:

Self-awareness, self-discover, self-actualization: These are often made to seem affairs of feeling, mainly, or of intuition. Teachers are asked to heighten their sensitivity, to tap the affective dimension of their lives, to trust, to love. Of course it is important to reach out, to feel, to experience love and concern. But I believe that, if teachers are truly to be present to them and to others, they need to exert effort in overcoming the weariness Camus described—a weariness all teachers, at some level, recognize. I believe that, for teachers as well as plague fighters, "health, integrity, purity," and the rest must be consciously chosen. So must interest and good faith (1978, p. 32).

CONCLUSION

During the past 20 years we have seen a revolution in the way that we understand the teaching and learning of mathematics in schools. Research on cognitive aspects of mathematics learning has led to the development of new instructional methods that can result in deep conceptual understanding in addition to the acquisition of knowledge of computational algorithms. More recently researchers have begun to realize that learning is not an individual process but rather it is situated in social contexts. As a result they have begun to look at the social and cultural aspects of learning, including discourse processes and the effects of gender and ethnicity. More recently, building on the work of researchers like Magdalene Lampert, the recognition of the complexity of learning has reached a new level by including the teacher as an active participant in the learning of mathematics, rather than just a deliverer of instruction.

In thinking about the complexity of teaching and learning mathematics in schools, and models such as Cohen and Ball's and Jaworski's, I am reminded of Joseph Schwab's commonplaces of education: An educational experience consists of someone teaching something to someone in some place and point in time (Schwab, 1978). Schwab emphasized the importance of each commonplace and that none has priority over the others. The teaching as a way of being perspective with its roots in existentialism asks us to go beyond Schwab's conception of separate commonplaces, and even beyond the interactional relationship among them proposed by Cohen and Ball. Instead, what the teaching as a way of being perspective asks us to acknowledge is that the commonplaces are all part of a dialectical whole that encompasses the educational situation in which they are immersed. Therefore, to effect changes in instruction we must change the educational situation. That can only be accomplished by asking teachers to not only change what they do, but who they are.

NOTES

1. While there is consensus among mathematics educators, there appears to be a large rift between their views of school mathematics and those of mathematicians (see Klein chapter in this volume).
2. All quotations are from Janice DeLuca's unpublished action research report.

REFERENCES

Askew, M., & Wiliam, D. (1995). *Recent research in mathematics education 5–16.* London: HMSO.

Black, P., & Wiliam, D. (1998). Inside the Black Box: Raising Standards through Classroom Assessment. *Phi Delta Kappan, 80*(2), 39–44.

Bowers, J., Cobb, P., & McClain, K. (1999). The evolution of mathematical practices: A case study. *Cognition & Instruction, 17*(1), 25–64.

Bransford, J.D., Brown, A.L., & Cocking, R.R. (Eds.). (1999). *How people learn: brain, mind, experience, and school.* Washington, DC: National Academy Press.

Brenner, M.E., Mayer, R.E., Moseley, B., Brar, T., Duran, R., Reed, B. S., & Webb, D. (1997). Learning by understanding: The role of multiple representations in learning algebra. *American Educational Research Journal, 34*(4), 663–689.

Buber, M. (1937). *I and thou* (Smith, Ronald Gregor, Trans.). Edinburgh: T. & T. Clark.

Carpenter, T., & Fennema, E. (1992). Cognitively guided instruction: Building on the knowledge of students and teachers. In W. Secada (Ed.), *Curriculum reform: The case of mathematics education in the United States* (pp. 457–470). Elmsford, NY: Pergamon Press.

Clandinin, D.J., & Connelly, F. (1992). Teacher as curriculum maker. In P. Jackson (Ed.), *Handbook of research on curriculum* (pp. 363–401). New York: Macmillan Publishing Company.

Cobb, P., & others. (1997). Reflective discourse and collective reflection. *Journal for Research in Mathematics Education, 28*(3), 258–277.

Cohen, D.K. (1991). A revolution in one classroom: The case of Mrs. Oublier. *Educational Evaluation and Policy Analysis, 12*(3), 327–345.

Cohen, D.K., & Ball, D.L. (1999). *Instruction, capacity and improvement* (RR-43). Philadelphia, PA: Consortium for Policy Research in Education.

Cohen, D.K., & Hill, H.C. (1998). *State policy and classroom performance: Mathematics reform in California.* Philadelphia, PA: Consortium for Policy Research in Education.

Cuban, L. (1993). *How teachers taught: constancy and change in American classrooms, 1890–1990.* New York: Teachers College Press.

Dewey, J. (1938). *Logic: The theory of inquiry.* New York: Henry Holt and Company.

Eisner, E. (1992). Curriculum ideologies. In P. Jackson (Ed.), *Handbook of research on curriculum* (pp. 302–326). New York: Macmillan Publishing Company.

Feldman, A. (1997). Varieties of wisdom in the practice of teachers. *Teaching and teacher education, 13*(7), 757–773.

Feldman, A., Kropf, A., & Alibrandi, M. (1998). Grading with points: The determination of report card grades by high school science teachers. *School Science & Mathematics, 98*(3), 40–48.

Fennema, E. (1974). Mathematics learning and sexes: A review. *Journal for Research in Mathematics Education, 5*(3), 126–139.

Fennema, E. (2000). *Gender equity for mathematics and science.* Madison, WI: National Center for Research in Mathematical Sciences Education.

Fennema, E. et al. (1993). Using children's mathematical knowledge in instruction. *American Educational Research Journal, 30*(3), 555–583.

Fosnot, C.F. (1996). *Constructivism: Theory, perspectives, and practice.* New York: Teachers College Press.

Fosnot, C.T. (1989). *Enquiring teachers, enquiring learners: a constructivist approach for teaching.* New York: Teachers College Press.

Fuson, K. C. (1992). Research on whole number addition and subtraction. In D.A. Grouws (Ed.), *Handbook of research on mathematics teaching and learning* (pp. 243–275). New York: Macmillan.

Gadamer, H.-G. (1992). *Truth and method* (2nd rev. ed.). New York: Crossroad.

Gee, J., & Crawford, V. (1998). Two kinds of teenagers: Language, identity, and social class. In D. Alverman, K. Hinchman, D. Moore, S. Phelps, & D. Warr (Eds.), *Reconceptualizing the literacies in adolescents' lives* (pp. 225–245). Hillsdale, NJ: Lawrence Erlbaum.

Greene, M. (Ed.). (1967). *Existential encounters for teachers.* New York: Random House.

Greene, M. (1973). *Teacher as stranger: Educational philosophy for the modern age.* Belmont, CA: Wadsworth Publishing Company.

Greene, M. (1978). Teaching: The question of personal reality. *Teachers College Record, 80*(1), 23–35.

Greene, M. (1988). *The dialectic of freedom.* New York: Teachers College Press.

Greer, B. (1992). Multiplication and division as models of situations. In D.A. Grouws (Ed.), *Handbook of research on mathematics teaching and learning* (pp. 276–295). New York: Macmillan.

Grouws, D. A. (Ed.). (1992). *Handbook of research on mathematics teaching and learning.* New York: Macmillan.

Heidegger, M. (1962). *Being and time* (J. Macquarrie & E. Robinson, Trans.). San Francisco: Harper San Francisco.

Herrera, T.A., & Ozgun-Koca, S.A. (1999). Promising practices in mathematics education. *The ERIC Review, 36*–39.

Hiebert, J., & Wearne, D. (1988). Instruction and cognitive change in mathematics. *Educational Psychologist, 23*(2), 105–117.

Jaworski, B. (1992). Mathematics teaching: What is it? *For the Learning of Mathematics: An International Journal of Mathematics Education, 12*(1), 8–14.

Koehler, M.S., & Grouws, D.A. (1992). Mathematics teaching practices and their effects. In D.A. Grouws (Ed.), *Handbook of research on mathematics teaching and learning* (pp. 115–126). New York: Macmillan.

Manouchehri, A., & Enderson, M. C. (1999). Promoting mathematical discourse: Learning from classroom examples. *Mathematics Teaching in the Middle School, 4*(4), 216–222.

May, R. (1983). *The discovery of being.* New York: W.W. Norton and Company.

McIntosh, M.E. (1997). Formative assessment in mathematics. *Clearing House, 71*(2), 92–96.

McLeod, D.B. (1992). Research on affect in mathematics education: A reconceptualization. In D.A. Grouws (Ed.), *Handbook of research on mathematics teaching and learning* (pp. 575–596). New York: Macmillan.

MMMP. (undated). *Missouri Middle School Mathematics Project Summary.*

NCTM. (1989). *Curriculum and evaluation standards for school mathematics.* Reston, VA: National Council of Teachers of Mathematics.

NCTM. (2000). *Principles and standards for school mathematics.* Reston, VA: The National Council of Teachers of Mathematics, Inc.

NISACA. (undated). *The educational system in the United States: Case study findings.* Washington, DC: National Institute on Student Achievement, Curriculum, and Assessment.

Pintrich, P.R., Marx, R.W., & Boyle, R.A. (1993). Beyond cold conceptual change: The role of motivational beliefs and classroom contextual factors in the process of conceptual change. *Review of Educational Research, 63*(2), 167–199.

Sartre, J. (1995). *Existentialism and human emotions.* New York: Carol Publishing Group.

Schoenfeld, A.H. (1994). What do we know about mathematics curricula? *Journal of Mathematical Behavior, 13*(1), 55–80.

Schwab, J. (1978). *Science, curriculum, and liberal education.* Chicago: University of Chicago Press.

Searle, J. (1984). *Minds, brains and science.* Cambridge, MA: Harvard University Press.

Shaughnessy, J.M. (1992). Research in probability and statistics: Reflections and directions. In D.A. Grouws (Ed.), *Handbook of research on mathematics teaching and learning* (pp. 465–494). New York: Macmillan.

Shulman, L. (1986). Those who understand; Knowledge growth in teaching. *Educational Researcher, 15*(2), 4–14.

Smith, C.M. (1998). A discourse on discourse: Wrestling with teaching rational equations. *The mathematics teacher, 91*(9), 749–753.

Steele, D.F. (1999). Learning mathematical language in the zone of proximal development. *Teaching children mathematics, 6*(1), 38–42.

Stengel, B. (1996, April 18–22). *Teaching epistemology through cell reproduction: A narrative exploration.* Paper presented at the Annual Meeting of the American Educational Research Association, New York.

Tobin, K., & McRobbie, C. (1996). Cultural myths as constraints to the enacted science curriculum. *Science Education, 80*(2), 223–241.

U.S. Department of Education. (2000). *Mathematics and science in the eight grade: Findings from the Third International Mathematics and Science Study.* Washington, DC: National Center for Educational Statistics.

Wilcox, S.K., & Zielinski, R.S. (1997). Using the assessment of students' learning to reshape teaching. *Mathematics Teacher, 90*(3), 223–229.

Yalom, I. (1980). *Existential psychology.* New York: Basic Books.

CHAPTER 7

A BRIEF HISTORY OF AMERICAN K–12 MATHEMATICS EDUCATION IN THE 20TH CENTURY

David Klein

ABSTRACT

This chapter describes and analyzes the major conflicts over K–12 mathematics education that erupted among professional educators, psychologists, mathematicians, and parents of school children in the U.S. during the twentieth century. The political struggles and policy changes in mathematics education in the 1980s and the 1990s are given special attention.

INTRODUCTION

In January 1998, when U.S. Education Secretary Richard Riley called for an end to the "math wars" in a speech before a joint meeting of the American Mathematical Society and the Mathematical Association of America, he could not have known that within two years, the department he directed

Mathematical Cognition, pages 175–225

would become the focus of the very math wars he sought to quell. In October 1999, the U.S. Department of Education recommended to the nation's 15,000 school districts a list of math books, including several that had been sharply criticized by mathematicians and parents of school children across the country for much of the preceding decade. Within a month of that release, 200 university mathematicians added their names to an open letter to Secretary Riley calling upon his department to withdraw those recommendations. The list of signatories included seven Nobel laureates and winners of the Fields Medal, the highest international award in mathematics, as well as math department chairs of many of the top universities in the country, and several state and national education leaders[1] (Riley 1998). By the end of the year 1999, the U.S. Secretary of Education had himself become embroiled in the nation's math wars.

Mathematics education policies and programs for U.S. public schools have never been more contentious than they were during the decade of the 1990s. The immediate cause of the math wars of the 90s was the introduction and widespread distribution of new math textbooks with radically diminished content, and a dearth of basic skills. This led to organized parental rebellions and criticisms of the new math curricula by mathematicians and other professionals.

In some respects the education wars of the 1990s have little to distinguish them from earlier periods. There is nothing new about disagreements over the best ways to educate the nation's school children. The periodic waves of education reform from the nation's colleges of education are more similar than they are different. The American education establishment has consistently advocated a progressivist education agenda for the bulk of the 20th century, and the mainstream views of the education community have enjoyed a commanding influence on public schools (Hirsch, 1996; Ravitch, 2000). Recognizing this dominion in the early part of the century, William Bagley in 1926 lamented:

> In no other country are the professional students of education so influential. In no other country is school practice so quickly responsive to the suggestions emanating from this group. We may stigmatize our schools as "static," "reactionary," "slow to change,"—reluctant to adopt what we, in our wisdom, prescribe. But compared to other countries, ours is the educational expert's paradise. (Ravitch, 2000, p. 193)

Colleges of education exert powerful direct influence on elementary and middle school teachers, and indirect influence on them through other organizations such as state level departments of education and professional teacher organizations. The influence on high school math teachers, while still powerful, has been less direct because of the subject matter specialization of the high school curriculum. The content demands of mathematics itself have limited the direct influence of some pedagogical fashions on high school math teachers. However, because of the hierarchical nature of mathematics and its heavy dependence at any level on prerequisites, high school and even college mathematics courses have at times been strongly affected by progressivist ideas, especially at the end of the 20th century.

The political struggles and policy changes in mathematics education in the 1980s, and especially the 1990s are the major topics of this chapter. However, the events of the final two decades of the 20th century are more easily understood in a historical context. Throughout the 20th century the "professional students of education" have militated for child centered discovery learning, and against systematic practice and teacher directed instruction. In some cases, progressivist math programs of the 1990s were intentionally without student textbooks, since books might interfere with student discovery. The essence of the dictum from educators of the 1990s and late 1980s, that the teacher should be "a guide on the side and not a sage on the stage," was already captured in a statement from the principal of one of John Dewey's "schools of tomorrow" from the 1920s:

> The teacher's arbitrary assignment of the next ten pages in history, or nine problems in arithmetic, or certain descriptions in geography, cannot be felt by the pupil as a real problem and a personal problem. (Ravitch, 2000, p. 179)

The next section provides a brief overview of some of the important historical trends and policies leading up to the events of the 1980s and 90s.

HISTORICAL OUTLINE: 1920 TO 1980

It would be a mistake to think of the major conflicts in education as disagreements over the most effective ways to teach. Broadly speaking, the education wars of the past century are best understood as a protracted struggle between content and pedagogy. At first glance, such a dichotomy seems unthinkable. There should no more be conflict between content and pedagogy than between one's right foot and left foot. They should work in tandem toward the same end, and avoid tripping each other. Content is the answer to the question of what to teach, while pedagogy answers the question of how to teach.

The trouble comes with the first step. Do we lead with the right foot or the left? If content decisions come first, then the choices of pedagogy may be limited. A choice of concentrated content precludes too much student centered, discovery learning, because that particular pedagogy requires more time than stiff content requirements would allow. In the same way, the choice of a pedagogy can naturally limit the amount of content that can be presented to students. Therein lies the source of the conflict.

With roots going back to Jean Jacques Rousseau and with the guidance of John Dewey, progressive education has dominated American schools since the early years of the 20th century. That is not to say that progressive education has gone unchallenged (see, Hirsch, 1996; Ravitch, 2000). Challenges increased in intensity starting in the 1950s, waxed and waned, and in the 1990s gained unprecedented strength. A consequence of the domination of progressivism during the first half of the 20th century was a predictable and remarkably steady decrease of academic content in public schools.

The prescriptions for the future of mathematics education were articulated early in the 20th century by one of the nation's most influential education leaders, William Heard Kilpatrick. According to E. D. Hirsch, Kilpatrick was "the most influential introducer of progressive ideas into American schools of education" (Hirsch, 1996, p. 52). Kilpatrick was an education professor at Teachers College at Columbia University, and a protege of John Dewey. According to Dewey, "In the best sense of the words, progressive education and the work of Dr. Kilpatrick are virtually synonymous" (Tennenbaum, 1951, p. vii). Kilpatrick majored in mathematics at Mercer College in Macon, Georgia. His mathematical education included some graduate work at Johns Hopkins University, but his interests changed and he eventually attended Teachers College and joined the faculty in 1911. In his 27 years at Teachers College, he taught some 35,000 students and was described by the New York Post as "the million-dollar professor" because the fees paid by his students to the college exceeded this amount. In some instances there were more than 650 students in a single one of his auditorium sized classes (Tennenbaum, 1951, p. 185). His book, *Foundations of Method*, written in 1925 became a standard text for teacher education courses across the country.

Reflecting mainstream views of progressive education, Kilpatrick rejected the notion that the study of mathematics contributed to mental discipline. His view was that subjects should be taught to students based on their direct practical value, or if students independently wanted to learn those subjects. This point of view toward education comported well with the pedagogical methods endorsed by progressive education. Limiting education primarily to utilitarian skills sharply limited academic content, and this helped to justify the slow pace of student centered, discovery learning, the centerpiece of progressivism. Kilpatrick proposed that the study of algebra and geometry in high school be discontinued "except as an intellectual luxury." According to Kilpatrick, mathematics is "harmful rather than helpful to the kind of thinking necessary for ordinary living." In an address before the student body at the University of Florida, Kilpatrick lectured, "We have in the past taught algebra and geometry to too many, not too few" (Tennenbaum, 1951, p. 105).

Progressivists drew support from the findings of psychologist Edward L. Thorndike. Thorndike conducted a series of experiments beginning in 1901 that cast doubt on the value of mental discipline and the possibility of transfer of training from one activity to another. These findings were used to challenge the justification for teaching mathematics as a form of mental discipline and contributed to the view that any mathematics education should be for purely utilitarian purposes (Osborne & Crosswhite, 1970, pp. 186–187). Thorndike stressed the importance of creating many "bonds" through repeated practice and championed a stimulus-response method of learning. This led to the fragmentation of arithmetic and the avoidance of teaching closely related ideas too close in time, for fear of establishing incorrect bonds. According to one writer, "For good or for ill, it was Thorndike who dealt the final blow to the 'science of arithmetic'" (Jones & Coxford, 1970, p. 38).

Kilpatrick's opinion that the teaching of algebra should be highly restricted was supported by other experts. According to David Snedden, the founder of educational sociology, and a prominent professor at Teachers College at the time, "Algebra . . . is a nonfunctional and nearly valueless subject for 90 percent of all boys and 99 percent of all girls—and no changes in method or content will change that" (Osborne & Crosswhite, 1970, p. 211). During part of his career, Snedden was Commissioner of Education for the state of Massachusetts (Ravitch, 2000, pp. 81–86).

In 1915 Kilpatrick was asked by the National Education Association's Commission on the Reorganization of Secondary Education to chair a committee to study the problem of teaching mathematics in the high schools. The committee included no mathematicians and was composed entirely of educators (Osborne & Crosswhite, 1970, p. 193). Kilpatrick directly challenged the use of mathematics to promote mental discipline. He wrote, "No longer should the force of tradition shield any subject from scrutiny . . . In probably no study did this older doctrine of mental discipline find larger scope than in mathematics, in arithmetic to an appreciable extent, more in algebra, and most of all in geometry" (Tennenbaum, 1951, p. 104). Kilpatrick maintained in his report, *The Problem of Mathematics in Secondary Education,* that nothing in mathematics should be taught unless its probable value could be shown, and recommended the traditional high school mathematics curriculum for only a select few (Ravitch, 2000, p. 126).

It was not surprising that mathematicians would object to Kilpatrick's report as an attack against the field of mathematics itself. David Eugene Smith, a mathematics professor at Teachers College and renowned historian of mathematics, tried to stop the publication of Kilpatrick's report as a part of the *Cardinal Principles of Secondary Education*, the full report of the Commission on the Reorganization of Secondary Education, and one of the most influential documents for education in the 20th century. Smith charged that there had been no meeting of the math committee and that Kilpatrick was the sole author of the report. Moreover, Kilpatrick's committee was not representative of teachers of mathematics or of mathematicians (Osborne & Crosswhite, 1970, pp. 194–195). Nevertheless, Kilpatrick's report was eventually published in 1920 by the U.S. Commissioner of Education, Philander P. Claxton, a friend of Kilpatrick (Ravitch, 2000, p. 126; Tennenbaum, 1951, p. 107).

The Kilpatrick committee and leading educational theoreticians had thrown the gauntlet, and the Mathematical Association of America (MAA) responded vigorously. Already in 1916, in anticipation of the Kilpatrick report, E. R. Hedrick, the first president of the MAA, appointed a committee called the National Committee on Mathematical Requirements. It was chaired by J. W. Young of Dartmouth and included mathematicians E. H. Moore, Oswald Veblen, and David E. Smith, in addition to several prominent teachers and administrators from the secondary school system. The reports of this committee were delayed because of World War I, but they were eventually collected into a 625-page volume entitled, *The Reorganization of Mathematics for Secondary Education*. The report was published in 1923 and is sometimes referred to as the *1923 Report*.

Meanwhile in 1920, the National Council of Teachers of Mathematics (NCTM) was founded, largely at the instigation of the MAA. The first NCTM president, C. M. Austin, made it clear that the organization would "keep the values and interests of mathematics before the educational world" and he urged that "curriculum studies and reforms and adjustments come from the teachers of mathematics rather than from the educational reformers." The NCTM was created in part to counter the progressivist educational agenda for mathematics, and it later played an important role in disseminating the *1923 Report* (Osborne & Crosswhite, 1970, pp. 194–196).

The *1923 Report* was perhaps the most comprehensive ever written on the topic of school mathematics. It included an extensive survey of secondary school curricula, and it documented the training of mathematics teachers in other countries. It discussed issues related to the psychology of learning mathematics, and justified the study of mathematics in terms of its applications as well as its intrinsic value. It even proposed curricula for the schools. In contradiction to the Kilpatrick report, the *1923 Report* underscored the importance of algebra to "every educated person" (Osborne & Crosswhite, 1970, p. 203). The *1923 Report* exerted some influence on public education. For example, some of the policies of the College Examination Board were based upon recommendations in the *1923 Report*. However, over the next two decades, the views expressed in the Kilpatrick report wielded greater influence than the *1923 Report* (Duren, 1989, p. 408). The NCTM also changed over time. It grew and gradually it "attracted to its membership and to its leadership those in positions much more subject to the influence and pressure of the professional reform movements" (Osborne & Crosswhite, 1970, p. 234).

In the 1930s the education journals, textbooks, and courses for administrators and teachers advocated the major themes of progressivism. The school curriculum would be determined by the needs and interests of children, as determined by professional educators, and not by academic subjects. It became a cliche in the 1930s, just as in the 1990s, for educators to say, "We teach children, not subject matter." The Activity Movement of the 1930s promoted the integration of subjects in elementary school, and argued against separate instruction in mathematics and other subjects. It drew its inspirations from Kilpatrick's writings. The Activity Movement spread rapidly into the nation's elementary schools. High schools were more resistant in part because the teachers were trained in specific subject areas and they were less willing to discard their specialties in favor of an ill-defined holism. Some proponents of the Activity Movement did not even acknowledge that reading and learning the multiplication tables were legitimate activities. As in the 1990s, there was public resistance to the education doctrines of this era. Among the critics were Walter Lippman, one of the nation's most widely respected commentators on public affairs, and literary critic, Howard Mumford Jones (Cremin, 1961, p. 326; Ravitch, 2000, pp. 238, 241, 311–312).

In the 1940s it became something of a public scandal that army recruits knew so little math that the army itself had to provide training in the arithmetic needed for basic bookkeeping and gunnery (Raimi, 2000). Admiral Nimitz complained of mathematical deficiencies of would-be officer candidates and navy volunteers. The basic skills of these military personnel should have been learned in the public schools but were not (Jones & Coxford, 1970, p. 59). As always, education doctrines did not sit well with much of the public. Nevertheless, by the mid-1940s, a new educational program called the Life Adjustment Movement emerged from the education community. The basic premise was that secondary schools were "too devoted to an academic curriculum." Education leaders presumed that 60% or more of all public school students lacked the intellectual capability for college work or even for skilled occupations, and those students would need a school program to prepare them for everyday living. They would need appropriate high school courses, including math programs, that focused purely on practical problems such as consumer buying, insurance, taxation, and home budgeting, but not on algebra, geometry, or trigonometry. The students in these courses would become unskilled or semiskilled laborers, or their wives, and they would not need an academic education. Instead they would be instructed in "home, shop, store, citizenship, and health."

By 1949 the Life Adjustment Movement had substantial support among educators, and was touted by numerous federal and state education agencies. Some educators even suggested that in order to avoid stigmatizing the students in these programs, non-academic studies should be available to all students. Life Adjustment could meet the needs of all American students (Ravitch, 2000, pp. 328–330).

However, many schools stubbornly clung to the teaching of academic subjects even when they offered life adjustment curricula as well. Moreover, parents of school children resisted these changes; they wanted their own children educated and not merely adjusted. They were sometimes joined by university professors and journalists who criticized the lack of academic content of the progressivist life adjustment programs. Changes in society at large also worked against the life adjustment agenda. Through the 1940s, the nation had witnessed tremendous scientific and engineering advances. By the end of the decade, the appearance of radar, cryptography, navigation, atomic energy, and other technological wonderments changed the economy and underscored the importance of mathematics in the modern world. This in turn caused a recognition of the importance of mathematics education in the schools. By the end of the 1940s, the public school system was the subject of a blizzard of criticisms, and the life adjustment movement fizzled out. Among the critics was Mortimer Smith. Reminiscent of Bagley's 1926 characterization of "students of education," he wrote in his 1949 book *Madly They Teach*:

> . . . those who make up the staffs of the schools and colleges of education, and the administrators and teachers whom they train to run the system, have a truly amazing uniformity of opinion regarding the aims, the content, and the methods of education. They constitute a cohesive body of believers with a clearly formulated set of dogmas and doctrines, and they are perpetuating the faith by seeing to it through state laws and the rules of state departments of education, that only those teachers and administrators are certified who have been trained in the correct dogma. (Cremin, 1961, p. 340)

As would be the case in the final decade of the century, critics of this period complained of a lack of attention to basic skills (Ravitch, 2000, p. 346).

Progressive education was forced into retreat in the 1950s, and even became the butt of jokes and vitriol (Ravitch, 2000, p. 361). During the previous half century, enrollment in advanced high school mathematics courses, and other academic subjects, had steadily decreased, thanks at least in part to progressive education. From 1933 to 1954 not only did the percentage of students taking high school geometry decrease, even the actual numbers of students decreased in spite of soaring enrollments.

Table 7.1 gives percentages of high school students enrolled in high school math courses (Jones & Coxford, 1970, p. 54).

Table 7.1.   Percentages of U.S. High School Students Enrolled in Various Courses

School Year	Algebra	Geometry	Trigonometry
1909 to 1910	56.9%	30.9%	1.9%
1914 to 1915	48.8%	26.5%	1.5%
1921 to 1922	40.2%	22.7%	1.5%
1927 to 1928	35.2%	19.8%	1.3%
1933 to 1934	30.4%	17.1%	1.3%
1948 to 1949	26.8%	12.8%	2.0%
1952 to 1953	24.6%	11.6%	1.7%
1954 to 1955	24.8%	11.4%	2.6%

The "New Math" period came into being in the early 1950s and lasted through the decade of the 1960s. New Math was not a monolithic movement. According to a director of one of the first New Math conferences, "The inception of the New Math was the collision between skills instruction and understanding . . . The disagreements between different entities of the New Math Movement were profound. Meetings between mathematicians and psychologists resulted only in determining that the two had nothing to say to each other" (Bosse, 1995, p. 180). However, in a 1960 paper delivered to the NCTM, Harvard psychologist Jerome Bruner wrote:

> I am struck by the fact that certain ideas in teaching mathematics that take a student away from the banal manipulation of natural numbers have the effect of freshening his eye to the possibility of discovery. I interpret such trends as the use of set theory in the early grades partly in this light—so too the Cuisenaire rods, the use of modular arithmetic, and other comparable devices. (Loveless, 2001)

In spite of disagreements, most projects of that period shared some general features. The New Math groups introduced curricula that emphasized coherent logical explanations for the mathematical procedures taught in the schools. New Math was clearly a move away from the anti-intellectualism of the previous half-century of progressivist doctrine. For the first time, mathematicians were actively involved in contributing to K–12 school mathematics curricula.

The University of Illinois Committee on School Mathematics headed by Max Beberman began in 1951 and was the first major project associated with the New Math era. Beberman's group published a series of high school math textbooks, and drew financial support from the Carnegie Corporation and the U.S. Office of Education. In 1955, the College Entrance Examination Board established a Commission on Mathematics to investigate the "mathematics needs of today's American youth." The Commission, consisting of high school teachers, math educators, and mathematicians, issued a report with recommendations for a curriculum to better prepare students for college, and produced a sample textbook for twelfth grade on probability and statistics (Bosse, 1995; Raimi, 200, p. 36; Wooton, 1965). The efforts of these and other early groups received little attention until the U.S.S.R. launched *Sputnik*, the first space satellite, in the fall of 1957. The American press treated *Sputnik* as a major humiliation, and called attention to the low quality of math and science instruction in the public schools. Congress responded by passing the 1958 National Defense Education Act to increase the number of science, math, and foreign language majors, and to contribute to school construction.

That same year, the American Mathematical Society set up the School Mathematics Study Group (SMSG), headed by Edward G. Begle, then at Yale University, to develop a new curriculum for high schools. Among the many curriculum groups of the New Math period, SMSG was the most influential. It created junior and senior high school math programs and eventually elementary school curricula as well. The original eight members of SMSG were appointed by the president of the American Mathematical Society, but thereafter the two organizations had no formal connection. SMSG subsequently appointed a 26 member advisory committee and a 45-member writing group which included 21 college and university mathematicians as well as 21 high school math teachers and supervisors (Wooton, 1965, pp. 9–16).

The National Council of Teachers of Mathematics set up its own curriculum committee, the Secondary School Curriculum Committee, which came out with its recommendations in 1959. Many other groups emerged during this period including, the Ball State Project, the University of Maryland Mathematics Project, the Minnesota School Science and Mathematics Center, and the Greater Cleveland Mathematics Program. In the late 1950s, individual high school and college teachers started to write their own texts along the lines suggested by the major curriculum groups (Kline, 1973, Ch. 3).

One of the contributions of the New Math movement was the introduction of calculus courses at the high school level (Bosse, 1995, p. 179). Although, there were important successes in the New Math period, some of the New Math curricula were excessively formal, with little attention to basic skills or to applications of mathematics. Programs that included treatments of number bases other than base ten, as well as relatively heavy emphases on set theory, or more exotic topics, tended to confuse and alienate even the most sympathetic parents of school children. There were instances in which abstractness for its own sake was overemphasized to the point of absurdity (Askey, 2001). Many teachers were not well equipped to deal with the demanding content of the New Math curricula. As a result public criticisms increased.

A substantial number of mathematicians had already expressed serious reservations relatively early in the New Math period. In 1962, a letter titled *On the Mathematics Curriculum of the High School,* signed by 64 prominent mathematicians, was published in the *American Mathematical Monthly* and *The Mathematics Teacher.* The letter criticized New Math and offered some general guidelines and principles for future curricula (Kline, 1973, Ch. 9).

By the early 1970s New Math was dead. The National Science Foundation discontinued funding programs of this type, and there was a call to go "back to the basics" in mathematics as well as in other subjects (Raimi, 2000; Ravitch, 2000). However, this direction for education did not go unchallenged. Progressive education had recovered from its doldrums of the 1950s, and by the late 1960s and early 1970s, it had regained its momentum. A. S. Niell's book *Summerhill,* published in 1960, is an account of an ultra progressive school in England. It was one of the most influential books on education of that decade. Founded in 1921 in Suffolk, England as a boarding school for relatively affluent children, Summerhill students determined completely what they would learn, and when. Niell wrote, "Whether a school has or has not a special method for teaching long division is of no significance, for long division is of no importance except to those who *want* to learn it. And the child who *wants* to learn long division *will* learn it no matter how it is taught." By 1970, some 200,000 copies of *Summerhill* were being sold per year, and it was required reading in 600 university courses (Ravitch, 2000, pp. 387–388).

Modeled on Summerhill, and supported by the challenges at that time of structures of authority, both within education and the larger society, "free schools" proliferated, and eventually helped give rise to the Open Education Movement. The Open Education Movement was nothing new; it was just a repetition of progressivist programs promoted in the 1920s, but the idea of letting children decide each day what they should learn at activity tables, play corners, or reading centers, was once again promoted as profound and revolutionary (Ravitch, 2000, p. 395).

The effects of the Open Education Movement were particularly devastating to children with limited resources, due to their lack of access to supplemental education from the home, or tutoring in basic skills outside of school. Lisa Delpit, an African American educator who taught in an inner city school in Philadelphia in the early 1970s wrote about the negative effects of this type of education on African American children. Relating a conversation with another African American teacher, she explained,

"White kids learn how to write a decent sentence. Even if they don't teach them in school, their parents make sure they get what they need. But what about our kids? They don't get it at home…" Summarizing the effects of the open classroom movement from her perspective in 1986, Professor Delpit wrote:

> I have come to believe that the "open classroom movement," despite its progressive intentions, faded in large part because it was not able to come to terms with the concerns of poor and minority communities. (Delpit, 1986)

Another prominent educator, Nancy Ichinaga, came to similar conclusions about the effects of the Open Education Movement on low income students, based on her experience as principal of Bennett-Kew Elementary school, in Inglewood, California. Ichinaga began a 24-year career as principal of Bennett-Kew in the Fall of 1974, one month before scores from the California's standardized test were released. At that time the school included only grades K–3 and it was called Bennett Elementary school. Bennett's 1974 third grade students ranked at the third percentile in the state, almost the absolute bottom. The school was then in its fourth year of the "Open Structure Program" and the student body throughout her tenure as principal was nearly 100 percent minority and low income. Reacting with shock and dismay at the test scores, Ichinaga confronted the teachers who admitted that their program was not working. The entire student body was illiterate and the student centered mathematics program was in shambles.

With the collaboration of her teachers, Nancy Ichinaga introduced clearly defined and well-structured reading and math programs which included practice in basic skills. After a few years, test scores increased to well beyond the 50th percentile, and by the end of the 20th century, her school had earned national acclaim and became a model for others to emulate (Armbrister, 2001; Carter, 2000; Helfand, 2000; Klein, 2000b). At an education conference held in May 1999, Principal Ichinaga described the situation in her school in 1974:

> My school had been patterned after *Summerhill.* And that's how bad it was! The kids used to make jello and bake cookies, and I used to tell the teachers, "Do you know what you've accomplished? You just gave them rotten teeth!"[2]

As in earlier periods of the 20th century, the agenda of progressivist educators was resisted by broad sectors of the public. The majority of states created minimum competency tests in basic skills starting in the mid-1970s, and almost half of them required students to pass these tests as a condition for graduation from high school. Due to public demand, some school districts created "fundamental schools" that emphasized traditional academics and promoted student discipline. While basic skills tests held the Open

Education Movement in check, by their nature they could not be used to hold students to very high standards, or to raise existing standards. During the 1970s, standardized test scores steadily decreased and bottomed out in the early 1980s (Ravitch, 2000, pp. 399, 406).

THE 1980S: PRELUDE TO NATIONAL STANDARDS

In the early 1980s, there was widespread recognition that the quality of math and science education had been deteriorating. A 1980 report by a presidential commission pointed to low enrollments in advanced mathematics and science courses and the general lowering of school expectations and college entrance requirements (Ravitch, 2000, p. 404). Among the various reports and commissions to investigate K–12 education in the early 1980s, two especially stand out: *An Agenda for Action* and *A Nation at Risk.* The different points of view and prescriptions for change expressed in these two reports characterize to some extent the opposing factions in the math wars of the 1990s.

The National Council of Teachers of Mathematics released *An Agenda for Action* in 1980. The report called for new directions in mathematics education which would later be codified in 1989 in the form of national standards. *An Agenda for Action* recommended that problem solving be the focus of school mathematics in the 1980s, along with new ways of teaching. The report asserted that "Requiring complete mastery of skills before allowing participation in challenging problem solving is counterproductive," and "Difficulty with paper-and-pencil computation should not interfere with the learning of problem-solving strategies." Technology would make problem solving available to students without basic skills. According to the report, "All students should have access to calculators and increasingly to computers throughout their school mathematics program." This included calculators "for use in elementary and secondary school classrooms." The report also warned, "It is dangerous to assume that skills from one era will suffice for another," and called for "decreased emphasis on such activities as . . . performing paper and pencil calculations with numbers of more than two digits." This would be possible because "The use of calculators has radically reduced the demand for some paper-and-pencil techniques." The report also recommended that "Team efforts in problem solving should be common place in elementary school classrooms," and encouraged "the use of manipulatives, where suited, to illustrate or develop a concept or skill." *An Agenda for Action* also called for "a wider range of measures than conventional testing." All of these directions would later become issues of contention in the math wars of the 1990s (National Council of Teachers of Math [NCTM], 1980).

Perhaps the boldest and most far reaching recommendation of *An Agenda for Action* was its proposal for "Mathematics educators and college mathematicians" to "reevaluate the role of calculus in the differentiated mathematics programs." The report argued that "Emerging programs that prepare users of mathematics in nontraditional areas of application may no longer demand the centrality of calculus that has traditionally been demanded for all students." The de-emphasis of calculus, when carried out on a large enough scale, would support the move away from the systematic development of the prerequisites of calculus: algebra, geometry, and trigonometry. The so-called "integrated" high school math books of the 1990s contributed to this tendency. While those books contained parts of algebra, geometry, and trigonometry, the developments of these traditional subjects were not systematic, and often depended on student "discoveries" that were incidental to solving "real world problems."

In spite of the NCTM's enthusiasm for the objectives of *An Agenda for Action*, the report received little attention. It was largely eclipsed by the 1983 report, *A Nation at Risk* (National Commission of Excellence in Education, 1983). This report was written by a commission appointed by Terrell Bell, the U.S. Secretary of Education, at that time. Unlike previous education reform efforts and reports by prestigious governmental bodies, this one captured the attention of the public. *A Nation at Risk* warned, "Our nation is at risk . . . the educational foundations of our society are presently being eroded by a rising tide of mediocrity that threatens our very future as a Nation and a people." Even sharper was the statement, "If an unfriendly foreign power had attempted to impose on America the mediocre educational performance that exits today, we might well have viewed it as an act of war."

A Nation at Risk addressed a wide variety of education issues, including specific shortcomings in mathematics education. Regarding remedial mathematics instruction, the report found that:

> Between 1975 and 1980, remedial mathematics courses in public 4-year colleges increased by 72 percent and now [in 1983] constitute one-quarter of all mathematics courses taught in those institutions.

> Business and military leaders complain that they are required to spend millions of dollars on costly remedial education and training programs in such basic skills as reading, writing, spelling, and computation.

Although the authors of *A Nation at Risk* did not attempt to analyze the causes of these deficiencies, the lack of attention to basic skills in elementary schools caught up in the Open Education Movement of the late 1960s and early 1970s surely contributed to the need for more remedial courses in the 1980s in high school and college.

A Nation at Risk described high school course offerings as a "curricular smorgasbord" and reported, "We offer intermediate algebra, but only 31 percent of our recent high school graduates complete it; we offer French I, but only 13 percent complete it; and we offer geography, but only 16 percent complete it. Calculus is available in schools enrolling about 60 percent of all students, but only 6 percent of all students complete it."

The importance of student assessment was also addressed. The report envisioned a role for standardized tests that foreshadowed a movement toward accountability in the late 1990s (Evers, 2001, Ch 9):

> Standardized tests of achievement (not to be confused with aptitude tests) should be administered at major transition points from one level of schooling to another and particularly from high school to college or work. The purposes of these tests would be to: (a) certify the student's credentials; (b) identify the need for remedial intervention; and (c) identify the opportunity for advanced or accelerated work. The tests should be administered as part of a nationwide (but not Federal) system of State and local standardized tests. This system should include other diagnostic procedures that assist teachers and students to evaluate student progress.

A Nation at Risk called attention to the quality of teachers and complained, "Too many teachers are being drawn from the bottom quarter of graduating high school and college students." Teacher training programs were also criticized in the report:

> The teacher preparation curriculum is weighted heavily with courses in "educational methods" at the expense of courses in subjects to be taught. A survey of 1,350 institutions training teachers indicated that 41 percent of the time of elementary school teacher candidates is spent in education courses, which reduces the amount of time available for subject matter courses.

The report also drew attention to teacher shortages, especially math and science teachers:

> The shortage of teachers in mathematics and science is particularly severe. A 1981 survey of 45 States revealed shortages of mathematics teachers in 43 States, critical shortages of earth sciences teachers in 33 States, and of physics teachers everywhere.

A Nation at Risk also addressed the question of textbooks, proposing that they be upgraded to include more rigorous content. It called upon "university scientists, scholars, and members of professional societies, in collaboration with master teachers, to help in this task, as they did in the post-Sputnik era. They should assist willing publishers in developing the products or publish their own alternatives where there are persistent inadequacies." The report addressed the textbook adoption process as well, suggesting that:

> In considering textbooks for adoption, States and school districts should: (a) evaluate texts and other materials on their ability to present rigorous and challenging material clearly; and (b) require publishers to furnish evaluation data on the material's effectiveness.

With widespread public concern about education, the release of *A Nation at Risk* resulted in newspaper headlines across the country. A number of states created task forces and commissions to measure their own state programs against the recommendations of *A Nation at Risk* (Ravitch, 2000, p. 413). It is illuminating to compare these recommendations to the California mathematics education polices of the late 1990s. As described below, California's mathematics policies in 1998 became the leading obstacle to progressivist domination in mathematics education. Yvonne Larson, the vice-chair of the Commission that released *A Nation at Risk* in 1983, served as the president of the California State Board of Education in 1997. Whether by intent or coincidence, the California policies conformed rather well with a number of the recommendations of the 1983 report.

THE 1989 NCTM STANDARDS

With public opinion in support of a strong focus on basic skills and clear high standards, the NCTM took steps to recast its own agenda under the label of standards. In 1986 the NCTM established the Commission on Standards for School Mathematics. The *Curriculum and Evaluation Standards for School Mathematics* was developed during the summer of 1987 and revised in 1988 by four working groups whose members were appointed by John Dossey, the president of the NCTM at that time. During the 1987–88 school year, input was sought from classroom teachers across the country. The project was coordinated by Thomas A. Romberg. The final document was published in 1989, and during the following decade it was commonly referred to as the *NCTM Standards*, or as the *Standards* (NCTM, 1989). Of the 24 working group members who had direct input into the writing of the *Standards*, none were mathematicians, and only two were concurrent K–12 teachers; the remainder were, for the most part, teacher education professors and instructors from universities. However, the NCTM successfully promoted the *Standards* as if they were developed through a grass-roots, bottom-up process (Bosse, 1995, pp. 184–185).

The *NCTM Standards* were not standards in the usual sense of the word. Harold Stevenson, a psychologist at the University of Michigan, described them as follows:

> In our view the *NCTM standards* present a vague, somewhat grandiose, readily misinterpreted view of what American children should learn in mathematics. Moreover, the view fails to meet what we would consider to be the meaning of "standards." Standards should involve a progression of accomplishments or competencies that are to be demonstrated at defined times in the child's schooling. The *NCTM standards* give no indication (beyond four-year intervals) of the sequence with which the content is to be presented and are not helpful to the classroom teacher in designing lessons that meet the standards.
>
> The *NCTM standards* list goals with which no one would be likely to disagree. Of course we want children to value mathematics, to be mathematics problem solvers, to be confident of their ability, and to be able to reason and communicate mathematically. Certainly students must develop a number sense, have concepts of whole number operations, and the other kinds of skills and knowledge indicated under NCTM's curriculum standards. But the published standards do not integrate these two important components: the general attitudes and mathematical skills.[3]

The 1989 NCTM *Curriculum and Evaluation Standards for School Mathematics* includes sections devoted to general standards for the bands of grades: K–4, 5–8, and 9–12. Another section is devoted to "Evaluation Standards." In many respects, the *1989 NCTM* standards promoted the views of *An Agenda for Action*, but with greater elaboration. The grade level bands included lists of topics that were to receive "increased attention" and lists of topics that should receive "decreased attention." For example, in the K–4 band, the *Standards* called for greater attention to "Meanings of operations," "Operation sense," "Mental computation," "Use of calculators for complex computation," "Collection and organization of data," "Pattern recognition and description," "Use of manipulative materials," and "Cooperative work."

Included on the list for decreased attention in the grades K–4 were "Complex paper-and-pencil computations," "Long division," "Paper and pencil fraction computation," "Use of rounding to estimate," "Rote practice," "Rote memorization of rules," and "Teaching by telling." For grades 5–8 the *Standards* were even more radical. The following were included on the list to be de-emphasized: "Relying on outside authority (teacher or an answer key)," "Manipulating symbols," "Memorizing rules and algorithms," "Practicing tedious paper-and-pencil computations," "Finding exact forms of answers."

As in *An Agenda for Action*, the *1989 NCTM Standards* put strong emphasis on the use of calculators throughout all grade levels. On page 8, the

Standards proclaimed, "The new technology not only has made calculations and graphing easier, it has changed the very nature of mathematics…" The NCTM therefore recommended that, "appropriate calculators should be available to all students at all times." The Standards did concede that "the availability of calculators does not eliminate the need for students to learn algorithms," and it did acknowledge the need for "some proficiency with paper and pencil algorithms." However, these concessions were not supported in the classroom scenarios, or other parts of the document.

The *NCTM Standards* reinforced the general themes of progressive education, dating back to the 1920s, by advocating student centered, discovery learning. The utilitarian justification of mathematics was so strong that both basic skills and general mathematical principles were to be learned almost invariably through "real world" problems. Mathematics for its own sake was not encouraged. The variant of progressivism favored by the NCTM during this time was called "constructivism" and the *NCTM Standards* were promoted under this banner (Bosse, 1995, pp. 182–183).

The term "constructivism" was adapted from cognitive psychology by educators, and its meaning in educational contexts is different from its use in psychology. E.D. Hirsch Jr. provided a useful definition in his book, *The Schools We Need: Why We Don't Have Them*, which begins as follows:

> **"Constructivism"** A psychological term used by educational specialists to sanction the practice of "self-paced learning" and "discovery learning." The term implies that only constructed knowledge—knowledge which one finds out for one's self—is truly integrated and understood. It is certainly true that such knowledge is very likely to be remembered and understood, but it is not the case, as constructivists imply, that *only* such self-discovered knowledge will be reliably understood and remembered. This incorrect claim plays on an ambiguity between the technical and nontechnical uses of the term "construct" in the psychological literature…

Hirsch elaborated further on the psychological meaning of constructivism in his book. A more general and technical discussion was given in a paper by John R. Anderson, Lynne M. Reder, Herbert A. Simon entitled, *Applications and Misapplications of Cognitive Psychology to Mathematics Education* (Anderson, Reder, & Simon, 1997). Criticisms of educational constructivism, as in this article, were not well received by the education community. In an address before the California State Board of Education in April 1997, Hirsch described the treatment of this paper. "After a so-called peer review, *Educational Researcher* turned down the article, and agreed to print only a section of its critique of situated learning. This decision would have been unremarkable except that the three authors of the article happened to be among the most distinguished cognitive scientists in the world, John Anderson and two other colleagues at Carnegie Mellon, Lynn Reder, and Herb Simon. The latter happens also to be a Nobel prize winner."[4]

Mathematics education leaders drew support for educational constructivism from the writings of Jean Piaget and Lev Semenovich Vygotsky. Piaget's ideas about developmental stages of learning, and Vygotsky's concept, "Zone of Proximal Development," seemed to be consistent with the child-centered, cooperative learning approaches to education long favored by colleges of education.

In the fall of 1989, President George H. W. Bush, then in his first year of office, was invited by the nation's governors to an education summit in Charlottesville, Virginia. A bipartisan call went out for national standards. Participants at the 1989 Education Summit made a commitment to make U.S. students first in the world in mathematics and science by the year 2000.

Political leaders in the late 1980s were motivated by employers' complaints about the costs of teaching basic skills to entry level workers, and by the low standing of U.S. students in comparisons with foreign students in an era of economic competition (Ravitch, 2000, pp. 431–432). The timing for the *NCTM Standards* could not have been better. The nation was looking for benchmarks that could improve education. The *NCTM Standards* had just been published, and by default they became the national model for standards. The *NCTM Standards* were immediately and perfunctorily endorsed by a long list of prominent organizations such as the American Mathematical Society, the Mathematical Association of America, and the Council of Scientific Society Presidents.

Within a few years, the NCTM produced two additional documents as part of its standards. One published in 1991 was narrowly focused on pedagogy and the other, published in 1995, was focused on testing (NCTM, 1991, 1995). By 1997 most state governments had adopted mathematics standards in close alignment with the NCTM standards (Raimi, 2000, p. 40).

THE NATIONAL SCIENCE FOUNDATION

The National Science Foundation (NSF) was the key to the implementation of the *NCTM Standards* across the nation. Without the massive support it received from the NSF, the sole effect of the *NCTM Standards* would have been to collect dust on bookshelves. Spurred by the 1989 Education Summit attended by President Bush and all of the nation's governors, the Education and Human Resources Division (EHR) of the NSF set about to make systemic changes in the way math and science were taught in U.S. schools. The blueprint for change in mathematics would be the *NCTM Standards*.

The NSF proceeded purposefully. The EHR developed a series of Systemic Initiative grants to promote fundamental changes in science and mathematics education in the nation's schools. The Statewide Systemic Initiatives were launched in 1991. These grants were designed in part to encourage state education agencies to align their state mathematics standards to the *NCTM Standards*. The result was a remarkable uniformity and adherence to the *NCTM Standards* at the state level (McKeown, Klein, & Patterson, 2000; Raimi, 2000).

Recognizing that education is largely a matter of local control, the NSF also launched its Urban Systemic Initiative (USI) program in 1994. These USI grants were designed to implement the NCTM agenda at the school district level in large cities. The USI grants were followed by a program for Rural Systemic Initiatives. By 1999, the USI had evolved into the Urban Systemic Program. This program allowed renewals of awards made under the USI program.

At first, the Systemic Initiative grants were awarded to proposals generally aligned to the educational views of the NSF, but awardees were allowed substantial freedom to develop their own strategies for reform. As the program evolved, so did the guidelines. By 1996, the NSF clarified its assumptions about what constitutes effective, standards-based education and asserted that:

- All children can learn by using and manipulating scientific and mathematical ideas that are meaningful and relate to real-world situations and to real problems.
- Mathematics and science are learned by doing rather than by passive methods of learning such as watching a teacher work at the chalkboard. Inquiry-based learning and hands-on learning more effectively engage students than lectures.
- The use and manipulation of scientific and mathematical ideas benefits from a variety of contributing perspectives and is, therefore, enhanced by cooperative problem solving.
- Technology can make learning easier, more comprehensive, and more lasting.
- This view of learning is reflected in the professional standards of the National Council of Teachers of Mathematics, the American Association for the Advancement of Science, and the National Research Council of the National Academy of Sciences (McKeown et al., 2000).

The NSF was clear in its support of the *NCTM Standards* and of progressive education. Children should learn through group-based discovery with the help of manipulatives and calculators. Earlier research funded by the NSF, such as "Project Follow Through," which reached very different conclusions about what works best in the classroom, would not be considered (Carnine, 2000; Coombs, 1998; *Effective School Practices*, 1995–6; Grossen,

1998). Regardless of what cognitive psychology might say about teaching methodologies, only constructivist programs would be supported.

Along with the Systemic Initiative awards, the NSF supported the creation and development of commercial mathematics curricula aligned to the *NCTM Standards*. In the decade of the 1990s, the National Science Foundation sponsored the creation of the following mathematics programs for K–12:

Elementary School
- Everyday Mathematics (K–6)
- TERC's Investigations in Number, Data, and Space (K–5)
- Math Trailblazers (TIMS) (K–5)

Middle School
- Connected Mathematics (6–8)
- Mathematics in Context (5–8)
- MathScape: Seeing and Thinking Mathematically (6–8)
- MATHThematics (STEM) (6–8)
- Pathways to Algebra and Geometry (MMAP) (6–7, or 7–8)

High School
- Contemporary Mathematics in Context (Core-Plus Mathematics Project) (9–12)
- Interactive Mathematics Program (9–12)
- MATH Connections: A Secondary Mathematics Core Curriculum (9–11)
- Mathematics: Modeling Our World (ARISE) (9–12)
- SIMMS Integrated Mathematics: A Modeling Approach Using Technology (9–12).

The development of NCTM aligned mathematics programs for K–12 was of obvious importance to the NSF (for a list of math programs explicitly endorsed by the NCTM, see the Appendix). How could the NCTM agenda be carried out without classroom materials that were specifically aligned to the *NCTM Standards?* An important component of the Systemic Initiatives was the aggressive distribution of NCTM aligned curricula for classroom use. The *NCTM Standards* were vague as to mathematical content, but specific in its support of constructivist pedagogy, the criterion that mattered most to the NSF. It should be noted that the Systemic Initiatives sometimes promoted curricula not on the list above, such as College Preparatory Mathematics, a high school program, and MathLand, a K–6 curriculum. MathLand was one of the most controversial of the widely used programs aligned to the *NCTM Standards* (Scharlemann, 1996).

In addition to aligning state math standards to the *NCTM standards* and creating and distributing math books and programs aligned to those standards, the NSF attempted with considerable success to push these approaches up to the university level. Most notable in this regard was the NSF's funding of a "reform calculus" book, often referred to as "Harvard Calculus," that relied heavily on calculators and discovery work by the students, and minimized the level of high school algebra required for the program (Hughes-Hallett, Gleason et al., 1994; Klein, 1999; Klein & Rosen, 1997).

The NSF also funded distribution centers to promote the curricular programs it had helped to create. For example, an NSF sponsored organization created in 1997 called, "The K–12 Mathematics Curriculum Center," had a mission statement "to support school districts as they build an effective mathematics education program using curriculum materials developed in response to the National Council of Teachers of Mathematics' *Curriculum and Evaluation Standards for School Mathematics.*"

The Education and Human Resources Division of the NSF faced a serious hurdle in carrying out its Systemic Initiatives. U.S. K–12 education collectively was a multibillion dollar operation and the huge budgets alone gave public education an inertia that would be hard to overcome. Even though the millions of dollars at its disposal made the EHR budget large in absolute terms, it was miniscule relative to the combined budgets of the school systems that the NSF sought to reform. It would not be easy to effect major changes in K–12 mathematics and science education without access to greater resources.

To some extent private foundations contributed to the goal of implementing the *NCTM Standards* through teacher training programs for the curricula supported by the NSF, and in other ways. The Noyce Foundation was especially active in promoting NCTM aligned math curricula in Massachusetts and parts of California. Others such as the W. M. Keck Foundation and Bank of America contributed as well. However, the NSF itself found ingenious ways to increase its influence. The strategy was to use small grants to leverage major changes in states and school districts. NSF Assistant Director Luther Williams, who was in charge of the Education and Human Resources Division, explained the strategy in a July 1998 Urban Systemic Initiative Summary Update:

> The NSF investment that promotes systemic reform will never exceed a small percentage of a given site's overall budget. The "converged" resources are not merely fiscal, but also strategic, in that they help induce a unitary . . . reform operation. The catalytic nature of the USI-led reform obligates systemwide policy and fiscal resources to embrace standards-based instruction and create conditions for helping assorted . . . expenditures to become organized and used in a single-purpose direction.

NSF Assistant Director Williams gave successful examples of this strategy. "Cleveland devoted half of its available bond referendum funding" for USI-related instructional material. "Los Angeles . . . is one of several cities in the USI portfolio that places all Title II funding resources under the control of the USI." "In the Fresno Unified School System, $31 million of Title 1 funds have been realigned in support of USI activities" (McKeown et al., 2000, p. 317).

The Systemic Initiatives were extraordinarily successful in promoting the *NCTM Standards* and implementing NCTM aligned curricula at the classroom level. Los Angeles Unified School District (LAUSD), the second largest school district in the nation, serves as an illustrative example.

LAUSD was awarded a five-year Urban Systemic Initiative grant in 1995 for $15 million. The $3 million per year from the Los Angeles Systemic Initiative (LASI) amounted to only one-twentieth of 1% of LAUSD's annual budget of $5.8 billion, or about $3.79 per student per year in the district. Yet, the LASI project exerted almost complete control over mathematics and science education in the district. In addition to Title II funds, LASI gained control of the school district's television station and its ten science and technology centers. According to Luther Williams' July 1998 Summary update, "[LASI] accountability became the framework for a major policy initiative establishing benchmarks and standards in all subject areas for the entire school system." LASI developed the district standards not only for math and science, but also English and social studies. All four sets of standards were adopted by the school district in 1996.

The Los Angeles School district math standards were so weak and vague that they were a source of controversy. One typical standard, without any sort of elaboration, asked students to "make connections among related mathematical concepts and apply these concepts to other content areas and the world of work." The LASI/LAUSD standards stipulated the use of calculators and "other appropriate technology" before the end of third grade, thus raising the possibility that students would not be required to master arithmetic. The word "triangle" did not even appear in the standards at any grade level. By design, trigonometry and all Algebra II topics were completely missing (McKeown et al., 2000). Like the *NCTM Standards*, the LAUSD/LASI standards were given only for bands of grades, rendering them at best useless, even if they had been otherwise competently written.

The 1996 LAUSD/LASI math standards paved the way for the dissemination of textbooks and curricula aligned to those standards, as well as staff development in their use. The LASI 1997 annual report explained:

LAUSD's urban systemic initiative is well under way with its efforts to renew and unify districtwide instruction using standards-based curricula. These curricula are characterized by hands-on, inquiry based, problem solving, integrated/coordinated, student-teacher interactive instruction in math, science, technology for grades K–12. These efforts are supported and strengthened by needs-based staff development, increased communication among teachers and staff, changes in administrative policies that are essential for student access to the systemic benefits, and checks on progress and process at preselected gates in the system's superstructure.

LASI was successful in distributing "hands-on, inquiry based" curricula aligned to the *NCTM Standards* to LAUSD schools. LASI specifically recommended NCTM aligned curricula for all grades, including MathLand for K–5. By July 1998, more than half of all LAUSD schools were using math curricula aligned to the *NCTM Standards*, and LASI publicly announced its plan to require all LAUSD high schools to use one of four "integrated math" curricula within five years: Core-Plus, Interactive Mathematics Program, College Preparatory Mathematics, or McDougal Littell's "Integrated Math" (Haynes, 1998; Klein, 1998; Mejia, 1998). Two of these were funded by the NSF. This plan was not carried out because of the adoption of a new set of mathematics standards by the state of California in December 1997. But long after these rigorous California State Mathematics Standards were adopted, LAUSD schools continued to use LASI endorsed material. At a meeting of the LAUSD school board on May 2, 2000, it was revealed that fewer than 3% of elementary schools in the district were using California state approved mathematics programs. MathLand was used by 45% of the 420 elementary schools in LAUSD, while Quest 2000, a similar NCTM aligned program, was used by another 24% of the district's elementary schools. Eventually, the 1997 California mathematics standards were accepted and implemented by LAUSD, but not before a generation of students was educationally disenfranchised by the NSF Systemic Initiative Program.

The NSF's Systemic Initiative programs in other parts of the country were similarly successful in promoting mathematics curricula funded by the NSF, or otherwise aligned to the *NCTM Standards*. El Paso, Texas serves as an example. The El Paso Urban Systemic Initiative grant was awarded in 1994 and administered under the direction of the El Paso Collaborative for Academic Excellence. This collaborative coordinated other NSF funded projects including the Partnership for Excellence in Teacher Education and Model Institutions for Excellence, as well as private foundation grants, including support from The Exxon Corporation, The Pew Charitable Trusts, and The Coca-Cola Foundation.

El Paso is geographically removed from other U.S. cities and is unusual in that it is a "closed system." The teachers trained at the University of Texas, El Paso (UTEP) teach almost exclusively in the El Paso school districts, and the teachers in the El Paso school districts almost exclusively undertook their university studies at UTEP. This made the effectiveness of the K–12 and university programs easier to assess. It also made the entire education system easier to control. During the 1990s, the K–16 education system in El Paso was highly coordinated and focused on implementing constructivist math and science education programs. For this reason, it became a model center for educators from other parts of the country to visit and study.[5]

The Collaborative in El Paso worked in close coordination with the Texas Statewide Systemic Initiative housed in the Charles A. Dana Center in Austin. The Texas SSI developed an *Instructional Materials Analysis and Selection Scoring Grid* for Texas school districts to use in selecting math textbooks. The recommended criteria for selecting K–8 mathematics curricula included:

- Materials provide opportunities for teaching students to work in collaborative and cooperative groups.
- Materials provide opportunity for the appropriate use of technology.
- Students are engaged in the development of mathematical understanding through the use of manipulatives.
- Multiple forms of assessment activities, such as student demonstrations, rubrics, self-reflections, observations, and oral and written work are used throughout the instructional materials.
- Technology is built into the assessment tools.
- Assessment activities take into account the ways in which students' unique qualities influence how they learn and how they communicate their understanding.
- The instructional materials reflect cultural diversities and address historical perspectives.
- Problem solving permeates the entire instructional material through investigative situations.

The curricula chosen for El Paso public schools by 1999 were all NSF sponsored: TERC's Investigations in Number, Data, and Space (K–5), Connected Mathematics (6–8), SIMMS Integrated Mathematics: A Modeling Approach Using Technology (9–12).

The El Paso Collaborative for Academic Excellence created a confidential student evaluation questionnaire to monitor teaching methods used in high school math classrooms in all of EL Paso's public high schools. The evaluation included the following questions to students:

- How often do MOST STUDENTS talk with each other to describe or justify the strategy they used to solve a problem?
- How often does THE CLASS go in depth on a few problems instead of covering a large number of problems in the class period?
- How often does THE TEACHER TALK during most of the period?
- How often do YOU show that you understand a solution to a problem by explaining it in writing?

- How often do YOU use math in science and science in math?
- How often does THE CLASS work in pairs or groups to explain solutions?
- How often do YOU use hand calculators or computers to analyze data or solve problems?

The NSF awarded the Texas Statewide Systemic Initiative $2 million per year beginning in 1994. Yet, in spite of the low funding, the Texas SSI "provides leadership for a vast array of agency partnerships, and influences all aspects of education in Texas. Curricula, instructional practices, textbooks, assessment, professional development of teachers, teacher evaluation, teacher certification, and pre-service teacher education all now fall under the purview of the Texas SSI" (McKeown et al., 2000, p. 337).

PUBLIC RESISTANCE TO THE NCTM STANDARDS

To understand the public backlash against the NCTM math programs of the 1990s, one needs to understand some of the mathematical shortcomings of these programs. The mathematics books and curricula that parents of school children resisted shared some general features. Those programs typically failed to develop fundamental arithmetic and algebra skills. Elementary school programs encouraged students to invent their own arithmetic algorithms, while discouraging the use of the superior standard algorithms for addition, subtraction, multiplication, and division. Calculator use was encouraged to excess, and in some cases calculators were even incorporated into kindergarten lesson plans. Student discovery group work was the preferred mode of learning, sometimes exclusively, and the guidelines for discovery projects were at best inefficient and often aimless. Topics from statistics and data analysis were redundant from one grade level to the next, and were overemphasized. Arithmetic and algebra were radically de-emphasized. Mathematical definitions and proofs for the higher grades were generally deficient, missing entirely, or even incorrect. Some of the elementary school programs did not even provide books for students, as they might interfere with student discovery. Written and published criticisms from many sources, including mathematicians, of specific mathematics programs were widespread in the 1990s and reinforced the convictions of dissatisfied parents.[6]

But not everyone viewed the near absence of the standard algorithms of arithmetic in NCTM aligned books as a shortcoming. Some prominent educational researchers were explicit in their opposition to the teaching of algorithms to children. An article in the 1998 Yearbook of the NCTM entitled, *The Harmful Effects of Algorithms in Grades 1–4* by Constance Kamii and Ann

Dominick provides examples. Citing earlier education research, the authors wrote, "By the 1980s, some researchers were seriously questioning the wisdom of teaching conventional algorithms," and then listed examples of such research. Tracing the history of this line of inquiry they added, "Some investigators went further in the 1990s and concluded that algorithms are harmful to children," with examples provided. Elaborating, they wrote:

> Piaget's constructivism, and the more than sixty years of scientific research by him and others all over the world led Kamii to a compelling hypothesis: Children in the primary grades should be able to invent their own arithmetic without the instruction they are now receiving from textbooks and workbooks. This hypothesis was amply verified . . .

Kamii co-authored another article in the 1999 Yearbook of the NCTM in which similar conclusions were reached about the algorithms for the arithmetic of fractions (Kamil & Dominick, 998; Kamil & Warrinton, 1999).

Opposition to conventional arithmetic algorithms was not restricted to academic researchers. Similar convictions were held by teacher trainers with substantial influence. In a 1994 article entitled, *Arithmetic: The Last Holdout*, Marilyn Burns wrote:

> I am a teacher who has embraced the call for change completely. I've made shifts in my teaching so that helping children learn to think, reason, and solve problems has become the primary objective of my math instruction . . . I do not give timed tests on basic facts. I make calculators available for students to use at all times. I incorporate a variety of manipulative materials into my instruction. I do not rely on textbooks because textbooks, for the most part, encourage "doing the page" rather than "doing mathematics." (Burns, 1994, pp. 471–476)

Parents of school children in the 1990s were directly confronted by policies based on these ideas. For example, the Los Angeles Times reported in 1997:

> One missionary in the Reform cause is consultant Ruth Parker, who rejects long division and multiplication tables as nonsensical leftovers from a precalculator age. She urges audiences to "let kids play with numbers," and they will figure out most any math concept. Parker has spoken before 20,000 people over the last six months at the behest of school districts. (Colvin, 1997a)

Parents who worried that their children were getting unsound educations from NCTM aligned mathematics programs did not give much credence to education research findings or the advice of education experts, and most mathematicians didn't either. Perhaps the general attitude of parents was best captured by Jaime Escalante, the nationally famous mathematics teacher immortalized in the film *Stand and Deliver*, when he said, "whoever wrote [the *NCTM Standards*] must be a physical education teacher" (Sykes, 1995, p. 122).

Sifting through the claims and counterclaims, journalists of the 1990s tended to portray the math wars as an extended disagreement between those who wanted basic skills versus those who favored conceptual understanding of mathematics. The parents and mathematicians who criticized the NCTM aligned curricula were portrayed as proponents of basic skills, while educational administrators, professors of education, and other defenders of these programs, were portrayed as proponents of conceptual understanding, and sometimes even "higher order thinking." This dichotomy is implausible. The parents leading the opposition to the NCTM Standards, as discussed below, had considerable expertise in mathematics, generally exceeding that of the education professionals. This was even more the case of the large number of mathematicians who criticized these programs. Among them were some of the world's most distinguished mathematicians, in some cases with mathematical capabilities near the very limits of human ability. By contrast, many of the education professionals who spoke of "conceptual understanding" lacked even a rudimentary knowledge of mathematics.

More fundamentally, the separation of conceptual understanding from basic skills in mathematics is misguided. It is not possible to teach conceptual understanding in mathematics without the supporting basic skills, and basic skills are weakened by a lack of understanding. The essential connection between basic skills and understanding of concepts in mathematics was perhaps most eloquently explained by U.C. Berkeley mathematician Hung-Hsi Wu in his paper, *Basic Skills Versus Conceptual Understanding: A Bogus Dichotomy in Mathematics Education* (Wu, 1999).

The obstacles faced by parents opposed to the NCTM programs for their children were formidable. The events leading to the creation of the Princeton Charter school illustrate some of the generic difficulties.

In 1991 a group of about 250 parents of school children in Princeton, New Jersey petitioned the board of education for a more systematic and challenging math program. They found the one in use to be vague and weak. Many of the teachers did not even use textbooks. When parents asked about what was being taught in the classrooms, they were told that the curriculum was not very important, that "one size does not fit all," and, repeating the dictum of 1930s Progressivists, that the teachers were there to "teach children, not curricula." When parents complained of deficiencies in what little curriculum even existed, they were treated as if their cases were new and unrelated to other complaints. These responses have been reported by parents in many other school districts as well.

Test scores in Princeton were among the highest in the state, but that was not the result of a well-designed academic program. Many highly educated parents, including Princeton University faculty, were providing tutoring and enrichment for their own children. Other children with limited resources in the Princeton Regional School system did not fare well in this highly progressivist environment.

Finding their requests ignored, the "Curriculumists," those parents favoring an organized coherent curriculum for all students, concentrated on winning school board seats. One of them, Chiara Nappi, a theoretical physicist at the Institute for Advanced Study in Princeton, won a seat in 1993. By 1994 the Curriculumists held a majority of positions on the school board. However, even with formal political power, the Curriculumists were unable to make substantive changes in the district. They eventually turned their attention to creating a charter school for grades K–8 whose focus would be the fundamental academic disciplines, and which would provide an atmosphere that affirmed academic achievement. However, even this effort was resisted by Progressivists in the district. Nevertheless, after considerable effort, the Princeton Charter School came into existence in 1997 and provided a genuine alternative to the educational philosophy of the school district (Nappi, 1999).

Parents in California were also alarmed by the mathematics programs their children were getting in school. California was ahead of the rest of the nation in implementing the approach to mathematics education envisioned in the *NCTM Standards* and *An Agenda for Action*. The 1985 *California Model Curriculum Standards, Grades Nine Through Twelve* already had prescriptions that closely resembled those in the *NCTM Standards* such as:

> The mathematics program must present to students problems that utilize acquired skills and require the use of problem-solving strategies. Examples of strategies that students should employ are: estimate, look for a pattern, write an equation, guess and test, work backward, draw a picture or diagram, make a list or table, use models, act out the problem, and solve a related but simpler problem. The use of calculators and computers should also be encouraged as an essential part of the problem-solving process. Students should be encouraged to devise their own plans and explore alternate approaches to problems.

As a consequence, mathematics reform along the lines of the weak *1989 NCTM Standards* was well underway in California in the early 1990s. California was one of the first states to embrace the *NCTM Standards*, producing a state mathematics framework in 1992 that closely resembled the *NCTM Standards*. By 1994, the California State Board of Education had approved math curricula for grades K–8 aligned to the 1992 California mathematics framework, and by extension, the *NCTM Standards*.

The first significant parental rebellion in California occurred in Palo Alto, a highly educated community that included Stanford University faculty and business leaders. In May 1994, more than 600 parents signed a petition asking that the school district retain a traditional pre-algebra curriculum at one of the middle schools in the Palo Alto Unified School District. The district was about to replace the remaining traditional courses with a math program aligned to California's 1992 math framework. Finding the district uncooperative, 25 parents in Palo Alto formed "Honest and Open Logical Debate," or HOLD in February 1995, put up a website the next month, and within a short period of time there were nearly 500 households on the HOLD mailing list. The already considerable math credentials of HOLD members were increased by the support and participation of Henry Alder, a professor of mathematics at UC Davis, a former president of the Mathematical Association of America, and a former member of the California State Board of Education. Alder had long been advocating themes similar to those of HOLD.

HOLD criticized the 1992 California math framework and the *NCTM Standards*, and pointed to a decrease in Stanford Achievement Test scores coinciding with the implementation of "whole math" in district schools. From 1992 to 1994 the average overall student score for 8th grade math students had decreased from the 91st national percentile rank to the 81st. The decrease was more dramatic on the portion of the exam that tested computation. On that portion the scores dropped from the 86th percentile in 1992 to the 58th percentile in 1994. Parents took steps to compensate for the lack of computational skills taught to their children in school. According to Bill Evers, one of the cofounders of HOLD:

> Palo Alto School District parents are sufficiently discontented with the district's math performance that in massive numbers they are resorting to outside math tutoring programs. Forty-eight percent of parents report providing outside help in math for their children (in the middle schools, this number rises to 63 percent). The math-basics group HOLD's own informal survey of the best-known commercial math programs shows that Palo Alto parents are spending at least $1 million a year for math tutoring. (Evers, 1995)

With the extra tutoring, the district scores partially rebounded the following school year.

At the southern end of the state, four parents, Paul Clopton, Larry Gipson, Mike McKeown, and Martha Schwartz came together in the Autumn of 1995 to form "Mathematically Correct." Their common nemesis was fuzzy math and in particular, College Preparatory Mathematics (CPM), a secondary, integrated math program. Martha Schwartz had just participated in a group of parents that had collected more than 1,000 signatures for a petition to a school district in Torrance, California asking for a traditional alternative to CPM. This same program had been introduced in San Diego schools in 1993, and the founding parents found common cause in confronting the problems this curriculum and others like it were causing school children.

The founders of Mathematically Correct had credentials in science and mathematics that could not easily be dismissed. Gipson was a professional engineer; Clopton a statistician working for the Department of Veterans Affairs in San Diego; Schwartz was finishing up a Ph.D. in geophysics; McKeown was a faculty member at the Salk Institute for Biological Studies in San Diego (a few years later, McKeown accepted a professorship in the Division of Biology and Medicine at Brown University). They were soon joined by others, notably Wayne Bishop, a professor and former chair of the Mathematics Department at California State University, Los Angeles, and Frank Allan, a former president of the NCTM. Both had many years of experience dealing with mathematics education issues, and both were critics of the *1989 NCTM Standards.*

Organized for the explicit purpose of assisting parents dissatisfied with "fuzzy math" in their children's schools, Mathematically Correct attracted a large number of supporters (including the author of this chapter). Like other groups of its type, Mathematically Correct charged no dues, had no annual budget, and there was no formal membership. Mathematically Correct was fueled entirely by the energy and dedication of its supporters, especially its webmaster, Paul Clopton. In the decade of the 1990s, Mathematically Correct emerged as the most influential and effective organization to challenge the NCTM agenda. It served as a national clearing house for information and advice on K–12 mathematics education. Its supporters entered the political process, met with reporters and politicians, served on California government panels and commissions related to mathematics education, and testified before national boards and the U.S. Congress. Mathematically Correct and HOLD played important roles in establishing the California mathematics standards in 1997, a topic taken up in the next section.

Mathematically Correct also came into contact with other like-minded parent organizations, such as Parents Raising Educational Standards in Schools (PRESS), based in Milwaukee, Wisconsin; Concerned Parents of Reading, Massachusetts; Concerned Parents in Petaluma, California; Mountain View Achievement; Santa Monicans Working for Equity and Excellence in Public Schools; as well as many others. All of these grassroots parents' organizations were opposed to NCTM aligned math curricula in the schools and had information or websites linked from the Mathematically Correct website. The Internet was a powerful organizing tool for parents of school children during the 1990s.

A parent group in Plano, Texas took the unusual step of suing the school district in order to find an alternative to one of the NSF funded math programs. In 1996, Plano Independent School District (PISD) began piloting Connected Math in four of its nine middle schools. By the summer of 1998, some parents were objecting to the program. One parent who criticized Connected Math was removed from a textbook advisory committee in the Fall of 1998. Another parent was prevented from passing out information critical of Connected Math at PISD informational meetings, and was also prevented from collecting signatures to a petition asking for an open discussion with parents about the merits of the program. As a result, parents formed the organization, MathChoice, in January 1999. Frustrated that the district continued to ignore parental complaints about the program, MathChoice started another petition drive in May 1999. The petition was really just a one page form that parents could fill out requesting an alternative math class for their children. Each form began with the sentence, "This petition is for the addition of a specific, traditional/conventional academic class in the course of study of math for the parent or guardian's child named:..." The district responded by sending letters to parents in the school district that countered the petition, effectively putting an end to the petition drive. However, by the end of May, 521 signatures had already been collected.

Finding their petitions ignored, the Plano parents turned to litigation. In October 1999, MathChoice incorporated as the Plano Parental Rights Council. They attained nonprofit status from the IRS the following spring and elected Susan Sarhady as president. Seeking class certification, six parents filed suit in federal court "against the Plano Independent School District for violations of the parent's constitutionally protected rights of free speech/expression, equal protection and the fundamental right as parents to direct the education and upbringing of their children."[7] In May 2000, a federal judge ruled that "Plano Independent School District cannot be compelled to offer an alternative middle-school math program despite the objections of some parents to the new Connected Math approach..." However, the judge "also found that certain allegations by the parents should go forward to trial . . . The lawsuit claim[ed] that the First Amendment rights of several parents were violated when they were prohibited from distributing or displaying materials opposing the Connected Math program at several meetings" (Jacobson, 2000).

Another important parents' organization emerged in 1999 in New York City. The New York City school system had been awarded an Urban Systemic Initiative grant from the NSF in 1994, and New York state had a Statewide Systemic Initiative grant. The New York Urban Systemic Initiative reported training 4,200 teachers in inquiry-based curricula, and more than 700 teachers in the use of calculators for high school mathematics courses.

According to posted reports to the NSF, the USI also implemented "exemplary curricula" in over 5,000 classrooms in New York City.

New York City Schools are grouped into 32 community school districts. Each has its own school board and superintendent. Community School District 2 consists of about 42 schools serving 22,000 racially diverse students. The district included relatively affluent neighborhoods as well as neighborhoods with substantial concentrations of lower income families and recent immigrants.

Beginning in 1993, teachers were trained in materials created by Marilyn Burns, a prominent teacher trainer cited earlier in this section. From 1995 to 1998 pilot programs in TERC's Investigations in Number, Data and Space and Connected Mathematics gradually expanded in District 2. By 1999 TERC and CMP were used district wide. The NSF funded curriculum, Mathematics: Modeling Our World (ARISE), was scaled up for use in all of the high schools in 2000 and 2001.

In May 1999, Elizabeth Carson, a concerned parent of a middle school student, began a search for allies to try to reverse the district wide implementation of weak NCTM aligned mathematics programs. The result was an alliance consisting of parents, teachers, City University of New York mathematics professors, and a substantial portion of the faculty of the math department of the Courant Institute of New York University. They named themselves "New York City HOLD" (NYC HOLD) after the Palo Alto group. Allies of NYC HOLD communicated with each other largely through the Internet, but many of them met weekly at New York University for planning sessions or discussions with interested visitors, including education journalists. On June 6, 2001, NYC HOLD held an open forum for parents and teachers in an auditorium in the New York University Law school. Approximately 350 people attended, and plans were subsequently made for other projects to challenge the nearly exclusive use of NCTM-aligned curricula in the schools.

In the decade of the 1990s, the parent organizations in California, especially Mathematically Correct, experienced the greatest successes, not only in blocking the use of dubious classroom materials, but also in implementing coherent, effective mathematics policies at the state level. The California program at the end of the 20th century included high quality mathematics textbooks and a testing system aligned to the California standards. However, parent organizations did not accomplish these changes unilaterally. Many other sectors of society and prominent individuals played critical roles. They included classroom teachers and principals, university mathematicians, legislators, state school board members, journalists, and two successive governors.

MATHEMATICIANS, CALIFORNIA, AND THE NATION

No state had so great a national impact as California on mathematics education during the 1990s. This was due in part to the fact that California was the most populous state, and as a consequence, the demands placed on textbook publishers to sell to the California market influenced what was available to the rest of the nation. But the effect of California's new educational policies during the middle and late 1990s went deeper. Perhaps the clearest indications of the importance of California's choices were the harsh public denunciations by both the NCTM and the NSF of California's 1997 mathematics standards immediately following their release. This will be contrasted with the strong support given by university mathematicians and parent groups, later in this section. By the end of the decade, it was clear that California's mathematics program threatened a century of progressivist domination in K–12 mathematics education.

Not since the New Math period of the 1960s had university mathematicians played such important roles in K–12 education as in California during the 1990s. Mathematicians were involved in developing the state mathematics standards, the California mathematics framework, and in evaluating textbooks and professional development programs for teachers in California. Some mathematicians also helped to write and develop textbooks for the textbook adoption process of 2001. During the decade of the 1990s, at the national level, there were extended discussions about K–12 mathematics among research mathematicians through their professional meetings and magazines (see, e.g., Askey, 1992, pp. 424–426; Wu, 1996, pp. 1531–1537, 2000, pp. 946–957). The result was a greater participation by university mathematicians nationally in matters related to mathematics education, including interactions with parent organizations.

In California, by the mid-1990s, the dramatic failures of "whole language learning" in teaching primary grade students to read had already cost the education establishment substantial credibility with the public. Analogous failures in mathematics education were opening opportunities for critics of constructivist education policies to make changes. Mathematicians and parent activists displaced, to a considerable degree, the education professionals and college of education faculty who would normally be entrusted to work out the policy details for K–12 mathematics education. As a consequence, mathematicians were naturally drawn into educational and political debates.

An early example was the participation of Professor Wayne Bishop on a Mathematics Task Force formed by the state Superintendent of Schools, Delaine Eastin, in 1995. The 25 member Task Force was charged with recommending ways to improve mathematics instruction in California. Bishop publicly resigned from the Task Force in order to make known his disagreement with the weak recommendations the Task Force was making.

Following the release of the Task Force report, Professor Henry Alder addressed the California State Board of Education in December 1995. He articulated the views of the emerging parent organizations in California and indirectly reinforced Bishop's symbolic resignation. Alder recommended "a revision or perhaps even a complete rewriting of the 1992 California Mathematics Framework rather than issue a supplement." Paving the way for broader participation in mathematics education policy making, Alder also recommended that a:

> new task force to be charged with your Board's directives be appointed in consultation with all affected constituencies, with an appropriate mix of expertise from all segments interested in and involved in mathematics education. This means, in particular, that its membership should not be dominated by those who prepared the 1992 California Mathematics Framework and those who constituted the Mathematics Task Force. (Alder, 1995)

The State Board of Education agreed with the critics and scheduled a rewrite of the 1992 Framework two years ahead of the normal time table. By this time there was considerable public pressure to improve the teaching of reading and mathematics in the schools. The legislature had just passed a bill that required school districts to include the teaching of basic skills in reading and math as part of their curriculum. Governor Wilson signed this "ABC Bill" in October 1995, and it became law in January 1996. The ABC laws had virtually no effect on school districts, which were generally run by committed constructivists, but political leaders felt compelled to do something about the mounting failures in education. Whole language and whole math—the math programs aligned to the NCTM Standards and 1992 California framework—were widely viewed as responsible for depriving children of fundamental skills.

At the national level during the mid-1990s much attention was focused on international comparisons of student mathematics achievement. The first available results of the Third International Mathematics and Science Study (TIMSS) were released in November 1996. U.S. 8th graders scored slightly below the international average in mathematics. The second TIMSS report comparing 4th grade students in math was released in June 1997. U.S. fourth grade students were slightly above the international average among the participating countries. The final report compared students at the end of high school and was released in 1998. The mathematics achievement of U.S. 12th graders was among the lowest of the participating nations. The TIMSS data contained valuable information, but it had relatively little political impact on the ensuing debates, as both sides cited the studies to reinforce their respective positions. However, TIMSS researchers did express support for the *NCTM Standards*. The eighth grade study found that:

> **Ninety-five percent of U.S. teachers stated that they were either "very aware" or "somewhat aware" of current ideas about teaching and learning mathematics.** When asked to list titles of books they read to stay informed about current ideas, one third of U.S. teachers wrote down the names of two important documents by the National Council of Teachers of Mathematics, Curriculum and Evaluation Standards and Professional Teaching Standards [bold in original].
>
> U.S. teachers believe that their lessons are already implementing the reform recommendations, but the findings described so far in this chapter suggest that their lessons are not. When asked to evaluate to what degree the videotaped lesson was in accord with current ideas about teaching and learning mathematics, almost 75 percent of the teachers respond either "a lot" or "a fair amount." This discrepancy between teachers' beliefs and the TIMSS findings leads us to wonder how teachers themselves understand the key goals of the reform movement, and apply them in the classroom. (U.S. Department of Education, 1996, Ch. 3)

The report suggests, without any experimental support, that if the U.S. teachers had properly followed the constructivist *NCTM Standards*, then U.S. students would have performed better in the study. However, it is possible that the teachers were correct in asserting that they were following "current ideas about teaching and learning mathematics," and there was no "discrepancy." The report went on to say:

> Over 80 percent of the teachers in the study referred to something other than a focus on thinking, which is the central message of the mathematics reform movement. The majority of the teachers cited examples of hands-on math or cooperative learning, which are techniques included among the reform recommendations. However, these techniques can be used either with or without engaging students in real mathematical thinking. In fact, the videotape study observed many examples of these techniques being conducted in the absence of high-quality mathematical content.

The authors of the report did not consider the possibility that the NCTM reform movement itself was a contributing cause of poor student performance. Even a cursory examination of the NCTM aligned math curricula would show a disturbing lack of "high quality mathematical content." Nevertheless, the TIMSS report prescribed still more of the same reform:

> **These findings suggest that the instructional habits and attitudes of U.S. mathematics teachers are only beginning to change in the direction of implementation of mathematics reform recommendations. Teachers' implementa-**

tion of the reform still concentrates on isolated techniques rather than the central message, which is to focus lessons on high-level mathematical thought. The finding that almost 20 percent of the teachers believed that they had implemented this focus on mathematical thinking, despite experts' judgments that a high-quality sequence of mathematical ideas was virtually absent in their lessons, suggests that teachers may not yet understand what the reform movement means by this term [bold in original].

The growing criticisms of NCTM aligned reform curricula coming from professional mathematicians raised the possibility that the real focus of the reform movement was constructivist classroom techniques rather than "high-level mathematical thought." This possibility was not considered by the authors of the TIMSS reports.

Results from National Assessment of Educational Progress (NAEP) were released in February 1996. While the nation as a whole made some improvements, California's fourth graders scored below their peers in 40 states and came out ahead of only those in Mississippi. A careful analysis of NAEP trends for the nation as a whole was published by the Brookings Institution later in September 2000, but California's relative downward slide reinforced the political will toward writing explicit mathematics standards and rectifying the 1992 framework to include more attention to basic skills (Loveless & DiPerna, 2000). Adding to California's concerns was a steady increase in remedial math courses on the 23 campus California State University (CSU) system. The percentage of entering freshmen failing an entry level math test used by the CSU steadily increased from 1989, when 23% of all entering freshmen required remedial math help, to 54% of the entering freshmen requiring remediation in math in each of 1997 and 1998. While there was no proof that the decrease in math skills was caused by the constructivist math programs in the schools, school mathematics seemed to be getting worse rather than better as the NCTM reform agenda expanded.

In January 1997, a committee called the Academic Content and Performance Standards Commission (Standards Commission) was charged with writing mathematics (and other subject matter) standards for California and submitting its draft to the State Board of Education for final approval. The committee consisted of non expert citizens appointed through a political process. The majority of the Standards Commissioners were largely in agreement with the constructivist policies of the past. The result was a set of standards submitted to the Board in the Fall of 1997 that not only embraced the constructivist methods that California was trying to escape, but was also incoherent and full of mathematical errors.

Members of the State Board asked for help from Stanford University mathematics professors Gunnar Carlsson, Ralph Cohen, Steve Kerckhoff, and R. James Milgram. In a few short weeks they rewrote the standards, corrected more than 100 mathematical errors, and eliminated all pedagogical directives, leaving the standards pedagogically neutral. The final revisions, including those made by the State Board itself, resulted in a document that would allow teachers to use constructivist methods or direct instruction, or whatever classroom techniques worked for them, so long as they taught all of the grade level content standards. The mathematics framework was regarded as the proper document for discussions of pedagogy, but not the standards themselves. This was what the State Board was looking for, and the mathematicians' standards were adopted by California in December 1997. These standards were clear, coherent, and met the criteria set by the California legislature to be competitive with math standards of the highest performing countries.

Professor Hung-Hsi Wu did a careful analysis of the California standards, that the board adopted, in comparison to the draft submitted by the Standards Commission which the Board rejected. Wu found numerous mathematical errors and lack of clarity and cohesion in the rejected standards, in contrast to an overall soundness and clarity in the adopted standards (Wu, 2000). In 1998, the Fordham Foundation conducted an independent review of the mathematics standards from 46 states and the District of Columbia, as well as Japan. California's new board approved mathematics standards received the highest score, outranking even those of Japan (Raimi & Braden, 1998).

The NCTM responded to the new California mathematics standards with denunciations. The cover story of the February 1998 News Bulletin of the NCTM began with:

> Mathematics education in California suffered a serious blow in December. Over protests from business, community, and education leaders, California's state board of education unanimously approved curriculum standards that emphasize basic skills and de-emphasize creative problem solving, procedural skills, and critical thinking.

NCTM President Gail Burrill used strong words in a letter to the president of the California Board of Education. She wrote, "Today's children cannot be prepared for tomorrow's increasingly technological world with yesterday's content . . . The vision of important school mathematics should not be one that bears no relation to reality, ignores technology, focuses on a limited set of procedures . . . California's children deserve more."

The NSF also condemned California's deviation from constructivism. Luther Williams, the National Science Foundation's Assistant Director for Education and Human Resources, wrote a letter to the Board on NSF letterhead stationary. Williams' letter, dated December 11, 1997, explained that the Board's decision to adopt the mathematics standards "vacates any serious commitment to elevating problem solving and critical thinking skills..." Williams added, "The Board action is, charitably, shortsighted and detrimental to the long-term mathematical literacy of children in California." Speaking for the National Science Foundation, he chastised, "We view the Board action in California with grave disappointment and as a lost opportunity for the cities we support–indeed, for the entire state."

The condemnations of the new California math standards by non mathematicians turned into an avalanche. Judy Codding, a vice president of the National Center on Education and the Economy (NCEE), had served on California's Standards Commission. She made no secret of her opposition to the new standards. Speaking at an NCEE conference, she declared "I will fight to see that California math standards are not implemented in the classroom." California Superintendent of Schools Delaine Eastin also denounced the math new standards written by the Stanford mathematicians as being "dumbed down." According to Eastin, the California standards represented "a decided shift toward less thinking and more rote memorization." Eastin also complained that with the new standards, "we're not even going to let [students] use a calculator before the sixth grade" (Colvin, 1997b; Wu, 2000). The statewide chairs of the Academic Senates of the UC, CSU, and California Community College systems, none of whom were mathematicians, also joined the chorus. They issued a joint statement condemning the adoption of California's math standards and falsely declared that "the consensus position of the mathematical community" was in opposition to the new standards, and generally in support of the rejected, standards, written by the Standards Commission.

California mathematicians put an end to the rumor that there was any consensus in the mathematics community against the new California standards. More than 100 mathematics professors from colleges and universities in California added their names to an open letter in support of the California mathematics standards. The signatories included chairs of the math departments at Caltech, Stanford, several UC and CSU campuses, as well as community college faculty. Jaime Escalante also added his name in support.[8] One of the flash points in the disagreement about the standards was whether long division should be taught in K–12 beyond the case of single digit divisors, and this was indicated in the open letter. A detailed explanation of the importance of the division algorithm by two mathematicians was later provided for the benefit of teachers (Klein & Milgram, 2000).

The criticisms of the California standards in the press diminished after a few months, and work proceeded on developing the *Mathematics Framework for California Schools*. R. James Milgram and Hung-Hsi Wu played fundamental roles in the many mathematical portions of the final document. Important contributions were also made by others, including cognitive psychologist David Geary of the University of Missouri and educational researcher Douglas Carnine together with other members of the National Center to Improve the Tools of Educators (NCITE) at the University of Oregon. The State Board of Education contracted with NCITE to perform a study "to locate high quality research about achievement in mathematics, review that research, and synthesize the findings . . . From a total of 8,727 published studies of mathematics education in elementary and secondary schools, the research team identified 956 experimental studies. Of those, 110 were deemed high quality research because they met tests of minimal construct and internal and external validity" (California Department of Education, 1999).

The *Framework* was adopted by the California State Board of Education in December 1998. A system was developed for textbook adoptions in California which included panels of mathematicians, as well as different panels whose membership consisted primarily of classroom teachers. The panels of mathematicians were charged with evaluating mathematics curricula submitted for statewide adoption, on the basis of the quality of mathematical content. This screening process by mathematicians contributed important voices to California's 1999 and 2001 textbook adoption process. Most of the panel members came from California universities, but not all. Richard Askey of the University of Wisconsin at Madison and Ralph Raimi of the University of Rochester participated on the 1999 panels.

Even after California identified textbooks aligned to its new state standards, resistance to the California standards at the local school district level was significant. Decisions at the district level were largely under the control of administrators who looked for guidance from the NCTM, the NSF, and sometimes the NCEE. The new content standards of California would not easily be accepted. In one case which received front page coverage in the Los Angeles Times, a critic of the California math standards threatened a hunger strike in order to increase the chances of classroom use of NCTM aligned math programs (Colvin, 2000; Mendieta, 2000). Nevertheless, as early as 1999 some school districts were coming to grips with the new guidelines. The Los Angeles Unified School District included Paul Clopton, Hung-Hsi Wu, Ze'ev Wurman, one of the co-founders of HOLD, and Barry Simon, the mathematics department chair at Caltech, on a textbook selection committee. While the recommendations of these highly knowledgeable participants were largely ignored, the mere fact of their participation was a departure from the past.

One of the signal events of 1999 was the release of Liping Ma's book, *Knowing and Teaching Elementary Mathematics* (Ma, 1999). Ma compared answers to elementary school math questions by 23 U.S. elementary school teachers to those by 72 Chinese elementary school math teachers. Of the U.S. teachers, 12 were participating in an NSF-sponsored program whose "goal was to prepare excellent classroom mathematics teachers to be in-service leaders in their own school districts or regions" (Ma, 1999, p. xxii). The remaining U.S. teachers were interns, each with one year experience teaching. The interns were to receive Masters Degrees at the end of the summer during which interviews took place. By contrast, most Chinese teachers had only 11 or 12 years of formal education, completing only the ninth grade in high school followed by two or three years of normal school. In spite of their fewer years of formal education, the Chinese teachers demonstrated much greater understanding of fundamental mathematics than did their U.S. counterparts. Ma masterfully explained the interrelationships of pedagogy and content at the elementary school level and drew important lessons from her investigations. Liping Ma's book was embraced by all sides in the math wars. That unique distinction offered at least some hope that the warring factions could at some point find substantive issues upon which to agree.

Other events in 1999 were less unifying. In October, the U.S. Department of Education released a list of ten recommended math programs, as indicated at the beginning of this chapter. The programs were designated as either "exemplary" or "promising," and those programs are listed in the appendix to this chapter. The *Open Letter to United States Secretary of Education Richard Riley* was published on November 18, 1999 as a full paid ad in the Washington Post, paid for by the Packard Humanities Institute. The authors of the letter were David Klein, Richard Askey, R. James Milgram, and Hung-Hsi Wu. Descriptions of some of the shortcomings of the "exemplary" and "promising" curricula were later published in the American School Board Journal (Klein, 2000a). The NCTM responded to the open letter by explicitly endorsing all ten of the "exemplary" and "promising" programs (see appendix).

The ten "exemplary" and "promising" math programs were chosen by an "Expert Panel" designated by the U.S. Department of Education. The one mathematician on the Expert Panel, Manuel Berriozabal, publicly distanced himself from its decisions. The *Christian Science Monitor* reported that "Berriozabal abstained or voted against all 10 programs," and:

"The panel was a good idea," Dr. Berriozabal says, "but we made some bad judgments. From the best I could tell, none of the programs we selected as 'promising' or 'exemplary' had any kind of long-term track record of achievement." After Berriozabal arrived in Washington, the panel began debating the criteria to determine a successful program. Berriozabal thought that long-term proof of achievement should top the list. Most others on the panel wanted to require programs to conform to NCTM standards—then gauge achievement. (Clayton, 2000)

Not all mathematicians were in agreement with the Open Letter. The most prominent critic of the Open Letter was Hyman Bass, the incoming president of the American Mathematical Society. Bass posted a message on a national listserve that denounced the Open Letter (Bass, 1999). The only program he defended in his message was Connected Math, though he did acknowledge that this grade 6–8 "exemplary" program did not include any treatment or explanation of division of fractions, as pointed out by Richard Askey. Bass complained that the Open Letter politicized the discussion. As reported in the *Notices of the American Mathematical Society:*

> Bass disagrees with many of the conclusions in the letter, but his main objection is that the letter has inserted the debate over mathematics curricula "into the world of journalism and politics, where . . . serious and balanced discussion will no longer be possible." He also expressed concern that "What appear to be very sensible reservations about what the Department of Education did [have] become in fact part of a veiled and systematic assault on the professional education community." (Jackson, 2000)

In his email message, Bass expanded on his political objections:

> Mathematically Correct, an important agent in promoting this Open Letter, has been politically active around the country. In Massachusetts it is allied with efforts of the Deputy Commissioner of Education, Sandra Stotsky, to review proposed revisions to the State Framework. Her ideological and uninformed opposition to "constructivist ideas" has reached the incredible state where she is opposed to inclusion of discussion of "Classical Greek constructions" as being "constructivist pedagogy." Is this what serious mathematicians want to associate themselves with?

Formerly a research associate at Harvard and an expert on children's reading, Dr. Sandra Stotsky was one of a handful of education leaders at the state or national level who endorsed the Open Letter. Chester Finn, a former U.S. Assistant Secretary of Education, and Lisa Graham Keegan, the Superintendent of Public Education of Arizona also endorsed the Open Letter to U.S. Secretary Riley. Bass' accusation that Stotsky was opposed to "Classical Greek constructions" in geometry was completely without basis, as she later informed him; Bass had unwittingly misinterpreted another person's sarcastic comments. Indeed, Stotsky was on record as wanting a strong set of high school geometry standards in the revision of the mathematics curriculum framework for Massachusetts and sought the advice of Harvard mathematics professor Wilfried Schmid. Schmid provided generous assistance in the development of the new mathematics framework for Massachusetts, which suffered from similar opposition as the one in California. The Massachusetts math framework, much like California's, deviated from the constructivist prescriptions of the NCTM.[9]

Schmid, who was critical of NCTM aligned curricula, also signed the Open Letter (Hartocollis, 2000).

Several months after the publication of the Open Letter to Secretary Riley, the U.S. Department of Education designated two more curricula as "promising": *I Can Learn* and *Growing With Mathematics*. The Department of Education praised these two programs, for their alignment to the *NCTM Standards*, among other reasons.

At the state level, California all but ignored the U.S. Department of Education recommendations. Of the 12 "exemplary" and "promising" math programs, only the UCSMP grade 7 and 8 textbooks were adopted in 1999 in California, and none were accepted for statewide adoption in 2001. Several NSF sponsored math curricular programs were submitted for statewide adoption in California in 1999 and 2001, but due to deficiencies in mathematical content, none were adopted in either year.

Given the size of the California textbook market, it is not surprising that there were heated debates between mathematicians, on the one hand, and the mathematics education community, on the other, about specific curricula and the influence of the California standards. As an illustration, the creators of one of the "exemplary" programs, Core-Plus, posted an article on their website from Western Michigan University that included as part of a rebuttal of criticisms of Core-Plus:

> ...Mr. Milgram also has a strong anti-reform agenda and was a leader in the campaign that led to the new California Mathematics Standards that have been widely criticized as retrograde by the mathematics education community. (Schoen, Hirsch, Coxford, & Fey, 1999)

The culminating event for mathematics education of the 1990s occurred in April 2000 when the NCTM released a new document entitled, *Principles and Standards for School Mathematics* (PSSM) (NTM, 2000). PSSM was a revision of the *1989 NCTM Standards* intended to address some of the criticisms of the earlier document. The writing teams for the year 2000 national standards began work on the PSSM in 1997, and many organizations were solicited for suggestions. The PSSM is a 402-page document organized into eight chapters, and it is similar in many respects to its predecessor, the *1989 NCTM Standards*. Some of the more radical declarations from the *1989 NCTM Standards* were eliminated, and slightly greater emphasis was given to the importance of arithmetic algorithms and computational fluency in the new document. The PSSM provided guidelines for spans of grades: pre-kindergarten to grade 2, 3–5, 6–8, and 9–12. As explained by Ralph Raimi who served on a committee of the American Mathematical Society to make recommendations for the new standards, the revisions fell short of what many of the critics would have preferred:

As Joan Ferrini-Mundy, its principal editor, explained in her September Notices [of the American Mathematical Society] article, NCTM this time commissioned the commentary of many mathematicians, including committees of AMS, MAA, and SIAM, upon an earlier draft prepared for us. I myself served on the AMS committee and (by commission) as an individual too. NCTM solicited public advice at large, and I know several who also attempted to link the mathematical world with the new document, but the effort was to little avail; the message—the "vision" of PSSM—remains, in my vision, much the same as that of the original 1989 Standards.

PSSM continues to abhor direct instruction in, among other things, standard algorithms, Euclidean geometry, and the uses of memory. Though like its predecessor it has the word "standards" in its title, it is not a set of standards in the usual meaning of the term, for it refuses to say what exactly a child should learn in thirteen years of schooling. Long division? Quadratic formula? How to compute the quotient of two fractions? (See p. 218 of PSSM for an enlightening discussion.) Proof of a theorem on inscribed angles? Trigonometric identities? PSSM will neither affirm or deny, lest it seem to dictate content (Raimi, 2001).

CONCLUDING REMARKS

At the end of the 20th century, mathematics education policies in U.S. public schools were in a state of flux. Disagreements between parents and mathematicians, on the one hand, and professional educators, on the other, continued without clear resolution. Wilfried Schmid described the disagreements at the end of the 1990s succinctly:

The disagreement extends over the entire mathematics curriculum, kindergarten through high school. It runs right through the National Council of Teachers of Mathematics (NCTM), the professional organization of mathematics teachers. The new NCTM curriculum guidelines, presented with great fanfare on April 12 [2000], represent an earnest effort at finding common ground, but barely manage to paper-over the differences.

Among teachers and mathematics educators, the avant-garde reformers are the most energetic, and their voices drown out those skeptical of extreme reforms. On the other side, among academic mathematicians and scientists who have reflected on these questions, a clear majority oppose the new trends in math education. The academics, mostly unfamiliar with education issues, have been reluctant to join the debate. But finally, some of them are speaking up.

Parents, for the most part, have also been silent, trusting the experts—the teachers' organizations and math educators. Several reform curricula do not provide textbooks in the usual sense, and this deprives parents of one important source of information. Yet, also among parents, attitudes may be changing.

The stakes are high in this argument. State curriculum frameworks need to be written, and these serve as basis for assessment tests; some of the reformers receive substantial educational research grants, consulting fees or textbook royalties. For now, the reformers have lost the battle in California. They are redoubling their efforts in Massachusetts, where the curriculum framework is being revised. The struggle is fierce, by academic standards. (Schmid, 2000)

The stakes are high not only for mathematics education in the public schools, but also for the nation's colleges and universities. Through a domino effect that begins in the elementary school grades and works its way up the educational ladder, the so-called reforms promoted by the NCTM, and other education organizations, are sure to affect university level mathematics education. Without adequate foundations in arithmetic skills and concepts from elementary school, entering middle school students will be unable to progress to algebra. Without strong foundations in algebraic skills and ideas, the doors to subsequent meaningful mathematics courses will be closed. University mathematicians are worried. As Hung-Hsi Wu explained in 1997:

This reform once again raises questions about the values of a mathematics education . . . by redefining what constitutes mathematics and by advocating pedagogical practices based on opinions rather than research data of large-scale studies from cognitive psychology.

The reform has the potential to change completely the undergraduate mathematics curriculum and to throttle the normal process of producing a competent corps of scientists, engineers, and mathematicians. In some institutions, this potential is already a reality. (Wu, 1997)

In an era of international competition, it is unlikely that the public will tolerate such trends indefinitely. It was the broad implementation of the NCTM reforms themselves that created the resistance to them. Ironically, the extraordinary success in disseminating progressivist mathematics programs may, in the long run, be the principal reason for the demise of progressivism in mathematics education.

APPENDIX

The letter below was written in response to the Open Letter sent to U.S. Education Secretary Richard Riley from more than 200 mathematicians and prominent individuals. That Open Letter was published on November 18, 1999 in the Washington Post. It called for the withdrawal of the U.S. Department of Education's recommendations of the following mathematics programs, labeled by the Education Department as "exemplary" or "promising":

Exemplary
- Cognitive Tutor Algebra
- College Preparatory Mathematics (CPM)
- Connected Mathematics Program (CMP)
- Core-Plus Mathematics Project
- Interactive Mathematics Program (IMP)

Promising
- Everyday Mathematics
- MathLand
- Middle-school Mathematics through Applications Project (MMAP)
- Number Power
- The University of Chicago School Mathematics Project (UCSMP)

November 30, 1999

Secretary Richard W. Riley
United States Secretary of Education
400 Maryland Avenue
Washington, DC 20202

Dear Mr. Secretary:

In light of the recent paid advertisement in the Washington Post requesting that you withdraw the list of exemplary and promising mathematics programs, the Board of Directors of the National Council of Teachers of Mathematics wishes to inform you of their unconditional support for the work of the Expert Panel, the criteria used by the Panel, the process employed by the Panel, and the quality and appropriateness of their final recommendations.

We are deeply disappointed that so many eminent and well-intentioned mathematicians and scientists have chosen to attack the work of the Panel. We note, however, that the advertisement represents the opinion of a small, but vocal, minority of mathematicians and scientists, many of whom have little direct knowledge of the elementary and secondary school mathematics curriculum nor how to make it responsive to the needs of all students.

Unfortunately, while NCTM is working diligently and successfully to engage mathematicians and mathematics teachers at all levels in the process of setting high standards for school mathematics, the authors of the Post advertisement seem determined unilaterally to undermine the programs that the

Expert Panel has found to be exemplary and promising. We believe that the Panel took a hard look at quality, alignment with sound standards, and most importantly, how the various programs affect student learning. The ten programs recommended by the Expert Panel have already had a positive influence on thousands of young people. Thanks to work of the Panel, these programs can be expected to have an equally positive impact on millions of young people in the coming years. For reasons that we do not understand, this fact appears to seriously bother many of the individuals who allowed their names to be associated with the Post ad.

Mr. Secretary, NCTM's Board of Directors believes that the Department has performed a great service by providing this list of programs. We thank you and your colleagues for supporting the work of the Expert Panel and look forward to continuing to work with you on behalf of the mathematics education of our nation's youth.

Sincerely,

John A. Thorpe
Executive Director

ACKNOWLEDGMENTS

The author would like to express his gratitude to Henry Alder, Richard Askey, Wayne Bishop, Williamson Evers, R. James Milgram, Chiara Nappi, Ralph Raimi, Diane Ravitch, Sandra Stotsky, and Edie Pistolesi for their helpful comments and suggestions on draft versions of this chapter.

NOTES

1. An Open Letter to United States Secretary of Education, Richard Riley, November 1999, http://www.mathematicallycorrect.com/riley.htm

2. Recorded remarks of Nancy Ichinaga at the 1999 Conference on Standards-Based K–12 Education, held at California State University, Northridge, May 21 and 22, 1999. http://www.csun.edu/~hcbio027/standards/conference.html/

3. Posted on the Mathematically Correct website at: http://mathematically-correct.com/hwsnctm.htm

4. Hirsch, http://mathematicallycorrect.com/edh2cal.htm

5. The author was one such visitor on February 11 and 12, 1999.

6. Mathematically Correct, http://www.mathematicallycorrect.com

7. Testimony of Susan Sarhady, U.S. House of Representatives Committee on Education and the Workforce Subcommittee on Early Childhood, Youth and Families & Subcommittee on Postsecondary Education, Training and Life-Long Learning, February 2, 2000. http://gopher.house.gov/ed_workforce/

hearings/106th/ecyf/fuzzymath2200/sarhady.htm;   Plano Parental Rights
Council, Susan Sarhady http://www.planoprc.org/index.html

8.   David Klein et al., *Open Letter to CSU Chancellor Charles Reed* http://www
.mathematicallycorrect.com/reed.htm

9.   For background information, see the Mathematically Correct website.
http://www.mathematicallycorrect.com/bassattack.htm

REFERENCES

Alder, H. (1995, December 7). Presentation to the State Board of Education. http://
mathematicallycorrect.com/alder1.htm

Anderson, J.R., Reder, L.M., & Simon, H.A. (1997). *Applications and misapplications
of cognitive psychology to mathematics education.* Unpublished paper. http://
act.psy.cmu.edu/ACT/papers/misapplied-abs-ja.html

Armbrister, T. (2001, February). Principals of success. *Reader's Digest.*

Askey, R. (2001). Good intentions are not enough. In T. Loveless (Ed.), *The great
curriculum debate: How should we teach reading and math?* Washington, DC: Brookings Institution.

Askey, R. (1992). Some comments on education. *Notices of the American Mathematical
Society, 39,* 424–426.

Bass, H. (1999, November 30). Views on the Open Letter. *The Math Forum.* http://
forum.swarthmore.edu/epigone/amte

Bosse, M.J. (1995). The NCTM standards in light of the new math movement: A
warning! *Journal of Mathematical Behavior, 14,* 171–201.

Burns, M. (1994, February). Arithmetic: The last holdout. *Phi Delta Kappan,*
471–476.

California Department of Education. (1999). *Mathematics framework for California
schools: Kindergarten through grade twelve.* Sacramento: Author.

Carnine, D. (2000). *Why education experts resist effective practices (and what it would take
to make education more like medicine).* Thomas B. Fordham Foundation, http://
www.edexcellence.net. Washington, DC.

Carter, S.C. (2000). *No excuses.* The Heritage Foundation, www.heritage.org. Washington, DC.

Clayton, M. (2000, May 23). How a new math program rose to the top. *Christian Science Monitor.* http://www.csmonitor.com/sections/learning/mathmelt/p-
2story052300.html

Colvin, R. (2000, March 17). Debate over how to teach math takes cultural turn. *Los
Angeles Times.*

Colvin, R. (1997a, January 5). Formulas for math problems. *Los Angeles Times,* column 1.

Colvin, R. (1997b, November 30). State Board may return math classes to the
basics. *Los Angeles Times.*

Coombs, M.K. (1998, March 24). Honest follow-through needed on this project.
The Washington Times. http://mathematicallycorrect.com/honestft.htm

Cremin, L.A. (1961). *The transformation of the school: Progressivism in American education, 1876–1957.* New York: Alfred A Knopf, Inc.

Delpit, L. (1986, November). Skills and other dilemmas of a progressive educator. *Harvard Educational Review*, 379–385. [Reprinted in *American Educator*, Fall, 1996]

Duren, W. (1989). Mathematics in American society. in P. Duren (Ed.), *A century of mathematics in America, Part II*. Providence, RI: American Mathematical Society.

Effective School Practices. (1995–6, Winter). Vol.15(1). http://darkwing.uoregon.edu/~adiep/ft/151toc.htm

Evers, W. (2001). Standards and accountability. In T. Moe (Ed.), *A primer on America's schools* (Ch. 9). Stanford, CA: Hoover Institution Press.

Evers, B. (1995, May 17). The need for choice. Letter to the Editor. *Palo Alto Weekly*.

Grossen, B. (1998). *What is wrong with American education?* In W.M. Evers (Ed.), *What's gone wrong in America's classrooms?* Stanford, CA: Hoover Institution Press.

Hartocollis, A. (2000, April 27). The new, flexible math meets parental rebellion. *The New York Times*.

Haynes, K. (1998, May 29). Parental equation. *Los Angeles Times*.

Helfand, D. (2000, April 30). Inglewood writes book on success. *Los Angeles Times*.

Hirsch, E.D., Jr. (1996). *The schools we need: Why we don't have them*. New York: Double Day.

Hughes-Hallett, D., Gleason, A., et al. (1994). *Calculus*. New York: John Wiley & Sons, Inc.

Jackson, A. (2000, February). Open Letter on mathematics curricula ignites debate. *Notices of the American Mathematical Society*. http://www.ams.org/notices/200002/fyi.pdf

Jacobson, S. (2000, May 13). Part of parents' lawsuit dismissed. *The Dallas Morning News*.

Jones, P., & Coxford, A., Jr., (1970). Mathematics in the evolving schools. In *A history of mathematics education in the United States and Canada*. Washington, DC: National Council of Teachers of Mathematics, Thirty-second year book.

Kamil, C., & Dominick, A. (1998). The harmful effects of algorithms in grades 1–4. In *The teaching and learning of algorithms in school mathematics*, 1998 Yearbook. Reston, VA: National Council of Teachers of Mathematics.

Kamil, C., & Warrington, M.A. (1999). Teaching fractions: Fostering children's own reasoning. In *Developing mathematical reasoning*, 1999 Yearbook. Reston, VA: National Council of Teachers of Mathematics.

Klein, D. (2000a, April). Math problems: Why the U.S. Department of Education's recommended math programs don't add up. *American School Board Journal*, 187(4), 52–57. http://www.mathematicallycorrect.com/usnoadd.htm

Klein, D. (2000b, August). *High achievement in mathematics: Lessons from three Los Angeles elementary schools*. A Report Commissioned by the Brookings Institution, Washington, DC: http://brookings.org/gs/brown/bc_report/2000/LosAngeles.PDF

Klein, D. (1999). Big business, race, and gender in mathematics reform. Appendix In S. Krantz (Ed.), *How to teach mathematics*. Providence, RI: American Mathematical Society.

Klein, D. (1998, July/August). The freedom to agree. *California Political Review*, 9(4).

Klein, D., & R. Milgram, J.R. (2000). *The role of long division in the K–12 curriculum.* ftp://math.stanford.edu/pub/papers/milgram/long-division/longdivsion-done.htm.

Klein, D., & Rosen, J. (1997, November). Calculus reform–For the $millions. *Notices of the American Mathematical Society.*

Kline, M. (1973). *Why Johnny can't add: The failure of the new math.* New York: St. Martin's Press.

Loveless, T. (2001). A tale of two math reforms: The politics of the new math and the NCTM standards. In T. Loveless (Ed.), *The great curriculum debate: How should we teach reading and math?* Washington, DC: Brookings Institution Press.

Loveless, T., & DiPerna, P. (2000). The Brown Center Report on American Education: How well are American students learning? *Focus on math achievement.* Washington, DC: The Brookings Institution.

Ma, L. (1999). *Knowing and teaching elementary mathematics.* Hillsdale, NJ: Lawrence Erlbaum Associates.

McKeown, M., Klein, D., & Patterson, C. (2000). National Science Foundation systemic initiatives. In S. Stotsky (Ed.), *What's at stake in the K–12 standards wars: A primer for educational policy makers.* New York: Peter Lang Publishing, Inc.

Mejia, V. (1998, March 31). Fuzzy fracas. *Los Angeles New Times.*

Mendieta, G. (2000, March 31). Math that's worth a hunger strike education: Algebra is a civil rights issue for poor and minority children. *Los Angeles Times,* Op-Ed.

Nappi, C. (1999, October). *Why charter schools? The Princeton story.* The Thomas B. Fordham Foundation. http://www.edexcellence.net/library/wcs/wcs.html. Washington, DC.

National Commission on Excellence in Education. (1983). *A nation at risk: The imperative for educational reform.* Washington, DC: U.S. Government Printing Office. http://www.ed.gov/pubs/NatAtRisk/index.html

National Council of Teachers of Mathematics. (2000). *Principles and standards for school mathematics.* Reston, VA: Author.

National Council of Teachers of Mathematics. (1980). *An agenda for action: Recommendations for school mathematics of the 1980s.* Reston, VA: Author.

National Council of Teachers of Mathematics. (1989). *Curriculum and evaluation standards.* Reston, VA: Author.

National Council of Teachers of Mathematics. (1991). *Professional standards for teaching school mathematics.* Reston, VA: Author.

National Council of Teachers of Mathematics. (1995). *Assessment standards for school mathematics.* Reston, VA: Author.

Osborne, A., & Crosswhite, F.J. (1970). Forces and issues related to curriculum and instruction, 7–12. In *A history of mathematics education in the United States and Canada.* Thirty-second year book. Reston, VA: National Council of Teachers of Mathematics.

Raimi, R. (2001, February). Standards in school mathematics. Letters to the Editor. *Notices of the American Mathematical Society.*

Raimi, R. (2000). Judging standards for K–12 mathematics. In S. Stotsky (Ed.), *What's at stake in the K–12 standards wars: A primer for educational policy makers.* New York: Peter Lang Publishing, Inc.

Raimi, R., & Braden, L.S. (1998, March). 1998 State Mathematics Standards. *Fordham Report, 2*(3). http://www.edexcellence.net/standards/math.html

Ravitch, D. (2000). *Left back: A century of failed school reforms.* New York: Simon and Schuster.

Riley, R.W. (1998, April). The state of mathematics education: Building a strong foundation for the 21st century. *Notices of the American Mathematical Society,* 487–491.

Scharlemann, M. (1996, October 11). Open letter on MathLand. http://mathematicallycorrect.com/ml1.htm

Schmid, W. (2000, May). New battles in the math wars. *The Harvard Crimson.*

Schoen, H.L., Hirsch, C.R., Coxford, A.F., & Fey, J.T. (1999). When political agendas get in the way of the facts: The case of Debra Saunders' column 3/12/99. Copyright 1999, Core-Plus Mathematics Project.

Sykes, C. (1995). *Dumbing down our kids: Why American children feel good about themselves but can't read, write, or add.* New York: St. Martin's Press.

Tennenbaum, S. (1951). *William Heard Kilpatrick.* New York: Harper & Brothers Publishers.

U.S. Department of Education, National Center for Education Statistics Pursuing Excellence. (1996). *A study of U.S. eighth grade mathematics and science teaching, learning, curriculum and achievement in international context* (Ch. 3) (NCES 97–198). Washington, DC: U.S. Government Printing Office.

Wooton, W. (1965). *SMSG: The making of a curriculum.* New Haven, CT: Yale University Press.

Wu, H-H. (2000). The 1997 mathematics standards war in California, In S. Stotsky (Ed.), *What's at stake in the K–12 standards wars: A primer for educational policy makers.* New York: Peter Lang Publishing, Inc., http://www.mathematicallycorrect.com/hwu.htm

Wu, H-H. (1999, Fall). Basic skills versus conceptual understanding: A bogus dichotomy in mathematics education. *American Educator,* American Federation of Teachers. http://www.aft.org/publications/american_educator/fall99/wu.pdf

Wu, H-H. (1997). The mathematics education reform: Why you should be concerned and what you can do. *American Mathematical Monthly, 104,* 946–954.

Wu, H-H. (1996). The mathematician and mathematics education reform. *Notices of the American Mathematical Society, 43,* 1531–1537.

CHAPTER 8

ASSESSMENT IN MATHEMATICS

A Developmental Approach

John Pegg

ABSTRACT

Assessment is an integral part of teaching and learning. However, as we enter the 21st century the nature, role, importance and place concerning assessment practices have never been under such rigorous debate and controversy. One view advocated by many educational researchers is that there is a need for new assessment practices to complement more traditional widely-used techniques. These newer practices are to be (i) more in tune with current curriculum content and goals, and (ii) more able to inform teaching initiatives. The philosophy towards assessment in this chapter is synchronous with this view but also adds a further dimension to the defining parameters. The additional focus is that an empirically-based theoretical perspective, which is sensitive to student cognitive development, should underpin assessment initiatives. This chapter addresses this issue by considering one such approach. It does this by first establishing how such a technique is consistent with newer approaches to assessment and then by describing the model in detail. Exam-

Mathematical Cognition, pages 227–259
Copyright © 2002 by Information Age Publishing

ples, taken from different mathematics topics are then used to illustrate the ideas advocated. Finally, experiences gained by teachers using the model are provided and discussed.

INTRODUCTION

The term "assessment" in Mathematics refers to the identification and appraisal of students' knowledge, insight, understanding, skills, achievement, performance, and capability in Mathematics. (Niss, 1998)

Unlike the broad view of assessment presented by Niss above, most assessment practices in mathematics throughout the world do not match this rhetoric (see, e.g., Dwyer, 1998). Instead, assessment is dominated by a focus on content (in the form of facts) and skills (associated with computational techniques), and the ability of learners to reproduce these on demand. This narrow focus has had, and continues to have, a sterile effect upon innovations and developments in mathematics curriculum and even on what it means for a person to think mathematically.

It has become almost axiomatic that for most of society (i) what is assessed and (ii) how it is assessed provide the clearest indication of what is important and valued about formal education (Cole, 1990). This type of thinking lies behind Ramsden's (1992, p. 187) comment: "Assessment always defines the actual curriculum."

In the case of mathematics, many potentially creative improvements to mathematics teaching and learning have foundered because of the assessment practices being used. Indeed, the failure of many innovative teaching reforms in mathematics of the last fifty years can be traced to a lack of synchronisation between intended curriculum changes in content and pedagogy, and the assessment practices teachers employ (Niss, 1993a).

Disappointingly, even when tests have been designed for particular assessment purposes in mathematics, they are often used inappropriately.

Unfortunately, tests in Mathematics education are rarely used in a manner appropriate to their design. Tests designed for diagnostic purposes are often used for evaluating programs; scores from self-selected populations are used to compare districts and states; and commonly used achievement tests stress simple skills rather than sophisticated tasks, not because such skills are more important, but because they are easier to measure. (National Research Council, 1989, p. 68)

Concerns such as described above have resulted in numerous calls for changing and reconceptualizing traditional assessment. Some important examples include the following. The first was the International Congress of

Mathematics Instruction Study held in Calonge, Spain in April 1991 with the theme *Assessment in Mathematics Education and its Effects.* The second was the Australian Council of Education Research conference held in Geelong, Australia in November 1991 with the theme *Reshaping Assessment Practices: Assessment in the Mathematical Sciences under challenge.* The third and most recent was the establishment in mid-2001 of an independent commission concerning assessment issues. This group, referred to as The Commission of Instructionally Supportive Assessment, was established by five National U.S. organizations of educators. The Commission has recently produced two reports, one for policymakers entitled *Building Tests That Support Instruction and Accountability: A Guide for Policymakers* and one for those who create high-stakes accountability tests entitled *Illustrative Language for an RFP to Build Tests that Support Instruction and Accountability.* Taken together, these three examples illustrate the widespread nature, and document the diversity, of the issues involved in current assessment in mathematics.

Many of the new approaches to assessment advocated in these forums can be placed under the general banner of the alternative assessment movement. These alternative assessment approaches have a common underlying philosophy. In general, such assessment practices are linked closely to the intended curriculum, assess a wide variety of skills and attributes including ones of higher order, elevate the importance of formative assessment practices, and provide advice to the teacher on the level of student understanding in a way that might encourage a more appropriately focused teaching approach. Hence, the "rationale for developing and using alternative assessment remains quite compelling . . . compared to traditional tests, (such approaches) offer the potential for greater 'ecological validity' and relevance, assessment of a wider range of skills and knowledge, and adaptability to a variety of response modes" (Wilson & Sloane, 2000, p. 182).

Despite such general consensus concerning both the philosophy behind, and the need for improvements in, assessment practices, the emphasis on assessment has not been without problems (McCallum, Gipps, McAlister, & Brown, 1995). The problems identified have to do with costs in acquainting teachers with the new techniques, costs in time by the teacher in the classroom to employ the procedures, difficulties in convincing various stakeholder groups that current traditional assessment practices have important drawbacks, and that new approaches are worth pursuing as they improve the learning opportunities for students. Hence, often associated with alternative assessment programs are detailed professional development and information programs. It is the purpose of this chapter to make a contribution to the literature in the area of alternative assessment in mathematics.

This chapter is directed to those involved in teaching mathematics, and for those who frame and develop mathematics curricula. The ideas advocated provide a basis for assessment practices, curriculum development, and teaching. The approach discussed presents possible ways forward that address the issues flagged above in a useful, relevant and practical way. The ideas have a strong psychological and theoretical perspective that can act as a backdrop against which informed teachers and curriculum planners may work. It brings together a consistent and empirically supported body of research knowledge concerning cognitive development and relates it directly to specific content areas in mathematics.

The sections to follow lay the groundwork for the innovative assessment model that is presented later in the chapter. The first section provides a brief overview of some current issues in mathematics assessment. The chapter then turns to an examination of current practices in mathematics assessment with a particular focus on the promises and pitfalls of the *outcomes-based education movement*. The middle sections present a different way of conceptualizing and conducting educational assessment in general and mathematics assessment in particular. Examples are provided of how this different procedure (utilizing the SOLO model) can be used to assess student progress and to inform educational decisions. The concluding sections of the paper discuss current initiatives in employing the model with cohorts of secondary and elementary teachers. Flowing from this are identified strengths of the SOLO model, and the results of recent attempts to establish professional development frameworks that support teachers in learning and applying the model in their classrooms.

SOME CURRENT ASSESSMENT ISSUES IN MATHEMATICS

The roots of current assessment initiatives in mathematics have been documented by numerous writers (e.g., Griffiths & Howson, 1974; Linn, 2000; Niss, 1993b; Romberg 1987). While various evolutionary paths can be discerned, these do not appear to have been greatly influenced by either research or the needs of the learner and teacher.

It would be nice to write that current assessment practices mirror evolving perceptions by the research and teaching community about (i) the nature and aims of teaching mathematics, (ii) the increased sophistication of the tools available to teachers to undertake assessment, and (iii) a growing awareness of how learners acquire competencies. Unfortunately, this writer believes that, except in small-scale studies, the application of systematic and research-based endeavors into assessment have not been widely implemented.

This seems particularly true of the assessment practices (often referred to as high-stakes testing) generally associated with the outcomes-based or standards-based education models currently dominating education practice worldwide. In high-stakes testing, past practices seem to have been reinvented and repackaged (sometimes using new language/jargon). However, the assumptions driving the procedures have not changed and, with a focus on selection, passing and failing, they usually remain incompatible with curriculum aims (Gipps, 1994; Taylor, 1994). The rationale for such stances is often political and is built upon calls to maintain community standards and traditions (Burton, 1992).

One further consequence of high-stakes testing practices is that much of the importance given to assessment in mathematics is only partially concerned with the learning of mathematics as presented in the curriculum. Instead, the results of assessment are used in a gatekeeper role for students' grade progression and/or career options. Given that traditional mathematics testing practices can be carried out cheaply for large numbers of students, the gatekeeping role is seen as a viable way to help social planning (control).

Confounding the assessment/testing scene further is a blurring of the distinction between the word's assessment and evaluation. As implied in the initial quote in this chapter, the word "assessment" relates to the process of collecting evidence on, and making judgements about, learners' needs, strengths, abilities and achievements. This description sets it apart from the meaning of the word "evaluation", which is best described as the process of collecting evidence on, and making judgements about, the effectiveness of curricula initiatives, educational policies, and teaching programs and procedures. This latter approach has more to do with external accountability concerns. Some of the current issues with assessment can be addressed more effectively if these two terms are separated and considered independently.

Interestingly, as we begin to proceed through a new century leaving the "industrial" period of our history behind, changes in western society highlights the need for a broader, more comprehensive view of learning and assessment. A view in stark contrast to much of current practice. As we enter a post-industrial (or information) age, the destructive use of certain mathematics tests is being openly challenged. Comments, such as those from Robert M. White, President of the U.S. National Academy of Engineering in 1987, are indicative of this awareness. He stated: "The national spotlight is turning on mathematics as we appreciate its central role in the economic growth of this country. . . . It must become a pump instead of a filter" (cited in the National Research Council publication *Everybody Counts*, 1989, p. 6).

The implication here is that mathematics is a necessary and important means for the development of an intellectual base for work knowledge and skills (Wake & Williams, 2000). More important, White challenges the use of assessment that uses mathematics as a limiter on what people can achieve rather than as a catalyst to provide openings to richer and more varied career options.

This message was repeated, but with a greater sense of urgency, in the 2000 publication, *Before It's Too Late: A Report to the Nation from the National Commission on Mathematics and Science Teaching for the 21st Century*. The Report (Glenn, 2000, p.7), directed at a U.S. readership, identified four important and enduring reasons for the need for students to achieve to their potential in mathematics and Science. These were:

1. The rapid pace of change in both the increasingly interdependent global economy and in the American workplace demands widespread mathematics- and science-related knowledge and abilities;

2. Our citizens need both mathematics and science for their every day decision making;

3. Mathematics and science are inextricably linked to the nation's security interests; and

4. The deeper, intrinsic value of mathematical and scientific knowledge shape and define our common life, and history, and culture. Mathematics and science are primary sources of lifelong learning and the progress of our civilization.

Unless assessment practices are made more relevant to the needs of learners and teachers then such high ideals as indicated above will not be reached.

Another issue for assessment in mathematics is the number of groups that see themselves as stakeholders in the education enterprise. There are governments—state and federal, education authorities, employer groups, schools, parents, teachers, learners, and researchers. Each of these groups deservedly should have a voice in how mathematics is taught and assessed. Assessment is carried out within a social context and has to serve the society in which it functions. However, substantive progress in reforming assessment is only going to be possible if some form of consensus can be achieved. This writer believes that any meaningful consensus should center on using assessment to improve the quality of teaching and learning, and that making problems in current assessment procedures explicit in a language stakeholders can understand.

It is clear to this writer that current methods of assessment do not satisfy societal needs. The most common current practice is to administer a norm-referenced test that assesses summative progress and then reports that progress in the form of a single mark. This mark then indicates how a given student has performed relative to other students who have taken the test. The problem for those who defend this approach is in explaining how it is possible for a single score to serve the needs of stakeholders. In particular, a single score does not provide the information most beneficial to students and teachers, the stakeholders most central to the educational process.

Therefore, by their very nature, traditional assessment practices are inadequate for guiding teacher actions in learning situations. At best, these practices represent only a partial picture of a learner's understanding, contribute very little advice concerning students' strengths and weaknesses, and the directions in which teaching should proceed. Hence, as a result of current assessment practices, teachers have little insight into what to do next with their students or how they might best address student concerns. This chapter adopts the stance that the major purpose of assessment activity should be to improve learning.

To begin to address this situation there is a need for the primary goal of assessment to be an educational one. There are important implications associated with this simple statement. First, and foremost, there has to be a "constructive alignment" (Biggs, 1996) of content (syllabus), pedagogy, and assessment. Only in this way can assessment be informative and useful for learner and teacher.

Implied within this primary goal for assessment is the importance of ongoing assessment as students learn during the teaching process. Traditional assessment procedures are carried out summatively, i.e., at the end of a topic providing an indication of what has been learnt. Alternatively, formative assessment is carried out during the learning process providing an indication of how the student is coping and where instruction may best proceed. While both forms of assessment can impact on teaching (Butler, 1988), it is formative assessment that appears to have the potential for greatest impact on learning (Black & William, 1998a, 1998b).

"Formative assessment practices seem, or are claimed to be, more sympathetic to a rich view of what it is to know mathematics (or to have mathematical power) than are the 'achievement' tests often required by society" (Stephens, 1992, p. viii). Significantly, Black and William (1998a, 1998b) identified in their review of research into assessment, from 1986 onward, that there were at least 20 quantitative studies that showed that programs which included a greater emphasis on formative assessment produced significant learning effect size gains of the order of .4 to .7.

Before taking up the idea of assessment practices that include both formative and summative aspects, as well as part of a three-way partnership with curriculum content and learning activities, the chapter considers briefly outcomes-based approaches to education/assessment. On the surface this approach appears, despite reservations (see, e.g., Wien & Dudley-

Marling, 1998), to have the potential to address many of the concerns highlighted above with traditional assessment.

OUTCOMES-BASED ASSESSMENT

Outcomes-based education is a general name used to describe an approach that attempts to provide a learning agenda. This approach is based on a set of hierarchically designed benchmarks or signposts (often referred to as levels or bands) which are used to describe the content of instruction. Students' understandings are judged according to where they are situated along a nominal developmental continuum at various times in their education.

When applied to a school curriculum, outcomes-based education has the aim of making education goals more explicit than has been the case in traditional syllabuses. As a result, it is anticipated that teachers, students and end-users are more in tune with what might be expected as a result of the education process, and, in so doing, standards are expected to be raised.

The reasons for the extensive adoption of outcomes-based education worldwide over the past twenty years are hard to identify. It seems to have emanated from a general movement by Governments, especially those in western societies, to require greater businesslike accountability and management techniques in education. Also, following the lead of the business sector, there was a move during this period from a focus on inputs to outputs, hopefully, quality outputs that could be quantifiable and demonstrable.

While research into students' learning seems to have played some role (at least in the beginning) for the establishment of this movement (Spady, 1993, 1994), direct research links appear tenuous. Consequently, for many, a key question concerning outcomes-based education remains "whether there is a strong research base that bears out the claimed benefits of establishing a large number of outcomes coupled with detailed assessment and reporting mechanisms at a number of levels" (Eltis, 1995).

Some Issues of Outcomes-based Education

The previous discussion provided the context for outcomes-based education in relatively global terms. This section looks more critically at the approach, under two broad categories. The first concerns the strong political support for the outcomes-based approach and two related issues concerning a top-down rushed implementation without fully addressing the tension evident between traditional assessment and outcomes-based assessment. The second broad category concerns the absence of a theoretical underpinning of outcomes-based assessment. It is this aspect which has most significance for this chapter.

Some developed countries such as the United States (and Australia) do not have a national curriculum. For both these countries, the outcomes-based education movement was one way of politically reducing the amount of curriculum diversity. If all students have to take the same test and there are consequences associated with test performance, it follows that the political entity responsible for test development will exert some degree of control over curriculum offerings. It also becomes a way of influencing control over teachers. Unfortunately, using outcomes-based assessment to monitor teachers places a heavy focus on short-term goals of education and this can often be at the expense of more important long-term priorities for the learner.

Associated with strong political imperatives, and maybe because of them, the implementation of outcomes-based education has been top-down and rushed. In every country where this approach has been adopted there has been complaints from the teaching profession concerning unacceptable increases in workload and poor teacher support concerning implementation. A major casualty has been teacher morale.

Part of the increase in workload of teachers has resulted because of the tension between traditional assessment and outcomes-based assessment. Traditional assessment can most commonly be referred to as norm-referenced while outcomes-based education has a criterion-referenced feel. While the main focus of these two approaches is different, they are not incompatible or in direct conflict.

In determining appropriate criterion levels of achievement, the decision must be taken as to what is reasonable and typical to expect from the given age cohort being investigated. Hence, the criteria are being defined within a norm-referenced context. This linking of the two types of assessment, however, does not stop here. While the purposes are different, the strategies employed need not be.

Recent developments in computer software have enabled aspects of latent trait scaling and item-response theory to be used to address this issue. The net result is that individual's ability and test difficulty of the item can be scaled on a single dimension, together with an estimate of the standard error for each student and item. The ordering of the items in difficulty can provide insight into the criteria, and the positioning of students on the same scale locates the students against those criteria and, at the same time, it has a norm-referenced character enabling comparisons to be made across the cohort.

However, these newer techniques require time and professional development for teachers to acquire and understand. This time and development has not been forthcoming, hence, the friction between the two approaches remains unresolved sufficiently for practising teachers who find they are currently caught midstream.

The second major issue concerns the absence of a sound theoretical underpinning to the outcomes-based movement. Outcomes-based education curriculums are commonly developed based on the personal experiences of members of writing teams with isolated aspects of research used to support the ordering of certain concepts or topics. Planning around general psychological principles is routinely absent. It is unclear to this writer why this is the case. Such an approach flies in the face of a substantial research basis concerning how students acquire understandings and the existence of several cognitive models which would serve to provide a theoretical grounding. This issue is the most profound concerning outcomes-based assessment and the one that has received little rigorous discussion.

More specifically, this writer has not found any of the outcomes-based syllabuses in any country to have an overarching theoretical cognitive underpinning. Without such a framework, no rationale can be provided for why material related to a certain content area can be arranged in order. There can be no justification of why certain outcomes are more difficult than others, and why different outcomes can be considered to be at the same level. There also can be no indication of what a "level" means unless the underlying framework is made clear.

Is a level or stage, for example, representative of a cognitive phase in thinking? Is the grouping of content into levels based on some underlying variables concerned with how students' learn? Alternatively, is the ordering of content a pragmatic splitting of material into some groupings based on idiosyncratic feelings (or experiences) of the writers of the syllabus? In the absence of a theoretical underpinning providing a basis for the answers to these questions, an outcomes-based approach can provide a feeling of student cognitive development but offer a sterile environment for learning as it may not mirror students' natural cognitive process concerned with developing understanding.

Missing from most, if not all, current syllabus frameworks in mathematics, is the vital need to sequence content in a developmentally justifiable way. Only when this is done, can any outcomes-based syllabus appropriately support learning. When empirically validated developmental considerations are not utilized, then there is the real chance of the content material being ordered inappropriately. Incorrect ordering of content places learners and teachers in a difficult situation, as needed conceptual prerequisites may not be in place.

In addition, the lack of a well-articulated framework means that teachers are unable to challenge or defend the ordering or placement of subject content. Without an articulated framework based on a set of cognitive principles, teachers are deprived of the opportunity to understand the thinking behind syllabus development. The only way for teachers to function in such a system is for them to remember the content associated with certain "levels" by rote. There is no ownership of the process or product. Difficulties in terms of syllabus structure will only be resolved by checking with what is written in a particular syllabus document. If these difficulties are checked with a syllabus prepared by a different group of people then the answers may most likely be different.

However, even in the rare occurrence that some theoretical framework is employed to drive the syllabus construction there can still be concerns. These concerns surface if the subject matter is too tightly defined, as can happen in mathematics. This can have the potential of institutionalising certain development patterns within a single tight boundary. The implication being that there is only one path of development for all students. As such, the outcomes represent a predetermined set of expectations provided in order and this pattern remains invariant. The problem here is that there is no recognition that different teaching contexts or initiatives may engender a different developmental path.

An approach is required that employs an explicit empirically verifiable framework, where the criteria are specific enough to provide support for teachers in planning their work and in allowing students to interpret their performance. However, the criteria should be flexible enough to encompass new ways of teaching (especially involving technology) which may mean that the fine specifics of a given level performance may vary but still hold within the framework.

One possible way forward, suggested in this chapter, is to incorporate an overarching theoretical basis for the categorizations and descriptions of cognitive growth, as well as a focus on the underlying structure of students' understanding. It would seem that this approach is more productive in the long-term for (i) the student, in terms of his/her learning potential, and (ii) teachers, in terms of their professional development.

ASSESSMENT FROM A COGNITION PERSPECTIVE

Flowing from the previous discussion is the importance of psychological perspectives providing a framework for assessment in mathematics. Surprisingly, cognition theories, which should be deeply embedded and reflected in the measurement of learning rarely make an overt contribution to assessment practices. There is little evidence of a systematic use of cognitive-based research to guide or influence wide-scale curriculum developments or their associated assessment practices. Significantly, and central to this chapter, if assessment is to influence teaching, then it must rest on a theoretical basis for learning which provides useable information to guide subsequent teaching directions.

It is this writer's belief that there are empirically determined models available which can be utilized to address these concerns, as the research community is now at a stage with cognitive theory where common fundamental views of the learning process seem to be available for application. Further, there appears to be a large degree of consensus emerging from different cognition approaches (e.g., Case & Edelstein, 1993; Demetriou, 1988).

In the case of mathematics, these views are able to draw on general theories, neo-Piagetian theories of epistemology belong to this category, as well as local theories of conceptual mathematical growth, such as the various models of process-object encapsulation (Tall, 1999). These local theories often offer more value for explanation and prediction and, although sometimes restrictive, are better suited for practical purposes. However, some theoretical positions are able to incorporate both general and local aspects. This chapter elaborates one such model that is directly focused on learner outcomes in the classroom.

Currently, at the University of New England in New South Wales, Australia, a process is being investigated and trailed as part of two major federally-funded research studies. The projects are referred to under the generic title of Developmental-based Assessment and Instruction (DBA). Underpinning these projects is a means of interpreting students' responses within a framework of cognitive growth. As a consequence, teachers (and students) are able to place learners on a developmental continuum and, at the same time, teachers are alerted to possible pathways for future teaching endeavors.

The basic assessment philosophy behind DBA is that the assessment practices must satisfy community demands for accountability and be educationally meaningful and valid. The basic principles of DBA can be summarized by five statements.

1. Students should be assessed so that the *quality* of their understanding and learning can be determined.

2. Assessment should give substance to the mantra "what a student knows, understands and can do" by providing a means of describing the learners' knowledge and skills.

3. Assessment should be linked to the aims and content of the syllabus.

4. Assessment results should provide insights into the teaching process, i.e., where might future instruction most profitably be directed.

5. Theoretical cognitive perspectives should offer a framework for assessment practice and, consequently, curriculum development.

In addition, the assessment practices associated with DBA can be used for both formative and summative assessment. As suggested by Biggs (1998), it is more beneficial if both formative and summative approaches utilize equivalent procedures and are not characterized differently. He talks about the positive "backlash" from summative assessment when it defines the parameters for formative assessment. Here "you get aligned instruction, where teaching to the test is exactly what you want because it is teaching the intended curriculum" (p. 108).

The DBA approach shares many of the strengths of outcomes-based education, for example, the indicators are linked with monitoring student practice. This can occur as the student is learning the material, i.e., providing formative data to inform the teacher and learner of the state of play and where it might be most opportune to head. It could also occur at the end of the learning period, i.e., providing summative details so that an overview can be obtained on what has been achieved and where instruction might most profitably commence for future work. This has clear appeal, especially if one takes the philosophical stance that a primary purpose for assessment is to provide support for teaching techniques that can improve learning.

The differences between DBA and outcomes-based assessment lie in three important areas. First, in DBA it is the mental structure of the understanding that is important, with the criteria being merely examples typical of the types of levels of performance expected. They represent examples that *highlight key underpinning principles.* The examples students provide could vary depending on different learning experiences and activities, or on the background experiences students bring with them. However, the underlying cognitive structures of the responses remain the same. In the case of outcomes-based education, the profiles established, based on student outcomes, *are the actual focus of instruction* and represent a single and possible narrow view of what students are expected to know.

Second, and of most significance, a DBA approach rests on an empirically established cognitive developmental model. The model used is referred to as SOLO, which stands for the **S**tructure of the **O**bserved **L**earning **O**utcome. This model provides the theoretical basis for the decisions taken concerning content ordering and placement.

Third, a related strength of the SOLO model is the support such a framework provides in helping teachers keep the list of criteria to an administratively manageable load, and, more important, not allowing isolated criteria to become ends in themselves. As such, the encouragement of short-term success strategies by teachers focusing narrowly on isolated clusters of criteria at the expense of long-term holistic understanding is reduced.

THE SOLO MODEL

The SOLO model (commonly referred to as the SOLO Taxonomy in earlier works) was first described as a general model of intellectual development in Biggs and Collis (1982) with later modifications occurring in numerous papers (e.g., Biggs & Collis, 1991; Collis, Romberg, & Jurdak, 1986; Pegg, 1992; Pegg & Davey, 1998). SOLO has its genesis in the stage development notions of Piaget and information processing concepts developed during the 1970s. It has much in common with the broad raft of neo-Piagetian formulations of writers such as Case (1992), Halford (1993) and Fischer and Knight (1990).

The model resulted from an analysis of students' responses to questions posed in a variety of subject/topic areas, including number and operations, history, geography, poetry, and so on. Over the past 20 years, SOLO has built a substantial empirical base with use made of the model in many hundred published articles and as a theoretical basis for analyzing and interpreting student responses in doctoral theses.

SOLO is particularly relevant for assessing achievement in school or tertiary settings. It is both hierarchical and structural in nature. It is a model for interpreting the responses of students in terms of structural characteristics and these are then used to determine the level in the hierarchy represented by the particular response. It is in the area of measuring the *quality* of assimilation and accommodation of concepts and ideas in terms of progressive structural complexity that SOLO has its main strength.

The model is concerned with specifying "how well" (qualitative) something is learned rather than "how much" (quantitative). This distinction is important in school subjects such as mathematics and science where demand in recent times has begun to place strong emphasis on understanding applications and developing problem-solving skills.

Similar to Piaget, SOLO acknowledges the qualitatively different nature of children's thinking from that of an adult, and the way in which understanding is constructed by the learner. For Piaget and SOLO, learners actively construct their understandings by building upon earlier experiences and understandings. In doing this, they pass through sequential qualitatively different "stages". Each of these stages represents a coherent view of their world. This development is a result of processes of interaction between the learner and his or her social and physical environment.

The focus of the SOLO categorization also follows Piaget in that the interest is on cognitive processes rather than the end products alone, i.e., the focus is on the quality and nature of student understanding. The task of the teacher/researcher is to analyze the pattern of ideas. This person must distinguish between culturally or individual variable content of the learner's thought and the reasoning pattern or structure of the learners' thought. The process is to distinguish between structure and content/context. There is a tension here. Too little reliance on content leaves descriptors without the detail for understanding learners and their development. Too much content provides a theory that is applicable and true for too few learners. SOLO offers a balanced theoretical perspective that has relevance to all individuals but which is able to be considered relevant to specific topic areas. This in turn provides insight into group understanding that is so critical for appropriate classroom instruction.

The fundamental difference in focus between SOLO and Piaget's theory is the move away from an emphasis on the internal construct of an individual's developmental stage to the quality of learning demonstrated by a person's response. From a SOLO perspective, understanding is viewed as a more individual characteristic that is both content and context specific. Hence, SOLO emerges as a means of describing the underlying structure of an individual's performance at a specific time that is measured purely from a response. Describing the structure of any response is seen as phenomenon in its own right, without representing a particular stage of intellectual development of the learner. SOLO is concerned with classifying outcomes not students (Biggs & Collis, 1982, p. 23).

The move to a focus on the response emerged from the belief that Piaget's "generalized cognitive structure" could not be measured and was therefore, hypothetical. Biggs and Collis (1982, p. 31) challenged the usefulness of the idea of stages, especially in classroom situations where there is considerable empirical evidence that levels of functioning in one area/topic do not readily transfer to another similar area/topic. The generalized cognitive structure may provide an indication of some upper limit of an individual's functioning but it is a difficult feature to tie down. Reasons for the problems with a notion of a generalized cognitive structure include the influence on performance due to extraneous factors, such as motivation, intention, and prior learning strategies, as well as the amount of information that can be retained, and features specific to the task. Each of these are important determining variables that affect the actual responses given by an individual. Hence, SOLO is in the social constructivist tradition (see for example, Ernest, 1992, 1993) that refers to the importance of context and environment in the manner and form of what students learn.

To state this point another way, SOLO differs from Piagetian stage theory in that "evenness" is not expected. It was considered that no necessary structural connection between learning one topic and learning another existed, so that students were likely to operate at different cognitive levels for different topic areas. Therefore, the stability of stage attainment is not considered within SOLO, as *décalages* are considered to be part of the normal cognitive functioning of an individual, not rare and uncommon occurrences as perceived by Piaget. These differences between Piaget's theory and SOLO initiated the development of terminology specific to the model.

SOLO Modes and Levels

In SOLO, development is described in two ways, namely, upon the nature or abstractness of the task/response (referred to as the mode) and based on a person's ability to handle, with increased sophistication, relevant cues (referred to as the level of response).

SOLO postulates that all learning occurs in one of five *modes of functioning* and these are referred to as sensori motor, ikonic, concrete symbolic, formal and post formal. The five modes of thinking are described (briefly) in Table 8.1 together with an indication of the age at which they generally begin to appear.

Table 8.1.   Description of Modes in the SOLO Model

Sensori-motor: (soon after birth)	A person reacts to the physical environment. For the very young child it is the mode in which motor skills are acquired. These play an important part in later life as skills associated with various sports evolve.
Ikonic: (from 2 years)	A person internalises actions in the form of images. It is in this mode that the young child develops words and images which can stand for objects and events. For the adult this mode of functioning assists in the appreciation of art and music and leads to a form of knowledge referred to as intuitive.
Concrete symbolic: (from 6 or 7 years)	A person thinks through use of a symbol system such as written language and number systems. This is the most common mode addressed in learning in the upper primary and secondary school.
Formal: (from 15 or 16 years)	A person considers more abstract concepts. This can be described as working in terms of 'principles' and 'theories'. Students are no longer restricted to a concrete referent. In its more advanced form it involves the development of disciplines.
Post Formal: (possibly at around 22 years)	A person is able to question or challenge the fundamental structure of theories or disciplines.

These modes correspond reasonably closely to Piaget's stages of development. The major modification to the original is in placing Piaget's *early formal* stage into the earlier group of stages covered by *concrete operations*. This is consistent with Collis' (1975) earlier work in which he claimed that most children between 13 and 15 years are "concrete generalizers" and not "formal thinkers." By this term he means to imply that students in this age range are, in general, still tied to their own concrete experience where, for example, a few specific instances satisfy them of the reliability of a rule.

It is important to note that the ages given indicate generally when these degrees of abstraction can be interpreted and is context dependent. There is no implication that a student who is able to respond in the concrete symbolic mode in one context is able or would wish to respond in the same mode in other contexts. Nevertheless, an implication of this table is that most students in elementary and secondary school are capable of operating within the concrete symbolic mode (Collis, 1975). This is usually the target mode for instruction in elementary and secondary school, and teaching techniques need to be adopted generally to suit learners at this level. However, some students may still respond to stimuli in the ikonic mode, while others may respond with formal reasoning in some topics. Paramount is that each mode has its own identity, its own specific idiosyncratic character.

Within each mode, responses become increasingly complex as the cycle of learning develops. This growth can be described in terms of levels using the same generic terms for each mode. A level refers to a pattern of thought revealed in what a learner says and does. There is an assumption that must be made when observing structural levels, i.e., there is a pattern or consistency to what the learner thinks that has logic, not necessarily a logic of the teacher/researcher.

Table 8.2 describes the three levels that form a cycle of development. These descriptions of levels indicate an increasing sophistication in a learner's ability to handle certain tasks that can be associated with a particular mode.

Table 8.2.   Description of Three Levels in the SOLO Model*

Unistructural	The student focuses on the domain/problem, but uses only one piece of relevant data and so may be inconsistent.
Multistructural	Two or more pieces of data are used without any relationships perceived between them. No integration occurs. Some inconsistency may be apparent.
Relational	All data are now available, with each piece woven into an overall mosaic of relationships. The whole has become a coherent structure. No inconsistency is present within the known system.

*Sometimes a fourth level is employed, referred to as prestructural. This coding is applied when the response is below the target mode. Here the learner is frequently distracted or misled by irrelevant aspects of the situation and is therefore operating in a lower mode. Prestructural responses represent no use of relevant aspects of the mode in question.

Markers for these three levels described in Table 8.2 are observed structural cognitive similarities in the patterns of thought revealed by what learners say and/or do. Unistructural responses represent the use of only one aspect of the mode; multistructural responses represent several disjoint aspects, often in sequence; relational responses represent an integration of the elements identified in the previous level.

Each level integrates the level before it and logically requires the elements of the prior level. At the same time each level forms a logical and empirically consistent structured whole. An important consequence is that all learner responses should be able to be allocated to a particular level, a mixture of levels, or a mixture of adjoining levels (referred to as transitional responses).

The strength of the SOLO model is the linking of the cyclical nature of learning and the hierarchical nature of cognitive development. Each level of functioning within a cycle has its own integrity, its own idiosyncratic selection and use of data. Nevertheless, it serves to provide building blocks for the next higher level.

Two Cycles of Levels Within a Model

Research into SOLO levels in the 1990s (e.g., Campbell, Watson, & Collis, 1992; Pegg, 1992) identified an earlier cycle of levels present within the concrete symbolic mode than had previously been discussed. This finding arose when students' responses were analyzed over a greater range of learning situations than had been undertaken in earlier research. The key finding was that this earlier cycle represented an interface between responses in the ikonic mode and those traditionally categorized as concrete symbolic. Consequently, the responses in this first cycle were characterized by strong visual elements combining over the three levels to give a focus on a single idea or concept.

This first cycle in the concrete symbolic mode is indicated diagrammatically in Figure 8.1 by the use of the terms U_1, M_1, R_1 standing for the levels unistructural, multistructural, and relational, respectively. A response more advanced than the relational level in the first cycle becomes a new unistructural level in a new (second) cycle of levels. This second cycle of levels, coded as U_2, M_2 and R_2, is the one that has been traditionally assigned to the concrete symbolic mode in articles published prior to 1991.

In both cycles in the concrete symbolic mode, the nature of the response, i.e., the degree of abstractness, remains the same. For example, in the concrete symbolic mode the first cycle $U_1M_1R_1$ and the second cycle $U_2M_2R_2$ are both distinguished from cycles in the formal mode by their dependence on empirical cues, development being marked by a lessening of dependence upon empirical support as responses move from U_1 to R_2. Reality for the child in the concrete symbolic mode is seen as bound up

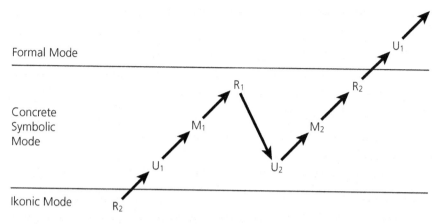

Figure 8.1.   Diagrammatic representation of levels associated with the concrete symbolic mode.

with the notion of closure and uniqueness which is related to both the nature of elements operated upon, and the number and type of operations involved.

Following from a relational response in the second cycle of the concrete symbolic mode is a unistructural response in the formal mode. Once again recent research in mathematics (Pegg & Coady, 1993; Pegg & Faithful, 1995) and in Science (Panizzon & Pegg, 1997) using SOLO has identified two cycles of growth in the formal mode. The pattern mirrors that identified in the concrete symbolic mode with the first cycle of levels representing a transition between the concrete symbolic mode and those responses traditionally coded as formal.

The transition to the new formal mode is interesting. The formal mode does not subsume the concrete symbolic mode, which remains available. The absorption of one mode by another is never complete as the learner always has the option of operating at a lower level than the one attained. This is an important issue when assessing student responses and lies at the insistence within the SOLO model that categorizations are of the response not the student.

Process-object Encapsulation Theories and SOLO

Over the past 10 years a range of learning theories have appeared in which certain cycles of learning have been used to describe development of mathematical (but mainly) algebraic ideas. These theories have a "local" flavor in that they have arisen to explain and predict cognitive development in specific topic domains in mathematics education. One group of theories can be described under the collective noun of process-object encapsulation. The writings of Dubinsky (Dubinsky et al., 1988; Czarnocha et al., 1999), Sfard (1991) and Gray and Tall (1994) belong to this perspective.

Each of these theories, founded essentially on the ideas of Piaget, sees cognitive growth through actions on existing objects that become interiorized into processes and then encapsulated as mental objects. This feature has been variously described (Tall, 1999) as *action, process, object* (Dubinsky), *interiorization, condensation, reification* (Sfard) and *procedure, process, concept* (Gray & Tall).

Dubinsky described this cycle as part of his APOS (action-process-object-schema) theory, although he later asserted that objects could also be formed by encapsulation of schemas as well as encapsulation of processes. Sfard (1991) proposed an operational growth through a cycle she termed interiorization-condensation-reification, which she complemented by a "structural" growth that focuses on the properties of the reified objects formed in an operational cycle.

In both cases these two theories are mainly based on experiences of students doing advanced mathematical thinking in senior secondary schools and at university. For this reason the emphasis is on formal (i.e., abstract) development rather than on earlier (i.e., concrete) acquired forms of understanding.

Gray and Tall (1994, 2001), focused more on the role of *symbols* acting as a pivot, switching from a process (such as addition of two numbers, say 3+4) to a concept (the sum 3+4, which is 7). The entity formed by a symbol and its pivotal link to *pro*cess or concept they named a *procept*. They observed that the growth of procepts occurred often through a sequence that they termed procedure-process-procept.

In this model, a procedure is a sequence of steps carried out by the individual, a process is where a number of procedures giving the same input-output are regarded as the same process, and the symbol shared by both becomes flexibly used to evoke process or concept. The work of Gray and Tall focuses more on symbol use in mathematics. This research is more appropriate to arithmetic and early algebra thinking.

While accepting that these three theories have been developed for different purposes and are also applied in somewhat distinct contexts, there is remarkable similarity in what each is reporting. This is surprising given that the abstractness of the mathematical understanding explored by the different models varies greatly in their difficulty and demands on working memory. However, these process-object theories describe in global terms an equivalent spectrum of development. It is not the purpose here to compare or contrast the different models. Of importance for this chapter is the links these models share with SOLO levels, and that SOLO can explain the obvious dilemma of similarities in level descriptors across markedly differing mathematically complex tasks.

A recent analysis of the model of Gray and Tall has offered new insights into the relationship between SOLO and process-object theories (Pegg & Tall, 2001). By seeing the multi-procedure level as distinct from the process level (and there are data to support this separation), we are presented with an apparently unassailable link in surface structure between the procept cycle in the model of Gray and Tall and the UMRU cycle in the SOLO model as shown in Table 8.3.

Table 8.3.   A comparison of process-object levels and those of the SOLO model

Process-Object Theory	SOLO Model
procedure	unistructural
multi-procedure	multistructural
process	relational
procept	unistructural (new cycle)

Hence, with the modification included, we can see that the process—object theories have identified what can be referred to as a "fundamental cycle of cognitive development." Hence, for each of the theories the cognitive construction identified can be compared with the UMRU sequences of SOLO.

Further, it is now possible to address the dilemma described above. The difference in complexity can be accounted for by considering the different modes of thinking identified in SOLO. For Gray and Tall, their focus is primarily in the concrete symbolic mode. Dubinsky and Sfard are concern with mathematics associated with the formal mode. As SOLO predicts the broad definition of unistructural, multistructural, and relational levels remains the same for all modes. It is the specific examples describing different content or contexts which changes within each mode.

Applications of SOLO in Mathematics

The discussion below considers responses to questions in each of the areas of arithmetic (fractions) and algebra (expressing generalization). Equivalent information on Geometry can be found in Pegg and Davey (1998).

Fractions

The following problem was asked of some several hundred students in the age range ten-to-fifteen years. This question was asked in mathematics lessons along with several other fraction-related questions. Students were asked:

> How much would each person receive if nine apple pies were divide between sixteen people so that each person receives the same amount?

In analyzing the student responses we can identify a first cycle of responses followed by two levels of a second cycle of responses within the concrete symbolic mode.

Early first cycle responses, which attempt to deal with the problem, focus on the need (the action) to cut the pies equitably, usually in halves. An issue emerged for some students when their action of cutting did not result in each person gaining an equal amount: "cut the pies into halves and you have two pieces left over" (for these students there was one pie too many). These students did not resolve this issue. This type of response was coded as U_1.

The next category of response (M_1) also has the cutting of the pies fairly as its focus, but the problem is seen in two parts with a new procedure employed to deal with the left over pie. "Cut one pie into 16 pieces and the rest into halves."

The third category (R_1) of response considers the effect of the cutting. The response moves on past the focus on equitable cutting to provide a summative view on how much each person would receive. "Cut each apple pie into sixteen pieces and each person gets 9 pieces each." Missing from this response is any use of standard fraction notation.

The next level of response, a new unistructural level (U_2) occurs as the response provided is more succinct and fraction notation is employed to express the different parts of the problem. "I would cut 8 pies in half and then cut the last pie into 16 pieces. So everyone gets 1/2 and 1/16 of a pie each." This response where students are comfortable to use fraction notation freely in their written language represents the beginning of the second cycle. This new cycle represents a development of fractions as numbers.

The second level (M_2) in this new cycle is on combining the fractions identified previously. The method employed is equivalent fractions whereby all fractions are rewritten with the same denominators before combining. "Cut 8 pies in half and give one half to each person. Then cut the last pie into 16 pieces and give one piece to each person. 1/2 + 1/16 = 8/16 + 1/16 = 9/16 each person ends up with 9/16 of a pie." Here, work with fractions takes on a more systematic and arithmetic process.

This was the highest level of response identified from the responses received. One could predict that the next level, a relational response within the second cycle, is when students can approach the task with considerable versatility. They can use a number of written approaches and are usually able to provide the answer efficiently in verbal form. These options of response were not available to the students in this study.

Expressing Generalization

The second example is the *tiles around square swimming pools problem* (Pegg, 1992). Several hundred students in Grades 7 to 10 (ages 12 to 15 years) were presented with six squares with side length starting at one unit and the largest having sides of 6 units. These diagrams represented "swimming pools" and were a visual aid for students.

The purpose of the activity was to find a rule for the number of tiles around any given square pool. The reason for this was so that the number of tiles for any given square pool could be worked out quickly and efficiently. The tiles were themselves squares of side one unit. Hence, for the first swimming pool which had a side length of one unit there are eight tiles needed, twelve for the next pool of side length two units, sixteen for the next, and so on. It was anticipated that students would provide an answer of the form, either in words or symbols, indicating that the number of tiles needed for any pool was four times the side length plus four.

Students had all taken part in similar generalisation-type exercises of finding rules governing number sequences, with and without diagrammatic support at some previous stage in their formal education. This type of activity is first encountered in Grade 7 (12 year olds) mathematics and is revisited several times in the period up to Grade 10.

As with the fraction concept, student responses were categorized into levels in the two cycles in the concrete symbolic mode. Included below are typical responses identified at each level. The spelling provided is how it was presented on student scripts.

The structure of the U_1 responses in the concrete symbolic mode in the first UMR cycle focused on counting the tiles around one pool. Answers provided include:

"There are 8 tiles around the pool"
"Each tile had numbers to get 8 altogether"
"You get on lot of tiles to go completely around the hole pool. The first one is 8 tiles go around it."

Some transitional responses between U_1 and M_1 were identified where the issue for the student was on counting the tiles around the first pool but also indicating that this should continue. "Well number one square is 8 tiles well you count the rest of the squares and add them up."

The next substantive level of responses was coded as M_1. Here student responses focused on counting the tiles on all the provided pools. Usually the student tabulated the data obtained in some way. "1. 8, 2. 12, 3. 16, 4. 20, 5. 24, 6. 28" and "1 pool = 8 tiles; 4 pools = 12 tiles; 9 pools = 16 tiles...."are two examples. In the latter case the student numbered the drawn tiles around all the pools showing the number of tiles needed. Note the "1 pool, 4 pools, 9 pools" refers to the pools of side 1, 2 and 3 units, respectively.

Relational level (R_1) responses in the first cycle indicated that the student had moved further than tabulating numbers of tiles. Here students identified a simple numeric relationship between the tiles of consecutive pools. Examples of student responses include: "because there's four between each one"; "The rule for the number of tiles surrounding the pool is every one goes 4"; Lists the tiles for each pool then "there is 4 more tiles in each one"; "Just add four more tiles to each swimming pool than the previous one had."

Responses in the second UMR cycle in the concrete symbolic mode were characterized be a lack of excessive counting and drawing of tiles on the diagrams provided. Second, the focus had moved past the reliance on the number of tiles on a previous pool influencing the next pool. Instead students, aware of the increase of four tiles between consecutive pools, moved to create a generalization about individual pools. The first level in this cycle U_2 was characterized by a focus on the perimeter of the pool. Here students reported the relationship between this property of the pools and the subsequent number of tiles. The response builds on the "four more tiles feature" that was significant in the R_1 response. Examples of student responses include "Find the perimeter in meters and add 4."

"Add 4 onto the perimeter."
"Add 4 tiles to each set of tiles on the edge of the pool.
"Perimeter + 4."

"The rule is the perimeter times 4." Here, the structure of the response is the same as other answers at this level except the student has chosen the incorrect operation.

The next level of responses was coded as M_2. Students responding at this level went further than the previous level by using a more basic and useful element than perimeter to establish a general rule, namely, side lengths. The rules provided are not particularly succinct and can be quite convoluted. The rules have a sequential feel to their development. Three examples are provided below.

"Count the number of tiles along one side plus 2 and multiply it by 4, then minus four."

"The length + 1 × 2 + Breadth + 1 × 2 – 4 = number of tiles."

"Take the length of the side and times that by two. Then take the length of the side again and add 2, then times that number by two and add the two sums together."

The final category of responses identified was coded as R_2. Students provided a rule that was succinct using minimum operations and using side length as a variable. Student responses included:

"The amount of squares around one side (inside) multiplied by 4 then add 4."

"Multiply the side length by 4 and add 4 more tiles in the same units and size."

"The number of tiles equals the length of the pool, times by four, then adding four."

Formal mode responses were not provided in this question. Nevertheless, one could hypothesize that it could concern the development of alternative rules formed by manipulating the rule, identified at the R_2 level, algebraically to form new rules.

Implications

In both of the examples provided above the evidence of two UMR cycles in the concrete symbolic mode was apparent. In both cases, the first cycle had a strong visual feature about it as the students developed the appropriate underlying concept. This concept then became a consolidated new unit that became the building block for the second cycle. During the second cycle the same structural development was noted except it was of a form that was more mathematical. However, there was still a "concreteness" about the procedures. This cycle concluded by students being able to obtain the correct response successfully.

This research supports the notion that mathematics in the middle primary to early secondary schools needs to be presented as a system of concretely based operations. Concretely based operations imply that the basic assumptions and reasoning procedures of the system should be firmly established in the learners' observable reality. It cannot, at this stage be axiomatic nor can new ideas be deductively established with meaning for the student. These ideas need to develop over time from a concrete activity whose outcomes are clearly determined and unambiguous. Different representations lead to different isolated systems, since a system is built on its referent, a concrete learner is not able to unify separate systems until the formal mode. In the formal mode the emphasis is removed from the actual real-world elements to the relationships between those elements.

As can be seen from the type of information obtained using SOLO, the model is suitable for both norm-referenced and criterion-referenced assessment, although it has most to contribute to the latter. In addition, it is useful in both formative and summative evaluation. This last point highlights a critical strength of SOLO, namely, its relevance to instruction. A SOLO level can indicate what a student knows, understands and can do. It also allows teachers an insight into where instruction might most profitable be directed. Hence, unlike most common assessment (quantitative) measures SOLO categorizations allow appropriate instructional decision making to occur.

In summary, SOLO is relevant to at least three areas of education. These are: assessment of student performance, curriculum analysis and providing a mechanism for enriching teaching procedures. An examination of the implications of the SOLO model for assessment is considered in the concluding section of this chapter following a discussion of how teachers reacted to professional development programs aimed at utilizing SOLO as an assessment tool in their classrooms.

APPLYING SOLO IN THE CLASSROOM

Currently, two projects are being undertaken to explore how teachers acquire SOLO skills and how they apply the model as an assessment framework in their classrooms. Of interest was the time needed by teachers who have a normal teaching load to acquire the skills, and what professional development support would be appropriate. In short, we were interested in how likely is it that the DBA technique can come to have a direct impact on teachers and education, and what might be the benefits of the approach?

The two projects received federal funding support in Australia and are currently in their last year. Both projects are looking at assessment in mathematics and Science. In one project groups of four teachers, two in mathematics and two in science have received one day a week leave from teaching to apply and use SOLO with their classes. These teachers meet every four weeks with university staff to discuss progress and they document their development through diaries.

The second program is more traditional in its approach. Here, more than 24 teachers of mathematics and science from elementary and secondary schools undertake a one-year professional development program each year. During this time the teachers meet as a group for three workshops undertaken away from the teachers' schools. One two-day meeting occurs early in the school year, another two-day meeting occurs midyear and the program finishes with a one-day meeting at the end of the school year. In between the workshops, schools are contacted by phone, e-mail, Web, etc. to maintain the momentum, along with at least two school visits by the tertiary team. All meetings are highly interactive with teachers reporting on their progress, findings, issues and concerns.

Although formal evaluation of the projects has not been completed, several positive features are emerging. In 90% of cases the work has had a profound effect on the teachers' view of testing, teaching, and the nature of student understanding. All teachers have reported coming out of the program thinking about their teaching and their students' learning more deeply than when they entered. They also report that other teachers on their staffs notice a difference in their approach to their classes. Interestingly this comment occurred whether the teachers were confident at coding responses.

A couple of comments from teacher reflections provide some insight into the effect of the programs on the participants after a year. One teacher reported "The acquisition of new skills has been an even slower process, and I did not feel it take place until later in the year. [Writing questions] took some time. The broader the question the harder it was to code. . . . I was 'softer' on my kids, so it was good to be working with others who could be more objective. In the end we all pretty much agreed on where to code each response. On the few occasions we argued, we all understood because we all used the same language. . . . Interaction with peers helped me to feel more comfortable with coding, I struggle on my own. It has changed my perspective on some of my kids; the poor kids can actually do better than I thought. Knowledge of SOLO is a powerful tool."

A second teacher commenting on one of the workshops stated:

I really enjoyed yesterday. It has given many insights into the frustration of teaching a different generation of students to the ones I first started teaching more than 20 years ago. The youth of today have far different demands and I am confident that this course will help me to meet these demands.

Later in the year the teacher commented. "I trailed some questions in the Grade 8 exam, and some of the other teachers commented on the 'different style.' They were concerned that some of their 'bright' students might not do so well. In the end, the brightest students did not necessarily give the highest responses. Now I need to learn how to give the students more time in the classroom to progress through the levels."

By the end of the Year the teacher had devised and tried many questions with various classes. The teacher seemed to love sharing successes and failures with other participants in the project. For example "I gave a question about how many ping-pong balls would fit into my classroom. I gave no other instructions. The students were really motivated . . . Some didn't even stop for lunch. They went about it in so many different ways. One girl took pages of words to explain her answer. One boy just gave some calculations. They both ended up with the same answer. SOLO helped me to reconcile both different types of responses. Other teachers are asking, "Why are students being asked to explain more?" They are curious; they see a change in my students (attitude). I have a different atmosphere in my classroom. It has changed the way I teach different topics. I now spend 'real time' preparing lessons. I want to be kept up to date next year, regular email contact?"

There were differences in how each teacher in the program reflected on their experiences. Nevertheless, the types of positive responses provided above were received from all the participants. Overall, the teachers' responses indicate that the ideas found resonance with them and that they were able to identify changes in their own practice as a result. While it is heartening to obtain such positive reports, teachers' enjoyment and valuing of the professional development program is necessary but not sufficient. More needs to be known about the influence of the programs on teacher actions and student learning. For example, a year after the support was provided are teachers in their classrooms still using DBA? If so, in what form is it being used? Is there evidence that students' performance/understanding has improved as result of the application of DBA? How have the teachers reconciled this alternative assessment with more traditional assessment practice? How have administrators, parents and students reacted to the changes? Answers to these types of questions are currently being sort.

CONCLUSION

As indicated in this chapter, the field of assessment is a fertile area in education and mathematics education research. Many reasons can be attributed to this phenomenon. One important reason is the recognition of the concerns by educational professionals that there is a need for better ways to describe, explore, and justify the findings and processes of assessment. At the heart of this view is the realization that the complex process of measuring and reporting the quality in students' understandings, while complex, need to be improved. Indeed, until new (better) assessment practices are widely implemented, real advances in teaching and learning mathematics will not be forthcoming. Further, the whole process is enhanced and the grade awarded becomes highly informative if the assessment is based on a qualitatively derived hierarchy that has its basis in a theory/taxonomy describing the evolution of learning (Biggs, 1998, p. 108).

Using SOLO, teachers have a tool to assist them in understanding (interpreting) the knowledge students possess, the nature of that knowledge, and also where it is most appropriate to direct the learning process. This idea has much in common with Vygotsky's (1978) notions of learning and his zone of proximal development. SOLO becomes a practical tool in providing a framework to help implement these ideas in a classroom setting.

SOLO also helps teachers avoid two problems associated with outcomes-based assessment of the insistence on a single path of learning. First, the levels in SOLO are seen as broad markers along a developmental journey. However, while the characteristics of each level remain constant, the actual detail of the student response will vary depending on the approach or methods used. This has the potential of discouraging teachers of the possibility that under pressure they may pursue inappropriate techniques (such as rote drill activities) which may provide some short-term successes by their students at the expense of long-term understandings.

Second, because SOLO levels form a coherent cycle of learning, there is less likelihood of teachers who use this model of being satisfied with dissecting learning into a number of small individual targets. Instead there is encouragement within the model for learners to acquire a relational understanding in any particular learning cycle. Such a level of understanding encompasses the "glue" that holds the elements identified individually at the multistructural level together and provides for a cohesive package of knowledge for the learner.

SOLO also allows educators a lens to see development through the eyes of learners as they construct their understandings. This allows teachers the chance to play a more explicit role so that assessment practices can better inform instruction. By observing and recognizing students' responses in terms of modes and levels, educators can close the gap between natural development and the outcomes of formal schooling. This view of human development provides the key for new assessment practices.

Hence, as a result, many student errors become recognized more accurately as a natural development phenomena, rather than carelessness. This should result in more appropriate development planning as well as better intervention and correction strategies by teachers. These teaching actions, guided by an empirically verifiable framework, will help teachers understand more about their students' progress and at the same time learn more about mathematics.

The application of developmentally-based assessment as advocated in this chapter with an emphasis on a strong cognitive theoretical model, there is the opportunity to at last help teachers match appropriately the needs and readiness of students at the level of functioning that is pedagogically appropriate. This way, such comments as offered by Evans below may no longer be relevant.

One can only be surprised at the extent to which children's genuine operative thinking in Mathematics lags behind the performances which we as teachers commonly teach them to make. (Evans, 1975, p. 2)

If this were the case, it would liberate learners of the need to be confronted by mathematics that they cannot understand and are unable to apply except through rote memorization.

Reform of assessment in mathematics is a necessary condition for any reform in the mathematics curriculum. Such assessment practices should be about measuring or describing the mathematical attainment of learners in demonstrably fair, valid and reliable ways. A way to proceed is for assessment practices to be designed to celebrate what the learner knows and understands. The ideas offered in this chapter seek to advance this approach in a way that genuinely supports and empowers learners and teachers.

REFERENCES

Biggs, J. (1996). Enhancing teaching through constructive alignment. *Higher Education, 32*, 347–364.

Biggs, J. (1998). A role for summative assessment. *Assessment in Education, 5*(1), 103–110.

Biggs, J., & Collis, K. (1982). *Evaluating the quality of learning: The SOLO taxonomy.* New York: Academic Press.

Biggs, J., & Collis, K. (1991). Multimodal learning and the quality of intelligent behaviour. In H. Rowe (Ed.), Intelligence, reconceptualization and measurement (pp. 57–76). Hillsdale, NJ: Laurence Erlbaum Assoc.

Black, P., & William, D. (1998a). Assessment and classroom learning. *Assessment in Education, 5*(1), 7–74.

Black, P., & William, D. (1998b). Inside the black box: raising standards through classroom assessment. *Phi Delta Kappan, 80*(2), 139–148.

Burton, L. (1992). Who assesses whom and to what purpose? In J. Izard & M. Stephens (Eds.), *Reshaping assessment practice: Assessment in the mathematical sciences under challenge* (pp.1–18). Melbourne: Australian Council of Educational Research.

Butler, R. (1988). Enhancing and undermining intrinsic motivation: the effects of task-involving and ego-involving evaluation on student interest and performance. *British Journal of Educational Psychology, 58*, 1–14.

Campbell, K., Watson, J., & Collis, K. (1992). Volume measurement and intellectual development. *Journal of Structural Learning and Intelligent Systems, 11*, 279–298.

Case, R. (1992). *The mind's staircase: Exploring the conceptual underpinnings of children's thought and knowledge.* Hillsdale: NJ: Laurence Erlbaum Assoc.

Case, R., & Edelstein, W. (Eds.). (1993). *The new structuralism in cognitive development.* Basel: Karger AG.

Cole, N.S. (1990). Conceptions of educational achievement. *Educational Researcher, 19*(3), 2–7.

Collis, K. (1975). *A study of concrete and formal operations in school mathematics: A Piagetian viewpoint.* Melbourne: Australian Council for Educational Research.

Collis, K.F.; Romberg, T.A., & Jurdak, M.E. (1986). A technique for assessing mathematical problem-solving ability. *Journal for Research in Mathematics Education, 17*(3), 206–221.

Czarnocha, B., Dubinsky, E., Prabhu, V., & Vidakovic, D. (1999). One theoretical perspective in undergraduate Mathematics education research. In O. Zaslavsky (Ed.), *Proceedings of the 23rd Conference of PME,* Haifa, *1,* 95–110.

Demetriou, A. (Ed.). (1988). *The neo-Piagetian theories of cognitive development: Toward an integration* Amsterdam: Elsevier Science Publishers B.V.

Dubinsky, E., Elterman, F., & Gong, C. (1988). The student's construction of quantification. *For the Learning of Mathematics 8,* 44–51.

Dwyer, C.A. (1998). Assessment and classroom learning: Theory and practice. *Assessment in Education, 5*(1), 131–137.

Eltis, K.J. (1995). *Focusing on learning: Report of the review of outcomes and profiles in New South Wales schooling.* Report to the State Government of NSW Australia on the implementation of an outcomes-based approach to curriculum development.

Ernest, P. (1992). The nature of mathematics: Towards a social constructivist account. *Science and Education, 1,* 89–100.

Ernest, P. (1993). Constructivism, the psychology of learning and the nature of Mathematics: Some critical issues. *Science and Education, 2,* 87–93.

Evans, G. (1975). Foreword. In K. Collis (1975). *A study of concrete and formal operations in school mathematics: A Piagetian viewpoint.* Melbourne: Australian Council for Educational Research.

Fischer, K.W., & Knight, C.C. (1990). Cognitive development in real children: Levels and variations. In B. Presseisen (Ed.), *Learning and thinking styles: Classroom interaction.* Washington, DC: National Education Association.

Gipps, C. (1994). *Beyond testing: Towards a theory of educational assessment.* London: Falmer.

Glenn, J. (Chair). (2000). *Before it's too late: A report to the nation from the National Commission on Mathematics and Science Teaching for the 21st Century.* Washington, DC: Education Publications Center, U.S. Department of Education.

Gray, E.M., & Tall, D.O. (1994). Duality, ambiguity and flexibility: A proceptual view of simple arithmetic. *Journal for Research in Mathematics Education, 26*(2), 115–141.

Gray, E.M., & Tall, D.O. (2001). Relationships between embodied objects and symbolic procepts: An explanatory theory of success and failure in mathematics. In M. van den Heuvel-Panhuizen (Ed.), *Proceedings of the 25th Conference of the International Group for the Psychology of Mathematics Education 3,* 65–72. Utrecht, The Netherlands.

Griffiths, H.B., & Howson, A.G. (1974). *Mathematics: Society and curricula.* London: Cambridge University Press.

Halford, G.S. (1993). *Children's understanding: The development of mental models.* Hillsdale, NJ: Lawrence Erlbaum

Linn, R.L. (2000). Assessments and accountability. *Educational Researcher, 29*(2), 4–16.

McCallum, B., Gipps, C., McAlister, S., & Brown, M. (1995). National curriculum assessment: Emerging models of teacher assessment in the classroom. In H.Torrence (Ed.) *Evaluating authentic assessment* (pp. 88–104). Philadelphia: Open University Press.

McNeir, G. (1993). *Outcome-based education*. ERIC Digest No. 85, ERIC ED 363914.

National Research Council, (1989). *Everybody counts: A report to the nation on the future of mathematics education*. Washington, DC: National Academy Press.

Niss, M. (Ed.) . (1993a). *Cases of assessment in mathematics education*. Dordrecht: Kluwer Academic Publishers.

Niss, M. (Ed.). (1993b). *Investigations into assessment in mathematics education*. Dordrecht: Kluwer Academic Publishers.

Niss, M. (1998). Assessment in geometry. In C. Mammana & V. Villani (Eds.), *Perspectives on the teaching of geometry for the 21st century* (pp. 263–274). Dordrecht: Kluwer Academic Publishers.

Panizzon, D., & Pegg, J. (1997). Investigating students' understandings of diffusion and osmosis: A post-piagetian analysis. In *Proceedings of the 1997 Annual Conference of the Australian Association for Research in Education*, Brisbane, November, available electronically, pp. 15.

Pegg, J. (1992). Assessing students' understanding at the primary and secondary level in the mathematical sciences. In J. Izard & M. Stephens (Eds.), *Reshaping assessment practice: Assessment in the mathematical sciences under challenge* (pp. 368–385). Melbourne: Australian Council of Educational Research.

Pegg, J., & Coady, C. (1993). Identifying SOLO levels in the formal mode. In I. Hirabayashi et al. (Eds.), *Proceedings of the 17th International Group for the Psychology of Mathematics Education Conference* (pp. 212–219). Japan: University of Tskuba.

Pegg, J., & Davey, G. (1998). A synthesis of two models: Interpreting student understanding in geometry. In R. Lehrer & C. Chazan, (Eds.), *Designing learning environments for developing understanding of geometry and space* (pp.109–135). Hillsdale, NJ: Lawrence Erlbaum.

Pegg, J., & Faithfull, M. (1995). Analysing higher order sills in deductive geometry. In A. Baturo (Ed.), *New directions in geometry education* (pp. 100–105). Brisbane: Queensland University of Technology Press.

Pegg, J., & Tall, D.O. (2001, December). *Fundamental cycles in learning algebra: An analysis*. Paper presented at the 12th International Congress of Mathematics Instruction Conference, The Future of the Teaching and Learning of Algebra, The University of Melbourne, Australia. Paper available electronically.

Ramsden, P. (1992). *Learning to teach in higher education*. London: Routledge.

Romberg, T.A. (1987). Measures of mathematical achievement. In T. Romberg & D. Stewart (Eds.), *The monitoring of school mathematics: Background papers, Vol. 2.: Implications from psychology; outcomes of instruction*. Madison, Wisconsin: Center for Education Research.

Sfard, A. (1991). On the dual nature of mathematical conceptions: reflections on processes and objects as different sides of the same coin. *Educational Studies in Mathematics*, 22(1), 1–36.

Spady, W.G. (1993). *Outcome-based education*. ACSA Workshop Report Number 5.

Spady, W.G. (1994). *Outcome-based education: Critical issues and answers.* ERIC No: ED 380910.

Stephens, M. (1992). Foreword. In J. Izard & M. Stephens (Eds.), *Reshaping assessment practice: Assessment in the mathematical sciences under challenge* (pp.vi-xiv). Melbourne: Australian Council of Educational Research.

Tall, D.O. (1999). Reflections on APOS theory in elementary and advanced mathematical thinking. In O. Zaslavsky (Ed.), *Proceedings of the 23rd Conference of PME, Haifa, Israel, 1,* 111–118.

Taylor, C. (1994). Assessment for measurement or standards: the peril and promise of large scale assessment reform. *American Educational Research Journal, 31,* 231–262.

Vygotsky, L.S. (1978). *Mind in society.* New York: Harvard University Press.

Wake, G., & Williams, J. (2000). Developing a new mathematics curriculum for post-compulsory education. In A. Bessot & J. Ridgway (Eds.), *Education for mathematics in the workplace* (pp.167–180). Dordrecht:: Kluwer Academic Publishers.

Wien, C.A., & Dudley-Marling, C. (1998). Limited vision: The Ontario curriculum and outcomes-based learning. *Canadian Journal of Education, 23*(4), 405–420.

Wilson, M., & Sloane, K. (2000). From principles to practice: An embedded assessment system, *Applied Measurement in Education, 13*(2), 181–208.